W9-DBL-518

E. D. Bradby (1827-1893) was a historian specialising in the Classics. He was a headmaster for twenty years, before retiring to do mission work in the east end of London.

PRAISE FOR E. D. BRADBY:

'Written with complete control . . . one could hardly wish for a more satisfactory treatment' – *The English Historical Review*

A History Of The French Revolution

E. D. Bradby

ENDEAVOURINK

AN ENDEAVOUR INK PAPERBACK

First published by Oxford University Press in 1926
This paperback edition published in 2017
by Endeavour Ink

Endeavour Ink is an imprint of Endeavour Press Ltd
Endeavour Press, 85-87 Borough High Street,
London, SE1 1NH

Copyright © E. D. Bradby 1926

The right of E. D. Bradby to be identified as the author of
this work has been asserted by him in accordance with the
Copyright, Design and Patents Act, 1988

All rights reserved. No part of this publication may be
reproduced, stored in a retrieval system, or transmitted, in
photocopying, recording or otherwise, without the prior
permission of the copyright owner

ISBN 978-1-911445-99-9

Typeset in Garamond 11.75/15.5 pt by
Palimpsest Book Production Ltd, Falkirk, Stirlingshire

Printed and bound in Great Britain by
Clays Ltd, St Ives plc

www.endeavourpress.com

CONTENTS

PREFACE

The aim of this book is to give some idea of the French Revolution to the general reader who is not an historical student, and more especially to the young reader. With thea causes which led up to it I have not attempted to deal,* as I wished to devote all my space to the Revolution itself. My narrative is based on many years' study of contemporary documents, and I have tried to embody the results of modern historical research. My object has been to present as accurate, clear, and truthful a picture as it lay in my power to draw, and I have striven after impartiality in my estimates of character, and have never condemned hastily. Many incidents I have omitted, often most reluctantly, since I was obliged to select those which seemed to me to have most bearing on the continuous narrative. I have endeavoured

* Among them, the influence of Freemasonry has been much exaggerated by some historians.

to explain political terms, remembering how often I was puzzled myself when I began my studies. For the same reason I have used the simplest forms of surnames, all the more willingly because it was the tendency of the Revolution to shorten, while it was the tendency of the *ancien régime* to pile one name on the top of the other. I have based my conclusions on the best evidence I could find, weighing one report against another; but in so large a subject there are departments, such as War and Diplomacy, which require expert knowledge, and these I have taken on trust, choosing my authorities with care.

It is painful to me, I must acknowledge, to be unable to mention in foot-notes my authorities and my obligations to historians. Pioneers publish documents and sift evidence, and those who come after use the results of their labours; therefore let me thank them here, and assure them of my deep and permanent gratitude.

Every book which contains original documents or serious research helps one to form a judgement, and this makes it hard to draw up a bibliography. But there is a large body of documents, common to all historians, upon which a solid first-hand knowledge must be founded; namely, the pamphlets and newspapers of the Revolution. Among the newspapers the *Moniteur*, which has been reprinted, stands supreme; but it has to be corrected and supplemented by the procès-verbaux of the three Assemblies, and by other papers.

Next in order come compilations of documents; e. g. the forty volumes of Buchez and Roux's *Histoire Parlementaire*, containing much that is inaccessible elsewhere; the great books on the history of Paris during the Revolution, M. Maurice Tourneux's *La Bibliographie de l'histoire de Paris pendant la Révolution Française*, and M. Alexandre Tuetey's *Repertoire general des sources manuscrites de l'histoire de Paris pendant la Révolution française*, containing careful inventories, the one of printed, the other of manuscript papers; M. Aulard's *Recueil des actes du Comité de Salut public*, containing the records of that Committee and its correspondence with Representatives on Mission; other, less voluminous works.

Mortimer-Ternaux's *Histoire de la Terreur*, 8 vols. (1862, &c.), though anything but impartial, is a mine of documents.

Letters are a great source of information, but it is well to make sure that they are genuine, as many historical letters have been forged.

Much may be learnt from Memoirs, though they can seldom be depended on if written long after the event.

For a bibliography on the first part of the Revolution, I may, perhaps, refer to my *Life of Bar nave*, ii. 371-8.

For special obligations I would mention here:

M. Aulard's *Orateurs de la Révolution*; *L'Assemblée*

Constituante, 1 vol., *L'Assemblée Législative et la Convention*, 2 vols.; an inspiring book which I would recommend to those who wish to push their studies further.

Also M. Albert Sorel's *L'Europe et la Révolution française*, vols. 1-4, in many ways a model history.

I owe much:

To two modern magazines: *La Révolution française*, long identified with M. Aulard's name, and M. Albert Mathiez's *Annales révolutionnaires*. In the second of these many of M. Mathiez's researches on Robespierre, Danton, &c., were originally published; some of these papers have been issued again in book form.

To the researches of M. Armand Brette on the Constituent Assembly.

To the researches of M. Charles Vatel on the Girondins and Charlotte Corday.

To the researches of M. Claude Perroud on the Girondins and Madame Roland.

For the wars, to M. Arthur Chuquet's *Guerres de la Révolution*, 11 vols. (1892, &c.); to Jomini's *Histoire critique et militaire des Guerres de la Révolution* (1820, &c.), and to F.-E. de Toulongeon's *Histoire de France depuis la Révolution de 1789* (1801, &c.).

For the war in la Vendée, to M. Ch.-L. Chassin's Études documentaires sur la Révolution française, *in 10 vols. under* various titles (1892, &c.), and to Savary's *Guerres des Vendéens et des Chou arts coutre la République* (1824, &c.).

For the history of the Revolutionary Tribunal, to M. Emile Campardon's *Le Tribunal révolutionnaire de Paris*, 2 vols. (1866), and to M. H. Wallon's *Histoire du Tribunal révolutionnaire de Paris*, 6 vols. (1880-2).

Among single books I owe much to:

de Tocqueville's *L'Ancien Regime et la Révolution*.

Léonce de Lavergne's *Les Assemblées Provinciales sous Louis XVI*.

For the siege of the Bastille, to M. Jules Flammermont's *La journée du 14 juillet 1789* (1892).

For the Commune of the Summer and Autumn of 1792, to M. F. Braesch's *La Commune du dix Août, 1792* (1911).

For the India Company business, to M. A. Mathiez's *L'Affaire de la Compagnie des Indes* (1920).

For the dissensions in the Comité de Salut public, in 1794, to M. Lévy-Schneider's paper in *La Révolution Française* (p. 97, vol. 38, 1900), called *Les démêles dans le Comité du Salut public avant le 9 thermidor*.

For the campaign resulting in the battle of Fleurus, to Comt. V. Dupuis' *Les Operations militaires sur la Sambre en 1794* (1907).

For the Jacobins on the 8th and 9th Thermidor, 1794, to M. Georges Michon's *Les séances des 8 et 9 thermidor au club des Jacobins*, in *Annales Historiques de la Révolution française*, Nov. 1924, p. 497.

For Robespierre on the 9th Thermidor, to M. A.

Mathiez's *Robespierre a la Commune le 9 thermidor*, in the same magazine, July 1924, p. 289.

For the revolt of the 1st Prairial, an III, to *Le Conventionnel Goujon*, by MM. L. Thénard and R. Guyot (1908).

For the revolt of Vendémiaire, an IV, to M. Henry Zivy's *Le treize Vendémiaire an IV*.

In conclusion, my debt to the British Museum and to the unfailing courtesy of its Staff is great, and I should like to record it; and also to offer thanks to all the friends who have helped me, especially to Mr. G. F. Bradby for invaluable advice and criticism, and to Mrs. H. C. Bradby for assistance with proofs.

E. D. BRADBY.
October, 1925.

PART I –

THE CONSTITUENT ASSEMBLY

I

THE CALLING OF THE STATES-GENERAL 1787 – 1789 (4TH MAY)

When the ordinary Englishman who has read the usual novels and magazine stories thinks of the French Revolution, it probably suggests to him, first of all, the guillotine, with scores of brave and handsome aristocrats rolling towards it in carts, amid the yells of a mob of fiends in red caps. But to the ordinary Frenchman the Revolution will probably suggest first of all 'the ideas of 1789' – ideas which have nothing to do with the guillotine.

To explain briefly what they were, we may say that in the year 1789 it was the common belief of enlightened Frenchmen:

That all men ought to be free and to enjoy equal rights, because men were born to be brothers and not masters and slaves; in other words: Liberty, Equality, and Fraternity.

That all questions in every department of life ought to be decided by justice and not by favour.

That every nation has a right to choose its own form of government, and no nation has a right to oppress another.

That every human being ought to be ready to sacrifice property, and hope of gain, and ease, and life, for the good of his country and because he loves it.

The Revolution was an attempt to put these ideas into practice. In the course of this attempt the French, as we shall see, met with great difficulties and made great mistakes; they were forced to fight for their existence against enemies both without and within, and in the heat of a tremendous conflict they forgot most of the ideas with which they had started. But the ideas, though for the time they seemed dead, did not perish; they have never ceased to inspire lovers of freedom, and a German Professor was right when, in 1914, he called the great War then opening: 'a struggle between Kultur* and the ideas of 1789.'

The causes of the Revolution were many and lay deep, and it is impossible in a short history such as this to deal with them fully, but in order to understand

* The German ideal of educated efficiency.

4

why a revolution of some kind had become necessary in France, we must take a glance at that country towards the close of the eighteenth century.

Old France was composed of a number of Provinces, great and small, which had come under the French Crown at different times, some by conquest, some by consent. The customs, the taxes, the privileges and even the laws of these Provinces varied, and it has often been said that they were more like a bundle of sticks tied together by the Monarchy than like branches growing out of a tree. Most of them had once possessed a sort of local Parliament, called the 'States', which managed their 'home affairs'; and besides this, the Provinces used to send representatives to a general assembly, called the States-General, which was summoned by the King from time to time and had the right to consent to taxes before he could levy them. But the Kings had grown despotic; they had ruled without the States-General since 1614, and the local 'States' only survived at all in about a quarter of the kingdom; the rest had long since ceased to exist or had been suppressed. The Provinces, regrouped into thirty-two divisions, were ruled by 'Intendants', who were supreme in all civil affairs and were responsible only to the King and his ministers; and as the King and his Ministers made all the laws, the Government was, in fact, an autocracy. Everything depended ultimately on what was called *le bon plaisir du roi*; good Ministers and good Intendants might rule well and wisely, but they might be succeeded, if the King so pleased, by bad ones, who could sweep away all their reforms.

In practice the King's power was limited by custom; moreover, when public opinion was strongly against a law, that law could not be enforced. Thus many laws became dead letters or were only enforced occasionally. This was the case with the laws against Protestants, who existed on sufferance merely, being forbidden to worship in their own way or to engage in any profession. These laws had at first been stringently enforced by the Courts, but before the Revolution persecution had ceased, and they were often able to evade such laws with the connivance of their enlightened Catholic neighbours.

It was hard enough on the French to have no part in making their laws, and this was not the only oppression under which they suffered. By ancient custom the nation was divided into three classes, called 'Estates' or 'Orders': the Clergy, the Nobles, and the 'third Estate' (Tiers-état). The first two were the 'privileged Orders'; they alone might hunt or keep pigeons, and, as chief privilege, they were excused payment of certain taxes and paid others at a light rate. Thus the burden of taxation fell almost entirely on the Tiers-état, the great bulk of the nation – peasants, workmen, soldiers, sailors, lawyers, doctors, every one engaged in any trade or industry. They were, besides, looked down upon as inferiors. High places were not for them; they could not become judges of the Superior Courts, nor, towards the end of the century, officers in Army or Navy;* they could only rise by favour of the great, and when they did thus rise they were made nobles. And as all the children of a noble were noble too and inherited the privileges of their father, the Orders were always kept apart and the nobles were encouraged to think themselves beings of a superior race.

The Clergy owned vast estates, and while the curés (the parish priests), who were poor, worked hard and were loved and respected, too many of the Bishops and higher Clergy led worldly and luxurious lives and brought Religion into contempt. Both Nobles and Clergy depended on the King for riches and promotion, and those who wished to gain his favour were obliged to dance attendance at Court; if they were successful they were rewarded with places and pensions for themselves and their friends – all at the expense of the nation.

The taxes, out of which these rewards were provided, seemed to have been devised to discourage industry and commerce and to press hardest on the poor. They

* This law was often evaded.

were of two kinds, the direct and the indirect. The most famous of the direct taxes was the *taille*, a heavy tax which carried other taxes in its train; levied in some Provinces on landed property and in others on income of any kind. The Nobles and Clergy were, in theory and often in practice, free from this tax. The indirect taxes were not collected by the Crown but let out to Farmers-General, who paid a fixed sum to the Treasury and made a profit out of them. The most famous was the *gabelle*, the salt tax,* light in some Provinces, heavy in others. Smuggling between the Provinces was frequent and could be punished with death. Another burden was the *corvée*, an obligation to which only the Tiers-état were subjected, by which, at this time, they were forced to make the roads and keep them in repair. In some Provinces they were allowed to pay a tax instead. Taxes were continually increased, as the Crown spent more and more lavishly and floundered deeper and deeper into debt, but no accounts were rendered to the nation.

The Tiers-état had not done with taxation when they had satisfied the King's demands; there were *dimes* (tithes) to be paid to the Clergy, and many kinds of 'feudal dues' were owed to the Nobles, relics of the days when the vassal paid his lord for protection. The Nobles, who

* Salt was of great importance as a means of preserving food.

had lost most of their power, had ceased to be protectors, and the peasants, who often owned land themselves,
had ceased to be vassals, but they still had to pay their
lord of the manor for the right to buy and to sell; they
had to grind their corn in his mills and to make their
wine in his presses; they had to pay him tolls on roads
and ferries. Sometimes, even, though this had become
rare, they had to work for him on occasion for nothing,
and to render him services such as beating the marshes
to keep the frogs quiet. Other taxes, tolls, and privileges,
of the same nature, vexed commerce in the towns. Thus
the industrious classes were hampered at every turn,
much land was ill-cultivated, and the condition of the
poor was often truly miserable.

Where rights and customs were so varied and so
complicated, difficult questions were always arising
which had to be settled by going to law. The French of
all classes were fond of going to law and took great
interest in all that went on in the Law Courts. There
were in France thirteen supreme Courts, called
Parlements, each independent of the other; the Parlement
of Paris, the most important of them, had jurisdiction
over one third of the kingdom. Under each Parlement
was a host of lesser Courts. There was no trial by jury,
everything was decided by the judges, and witnesses
were only heard in the lower Courts; the higher Courts
heard written reports of what the witnesses had said

and the arguments of advocates. Punishments were cruel, torture was still legal and criminals were still broken on the wheel. The people had learnt from the Code of the Law that property mattered more than life, and were accustomed to look on at lengthy and barbarous executions. Yet, in spite of drawbacks, the Law was in general well administered, the judges were often upright and honourable men, and the weak and oppressed found brave and generous defenders among the advocates. The Government had, however, found two means of over-riding the Law; first, the King had the power of removing any offender from the jurisdiction of the Court which was about to try him and of sending him to be tried elsewhere, or by a special commission. Secondly, the King could grant writs, called *lettres de cachet*, by virtue of which any person could be sent to any place in France, including prison, and could be kept there, without inquiry or trial, as long as the King pleased. Any man who opposed the Government could be got rid of in this manner, and the Ministers could oblige great families by putting away their inconvenient members quietly and without scandal.

The French who had to endure these ignominies were never a servile and backward race, like their neighbours the Germans; on the contrary they were bold and independent, quick to turn their Government into ridicule in song and epigram, advanced in all arts and sciences. Their good society was the wittiest and most brilliant in Europe, their authors the most renowned. Many observers, who found the French always polite, lively, cheerful and ready to be amused with trifles, thought them frivolous, and it is true that Court circles were frivolous and thoughtless. But all over France, before the Revolution, a very serious generation had grown up. Its members had come under the influence of the 'Philosophers', writers of whom the three greatest were Voltaire, the sceptic who hated tyranny and superstition and scoffed at the Religion of his day; Rousseau, fiery and sentimental, whose doctrine it was that men were happiest and best when they lived most naturally, and that all government depended on a mutual agreement between the King and his people; Montesquieu who taught the meaning and reason of Laws. These authors had led Frenchmen to think deeply on politics, and educated men, in almost every town, were aware that they were living in servitude and were sighing after liberty. The desire for liberty was not confined to the men of the Tiers-état, many of the younger Nobles shared it. During the War of Independence waged against Britain by the United States of America, a young enthusiast for Republics, the marquis de Lafayette, had crossed the Atlantic to fight as a volunteer for the Americans; his action was admired and his example followed. The

French Government afterwards joined in the war, not from sympathy with America but from a wish to cripple England; and many Nobles served in the army with distinction and came back with ideas about free governments and the rights of man which they spread through high society.

But however much thinking men might desire a change of government, there were obstacles in the way, so great that they seemed insuperable. The first and greatest was the difficulty of taking common action. Political meetings were not allowed, and the Press was not free, for the Government regulated what people might read. No book or pamphlet might be printed till it had passed the censors. Newspapers had to obtain a licence and each number was liable to be censored; very few papers were allowed, and in these few part of the space was filled with bad poetry and acrostics. It may be imagined how bitterly thinking men felt these restrictions.

Another obstacle lay in the fact that the bulk of the nation was not unhappy enough to rebel; and this was especially the case with the educated classes who were the natural leaders of the poor and ignorant masses. In times of famine there were revolts and riots, but disorders were always put down and things went on as before. It was an age of progress too; in spite of bad government, the Tiers-état was growing richer and more prosperous, and the Nobles were growing less exclusive. Reform was also made difficult by a curious abuse called the 'venality of offices', which interested large numbers of the well-to-do in maintaining the existing state of things and gave them a kind of independence. The Crown had long been accustomed to sell public offices, it was one of many expedients used to raise money. Thus, an office was 'created' – it might be that of a judge, or a town-councillor, or a minor administrator – and the right to hold it was sold, not to any one indiscriminately, but to a person who possessed certain qualifications, sometimes to the man who already filled it. And, in order to obtain a higher price, it was sold in perpetuity, so that the holder could sell it again, or leave it by will – always to a duly qualified person. In this manner offices passed from holder to holder like goods, and large sums of money were invested in them. The men who had bought them could not be removed without great difficulty, and owed no gratitude to the Crown.

Another circumstance which tended to delay change was the affection felt for the King. The French, who prided themselves on their loyalty, had always loved their Kings whenever their Kings gave them a chance. They had almost contrived to love the last King, Louis XV, one of the most heartless, selfish old sinners who ever lived, though there was nothing about him to love but a handsome face and a kingly presence; and their affection for his young grandson, Louis XVI, who succeeded him in 1774, was enthusiastic. There was, indeed, much to admire in Louis XVI; his life was pure and virtuous, his tastes were simple, he was a truly religious man who desired what he thought to be the good of his people and followed his conscience. Unfortunately his conscience was not an enlightened guide, and though he was naturally truthful, he had been brought up with the idea that it is lawful to resort to lying when other means of gaining a good object fail. He was also slow, timid, rather stupid, and instead of trusting to his own honest judgement, he let himself be influenced by the last person who had given him advice, persuaded each time that he had at length discovered the right course to pursue. This habit made his conduct unstable, and though he did not intend to deceive and betray he ended by doing both. His subjects, who knew his good qualities, blamed his ministers for all the bad measures that were taken, and continued to believe in him. In appearance Louis was neither ill-looking nor handsome; his face was large, his features heavy and his air stolid. His two chief amusements were hunting and the making of locks for doors. He was a poor talker, he had none of the small gracious ways of a king, and the aristocracy despised him, thinking him undignified and unroyal.

One royal quality, however, he had; he was firmly convinced that God alone had placed him on his throne, and that he was responsible for what he did to God, and not to his people. His people, on their part, were growing to believe, as firmly, that he was King because they willed it, and that he was therefore responsible to them. In spite of all drawbacks Louis might have done well and survived the Revolution, had he not had always at his side his evil angel, in the shape of the Queen whom he loved and admired.

Queen Marie-Antoinette, a daughter of the Empress Maria-Theresa of Austria, had been brought to France at the age of fifteen, and married to Louis, a shy, boorish youth, who was then Dauphin.* The little Dauphine found herself planted alone in a corrupt Court, where her one link with home was the Austrian Ambassador, Mercy, a wily diplomatist who taught her to put Austria secretly first and France second. Marie-Antoinette cared neither for Austria nor for France, but she learnt to be deceitful, though thanks to her proud and open nature she was never half as deceitful as her advisers wished. The lively girl grew up into a fascinating woman; handsome, graceful, dignified, with the air and carriage of a queen, a charming manner, and a heart kind enough to wish every one round her

* The heir to the Crown of France was called the Dauphin.

to be happy. For many years she had no children, her husband was nothing of a companion, and she tried to fill her empty life with a round of pleasures. She cast aside much of the burdensome and foolish Court etiquette, and as, at the same time, she associated chiefly with a set of dissolute nobles and was imprudent in her conduct, it is small wonder that she was thought to be wicked when she was only careless and giddy. Worse still, at a time when the Finances were in a bad state and there was much suffering, she was grossly extravagant. She spent much on herself and she could refuse nothing to her friends, who profited by her weakness to get all they could out of her. Unending gifts, at the expense of the nation, were lavished on her two chief friends, the princesse de Lamballe, a young widow, and the duchesse de Polignac, who brought a rapacious family to Court with her. The Queen, once popular, had completely lost the nation's heart, and at the time of the Revolution she was bitterly hated in France, while her reputation stood low in other countries. So ill did people think of her that a story of how a depraved Cardinal, whom she detested, had bribed her with a diamond necklace to admit him to Court favour, was believed. This tale, quite untrue as far as she was concerned,* made a great scandal

* Some swindlers got the diamond necklace from the Cardinal by forging letters from the Queen and impersonating her.

and did her much harm. Yet before 1789 she had finished with youthful follies, was a fond mother to her children and had become attached to her husband. Her influence over him was strong and she used it to make and unmake ministers and to block reforms. Her ambition was to transmit the power of the Crown undiminished to her son.

In May 1789 she had three children living, but the second, a sickly boy, died in the summer, leaving her with a girl of ten, known as Madame Royale, and Louis-Charles, a pretty, healthy boy of four, who succeeded his brother as Dauphin. The King had two brothers, both married to dull wives: Louis, comte de Provence, always called Monsieur, who was stout, fairly clever, and untrustworthy, and Charles, comte d'Artois, a gay, dissipated young spark, who prided himself on being the height of fashion. A young sister who lived with the King, Madame Elisabeth, a good and pious princess, and two old and rather disagreeable aunts completed the family. There were other princes of the royal house of Bourbon, notably the heads of two distant branches, the Princes of Conde and Conti, and the King's distant cousin, the duc d'Orléans: a man with a round, moon-like, blotchy face, good-natured, immoral and contemptible, yet immensely popular, because he took the side of the people. He squandered his enormous fortune and, in order to make money, cut down the trees in the garden of his palace in Paris, called the Palais-Royal, and built round it arcades of shops which he let. The garden, thus transformed, and replanted, became one of the most crowded resorts of Paris.

The King, like almost every one else, felt that reforms were necessary, and from time to time they were attempted. But little could be done without setting the Finances in order, and as soon as a minister began to economize, he roused the enmity of the courtiers, who were accustomed to get what they wanted for the asking. One reforming Minister, the great and wise Turgot, fell early in the reign after less than two years in office. Soon after Turgot's fall, the Genevese Banker, Necker, an excellent man of business, was appointed Minister, though he was a Swiss and a Protestant. Necker was an honest man, indifferent to riches, and as both he and his friends knew how to make the most of his real virtues, he had the confidence of the public. He partly restored credit, he carried out some reforms, and he even published accounts. But after nearly five years in office, he too fell, in 1781. His successor in 1783, the light-hearted and plausible Calonne, pursued a different plan; he went on borrowing and spending without heed to the future, and piled up a deficit in the Finances which he cleverly concealed. This reck-lessness hastened a crisis.

One slight if vexatious check on the powers of the Kings of France remained; they had ceased to summon the States-General, but it was still necessary to present new laws to the Parlements to be registered in their records; and until a Parlement had thus registered a law, it could not be enforced in the territory over which that Parlement had jurisdiction. The Parlements also had the right of presenting remonstrances to the King. Now the Judges, who had bought their places and could not be removed, had a strong sense of the authority of the Parlements with no fear of angering the King, and the Parlements were in the habit of making themselves troublesome to the Government by criticizing and opposing good laws and bad laws alike; sometimes they even refused to register them. Various means had been used to silence the Parlements; they were forced to register at sittings called 'Beds of Justice', at which the King issued his orders in person; they were 'exiled', i.e. sent away to other places, by *lettres de cachet*; Louis XV had actually dismissed them and put new, reformed, Parlements in their place. But the Parlements were tenacious, the lawyers supported them, the people applauded their resistance, and in the long run they had always got the best of it and had returned in triumph.

In 1786 an increase of revenue to fill up the growing deficit was urgently needed, and the obvious way of raising it was to make Clergy and Nobles pay their share of the taxes, and to call the States-General to sanction this important change in the laws. But the King and his Ministers were determined to go on ruling without the States-General, and Calonne, who knew that the Parlements would oppose fresh taxation, persuaded Louis to summon an Assembly of the 'Notables', believing that if the Notables agreed to his taxes, the Parlements must needs agree too. The Notables were Princes, Bishops, great Nobles, Presidents of Parlements and other dignitaries, and a few Mayors of towns. The King nominated them, therefore this meeting was not a great step forward; yet it was a step, and at the news of it France began to rouse herself as if from a long sleep, and lovers of freedom saw the dawn of hope.

The Notables met in February 1787 and sat till May. Calonne laid his new taxes before them, with other measures of much-needed reform, one of the chief being the establishment of Provincial Assemblies – a sort of County Council – in the Provinces which had lost their 'States'. At the same time he was obliged to reveal the deficit in the Finances, and the indignation excited both by his reforms and his recklessness was so great that the King was constrained to dismiss him. The Notables accepted many of the reforms, but made it clear that the majority would resist the moderate taxation of the privileged Orders which Calonne had proposed, and Calonne's successor, Loménie de Brienne, an Archbishop, afterwards a Cardinal, who adopted Calonne's plans, was compelled to turn to the Parlements for the registration of the new edicts. The Parlement of Paris registered certain edicts quietly, but when two edicts imposing taxes were presented, a stamp tax and the new land-tax to which the Nobles were to be subject, the Judges refused to register them on the ground that the Parlements were incompetent in this matter, and appealed to the King to summon the States-General which alone had the power of legalizing taxes.

The King held a 'Bed of Justice' on August 6th, at which the Parlement was forced to register. But the Judges protested strongly, and as they continued to protest and ordered the prosecution of Calonne, Brienne had them all sent off to Troyes by *lettres de cachet*. They went, loaded with the blessings of an admiring people; but Troyes was dull after Paris and, against the wishes of their leaders, they soon made their peace with Brienne. The two obnoxious new taxes were withdrawn, the Parlement registered an edict continuing an old tax, and was recalled to Paris.

Brienne, however, was badly in want of money, and as he could not raise it by taxes he determined to try a loan. This too had to be registered by the Parlement, and to ensure obedience a 'Royal Sitting' was held, – a sitting at which the King was supposed to consult his Parlement and not merely to issue orders. On grand occasions the Princes of the Blood Royal and certain great Lords, called the Peers, sat with the Parlement, and they were present at the 'Royal Sitting' of the 19th November 1787. The Chancellor presented the edict for the loan and made an announcement: all power, he said, belonged to the King, who was responsible to God alone; the country had done very well without the States-General for a century and a half, and the Provincial Assemblies would be far more useful than any States-General could be; nevertheless, the King would be graciously pleased to summon the States-General in five years' time. Several Judges then spoke, pleading earnestly with the King to grant the desire of all and summon the States-General at once. One of them, d'Eprémesnil, a dark, fiery man with a silvery voice, was so eloquent that Louis began to hesitate; but the Chancellor whispered something in his ear, and he ordered the registration of the loan. The duc d'Orléans protested that this was illegal; the Judges protested. It was all in vain, and a few days later two Judges were sent to distant fortresses while the Duke was ordered into the country.

The Parlement continued to protest, remonstrating against the use of *lettres de cachet*, and demanding the return of the Duke and the two Judges. The other Parlements joined in, and now there was a chorus of Parlements declaring that they had no power to register taxes which had not been sanctioned by the States-General, and claiming to speak for the nation. They had no legal right to speak for the nation, but the Tiers-état were glad to hear voices raised for the old rights of France, and the Nobles and Clergy, many of whom were strongly opposed to the encroachments of the Crown, felt much the same. It was clearly the wish of the whole nation that the States-General should be summoned.

By the spring of 1788 the continuous resistance of the Parlements was putting the Government in a difficult position, and Brienne resolved to end resistance by a sudden stroke. He prepared secretly edicts which were to be forced upon all the Parlements on the same day; edicts by which they were shorn of most of their powers, by which their prime power, the right of registering the laws, was taken from them and given to a new Court of Grandees. As usual, various reforms were to be made at the same time, in order to pacify the public.

D'Eprémesnil found out what the edicts were to be, and reported at once to the Parlement. At his proposal a protest was drawn up, and all present, including the Peers, took an oath that they would never sit in any new Court holding the rights which belonged to the Parlement. When the Ministers heard of this protest, they ordered the arrest of d'Eprémesnil and of another resisting Judge named Goislard, both of whom took refuge with the Parlement. Soldiers were then sent to surround the Palais de Justice where the Parlement sat, and during the night an officer of the Gardes-françaises, one of the King's special regiments, came into the hall, among the red-robed Judges, to make the arrests. The President refused to give up his colleagues, and told the officer that he must carry out the King's orders on his own responsibility. The officer answered that he did not know d'Eprémesnil and Goislard by sight, and demanded that they should be pointed out to him. At this, the Judges cried with one voice: "We are all d'Eprémesnil and Goislard!" and the officer had to retire discomfited. He came again in the morning (6th May) with an official of the Parlement, and ordered him to point out d'Eprémesnil and Goislard. The official, who knew them well, looked round the room, and said that he did not see d'Eprémesnil, and once more the officer of the Guards had to retire. But the two Judges gave themselves up to save the generous official from punishment, and were sent away to fortresses in the South.

Two days after, on May 8th, 1788, the King held a 'Bed of Justice' in the Paris Parlement; as for the others, the military took possession of their Courts and kept them prisoners till the registers had been signed.

This measure set the whole kingdom in a ferment. The Parlements had been forbidden to meet or to speak, but they still met privately and still protested; remonstrances and petitions for the recall of the Parlements and the convocation of the States-General poured in upon the King from every side, and in several Provinces the Government was defied and a movement was set on foot to claim the old rights of the Province. Two things must be noted with regard to these movements: first, that those who took part in them were risking their heads, and next, that the King was always addressed with loyalty and affection, blame being given to his Ministers alone. "Give us the greatest of benefits, that of being always able to love you", said one very daring and outspoken address.

The two most important movements were in Brittany and Dauphine. In Brittany the ill-treatment of the Parlement of Rennes led to riots among the people, which were suppressed by the military. A large number of Nobles met to protest, and sent deputies to Paris with a letter for the King. The King did not receive the letter, and the deputies were clapped into the Bastille, the great fortress of Paris, used as a State prison.

In Dauphine there was something like a revolution.

One of the reforms by which Brienne set most store was the creation of Provincial Assemblies to take the place of the lost 'States'. Most of the Parlements had registered this edict without demur; but three, one of which was the Parlement of Grenoble (the capital of Dauphine), had refused. The men of Dauphine did not want a Provincial Assembly as a gift from the King, they wanted to get back their own 'States' which existed as the right of the people.

After the 8th May, the Parlement of Grenoble, which continued to protest, was sent into the country by *lettres de cachet*. But this Parlement was specially beloved, and when the day came for its departure, the people suddenly rose, took the horses from the Judges' carriages, defied the troops of the garrison who were called out to disperse them, and refused to move till the Parlement had held a sitting in the Palace. This insurrection (7th June 1788), in which blood was shed, is known as 'the day of tiles', because tiles were torn from the house-roofs and hurled at the soldiers in the streets.

The better-educated people conducted a resistance equally bold but legal and peaceable. The 'Notables' of Grenoble met, though the authorities forbade it, and called upon the Province to send representatives to a meeting of the Three Orders. In vain the Government threatened and sent troops, the whole population, Clergy, Nobles and Tiers-état, was as one man. On July 21st, 1788 the meeting of the Three Orders was held at Vizille, near Grenoble, under the eyes of the troops, and resolutions were passed to beg the King for the convocation of the States-General, the recall of the Parlement, and the restoration of their own 'States'. The Three Orders also resolved that they would never separate their cause from that of the other Provinces, or abandon the rights of the nation.

The effect of this meeting, on the top of the general outcry, was so potent that the Government changed its tactics, and on August 8th an edict suspended the new Court for the registration of laws, and fixed May 1st, 1789 for the meeting of the States-General.* Brienne, who had attempted fresh repressive measures in Dauphine, was dismissed at the end of the month and, to the joy of all France, the popular Necker became Minister once more; the prisoners were released, the Parlements recalled and the edicts they had been forced to register were withdrawn.

This was not the only service done by the Three Orders of Dauphine. They wrung their 'States' out of the Government by steady persistence, and in all their meetings set an example of unity; Clergy and Nobles readily giving up their privileges and all three Orders voting together.

---

* The date was afterwards altered more than once.

The States-General having been definitely promised, the attention of the country was now directed to the question of how they should be formed. There were two main questions on which precedents set in former States-General varied. One: should there be as many deputies for the Tiers-état as for the two other Orders together? The other: should the Orders all vote together – the 'vote by head' this was called – or should each vote separately? The Tiers-état being by far the largest Order, it seemed only fair that it should have most deputies; but if the Orders voted separately this would be of no avail, for in that case the vote of each Order would only count as one in the final decision, and the 'Privileged Orders' could always join together and out-vote the Tiers-état. This would not be just, but it was what many of the Nobles desired; so did the Parlement of Paris, which had begun to be afraid that things were going too far; so did a second Assembly of the Notables, which sat in the winter.

But the Tiers-état had long been considered the natural ally of the Crown against the hostility of Clergy and Nobles, the King and Queen were in favour of trying conciliation, and Necker wished to engage the gratitude of the people; so on December 27th, the "double representation" of the Tiers-état was ordered. The question of the 'vote by head' was left unsettled. At the end of January 1789, the States-General was convoked and the elections ordered; the 'States' of Dauphine had already elected their deputies without waiting for orders.

The winter was one of the coldest ever known, and since much of the harvest had been ruined by a fierce July hailstorm, the sufferings of the poor were severe; but hope was in the air, better days were coming, so they believed, the States-General would set things to rights and give them bread. From one end to another France was humming with discussion and men were aflame with aspirations and lofty thoughts. Ladies talked about the affairs of the nation in their drawing-rooms, gentlemen in newly-founded Clubs and Societies, and there was a perfect rain of pamphlets about the States-General and the Constitution it might, could, and should give the country. For in the previous July, Brienne, in one of his attempts to quiet the kingdom, had invited every one to discuss the States-General, and by the winter every man of mark who had views on the subject was publishing them, as were also a great many nobodies. The most famous of these pamphlets was one written by the Abbé Siéyes, called, *Qu'est-ce que le Tiers-état?* which opened thus: "What is the Tiers-état? – Everything – What has it been in the political order up to the present? – Nothing – What does it ask? – To become something."

The elections, which filled the spring months with

excitement, were held in a complicated way. France was divided into many constituencies of every variety of size and importance, and in each of these the Tiers-état held 'Primary Assemblies'* in the towns and parishes of the district. Any Frenchman of twenty-five and upwards who lived in the place and paid taxes, could vote in these Assemblies. The 'Primary Assemblies' chose 'Electors' and all the 'Electors' of a constituency met together and chose deputies to the States-General. At the election of deputies, votes were taken by ballot in a lengthy way. The Nobles and Clergy chose their own deputies, each Order in meetings of its own, except in Dauphine where the three Orders voted together for all the deputies. Each Assembly drew up what were called *cahiers*: books in which they wrote what reforms they most wanted, what they wished their deputies to do, and what sort of a constitution they hoped to see set up. The honour of becoming a deputy was much coveted, and in general the best and ablest men were chosen, men of worth and character, who were not only clever but trusted and respected by their neighbours. A large number of deputies were lawyers, for the lawyers had been foremost in the cause of liberty; there were also a good many doctors.

As the time for the meeting of the States-General

* This term was not used till a little later.

drew near, hopes and fears about what was going to happen grew more definite. The King, who was a good deal under Necker's influence, was ready to consent to reforms and knew that he must part with some of his power; but as he was also under the influence of the Queen and the Court party, he did not mean to part with a jot more than he could help. The Queen had formerly protected Necker, but at this time she and all her friends and favourites, together with the comte d'Artois and some of the Princes, were set against any concessions.

Necker was friendly to reforms, but he imagined that the Tiers-état, grateful for what he had done, would be easily led, and he did not mean them to go too far. The great majority of the deputies of the Tiers-état was resolved to win the 'vote by head' first, and then that the States-General should establish a free and just constitution and put an end to despotic rule. Among the deputies of the Nobles, the majority was resolved against the 'vote by head' and wanted as few reforms made as possible, and this was the case with the Bishops and higher Clergy. But a minority of the Nobles, Lafayette being one, entirely agreed with the Tiers-état, and the 'low Clergy' as they were called, i.e. the curés, many of whom had been elected deputies, were favourably disposed.

The States-General had been summoned to meet at

Versailles at the end of April, and the deputies travelled thither in little bands of friends, many of them making the long journey away from home and family with reluctance, but settling into their lodgings in full confidence that they would soon be back, with their task done. There were, roughly, 300 deputies of the Clergy, 300 of the Nobles, and 600 of the Tiers-état, but all did not arrive in time for the opening, indeed the Paris elections were not yet over. The huge and beautiful Palace of Versailles, the King's habitual residence, had been built by Louis XIV. It stood at one end of the town, with great gardens and magnificent terraces, all open to the public, stretching behind it, and large courts in front, shut off by tall iron railings from a still larger open space called the 'place d'Armes'. From this 'place' branched out, like fan-sticks, three wide streets planted with avenues of trees; streets of palaces and fine stone houses. The central avenue led to Paris, eleven miles distant, and some way down it stood a vast hall called the 'Salle des Menus Plaisirs', flimsily built as a store-house for the properties used at the Palace in theatrical and other shows. This hall had been fitted up for the States-General with classic columns and wide galleries for spectators; it was suitably decorated with carpets and hangings and made a most imposing meeting place.

The deputies of the Tiers-état soon found that the

Court and the Court officials meant to keep them in their place. They were annoyed at the costume they were instructed to wear by the Master of the Ceremonies, the young marquis de Brézé; for while the Clergy wore their own best robes and the Nobles were splendid in black and cloth of gold, with lace cravats and white-plumed hats, the Tiers-état were in plain black, with muslin cravats, short lawyers' mantles and clergymen's hats – a kind of fancy dress. Again, when all the deputies were presented to the King on May 2nd, the Clergy and Nobles were received at once, but the Tiers-état were kept waiting for hours, and when they were at last admitted the Court ladies stared contemptuously at them as they were marched through the long gallery and halls of the Palace, and the King took hardly any notice of them beyond saying a kind word to a Breton farmer who wore his country clothes. The deputies, who had come with their hearts full of love and enthusiasm for the King, were somewhat chilled by this reception.

It was the custom for every assembly to hear mass in state, and this ceremony was celebrated with a pomp worthy of the occasion on Monday May 4th, a beautiful spring day. All Paris had come out to see the procession of the States-General escorting the Holy Sacrament across Versailles; the streets were lined by the King's Guards, every window was full and every house hung with tapestry or carpets. The deputies assembled in the church of Notre-Dame soon after seven o'clock, and waited for three hours before the King came with the Royal Family and the Court. After a short service the procession began to form; the clergy of Versailles led off, next came the Tiers-état, four abreast. They had embarrassed de Brézé sadly, when he tried to arrange them in correct order of precedence, by insisting that they would walk just as they happened to come out of church, and they had to wait outside in the hot sun for an hour and a half while he marshalled the Nobles, who came next. After the Nobles came the Clergy, the Bishops last, with the Holy Sacrament under a canopy, and with bands of music; then the Royal Family and the Court, in gorgeous array, followed by some of the Guards. The whole procession marched across the 'place' in front of the Palace, and on to the Cathedral of Saint-Louis, each man carrying a taper in his hand, and all the way the watching crowds greeted the Tiers-état with ringing cheers, received the Nobles and Clergy coldly, but applauded the duc d'Orléans, cheered Necker and acclaimed the King, whose face beamed with happiness. The Queen was not cheered, but her dignity and grace were much admired by the deputies of the Tiers-état. In Saint-Louis the Tiers-état again gave trouble to de Brézé by refusing to move from back seats where they had taken their places into seats still further back.

Mass was sung and a Bishop preached for an hour and three quarters; it was not a good sermon, but at one point he drew a picture of the sufferings of the poor under the taxes, so touching that many of the congregation were carried away and clapped vigorously. The service was not over till four o'clock.

It was a long day, full of joyful expectation; to-morrow the States-General would open, the Assembly that was to save France.

II

The Struggle with The King 5th May – 15th October 1789

On the morning of May 5th the galleries of the great Hall were packed with well-dressed spectators, watching with eager interest the entrance of the deputies, who were summoned in correct order from adjoining rooms, where they had assembled, and marshalled with due ceremony to their appointed places. De Brézé was in his glory, and the proceedings took several hours. At 12.30 the King arrived, with the Queen and the Court. Louis was welcomed with enthusiastic cheers as he took his place on the dais at one end of the Hall and looked down benignantly at his States-General. The Clergy were ranged along the wall on his right, the Nobles on his left, and the Tiers-état faced him at the other end of the Hall. All the deputies were seated on benches without backs, for whenever the King was present the use of seats with backs was forbidden by etiquette.

Louis opened the States-General in a short and much applauded speech; the Chancellor, whom no one could hear, followed; then came Necker, whose speech took two and a half hours to read. Every one was expecting the announcement of a decision about the 'vote by head', but it appeared from the speeches that the King was leaving the question for the States-General to decide themselves. Necker said explicitly that the Orders must begin by sitting apart, and that later on they might meet to discuss certain questions together, and his speech was a disappointment to the Tiers-état. It was the custom for deputies elected to any assembly to bring with them papers (credentials) to show that they had been properly elected, and the first task of an assembly was to see that these papers were in order; this was called 'verifying the credentials'. The three Orders were bidden to meet separately next day to do this, and the great Hall was assigned to the Tiers-état, while the Clergy and Nobles were given smaller halls close by.

When the Tiers-état, or the Commons, as they now began to call themselves, assembled in the morning, they found nothing ready for them; the Hall was being swept and the dais was being taken down. So, amid brooms and brushes and the noise of workmen, met

the six hundred men in whose hands the destiny of
France had been placed. Never were men in a more
difficult position; the Hall was remarkably bad for sound,
they had no platform to speak from, no rules to guide
them and hardly any political experience, and with all
this against them, they had to force the unwilling Clergy
and Nobles to join them, and to establish the 'vote by
head'. A single mistake might have ruined their cause;
but they made none. The Commons knew that many
of the poorer Clergy and a minority of the Nobles were
anxious to join them, and the position they took up
was this: there ought not to be, and there are not, three
separate Chambers in this States-General, but one; therefore the Commons, sitting in the great Hall, are only
the largest part of the assembly of the representatives
of the nation, waiting for the return of the two other
parts before they can begin to act. Many of the deputies had made up their minds that if the other Orders
refused to join, the Commons must act without them;
but not before every attempt had been made to bring
Clergy and Nobles in. Meanwhile the Commons had
to be careful to do nothing which would enable Clergy
or Nobles to say that they were acting like a separate
Chamber. So they did not verify their credentials and
they did not elect a President to keep order, as a complete
Chamber should do; they elected only a 'Dean', who
had but limited authority. There was, in fact, hardly

anything that they could do, and here too lay danger, for the people looked to the Commons for bread and for reforms, and if they lost the people's confidence, their power was gone. Nevertheless they had the courage to do almost nothing for five weeks. They were helped by sitting in the great Hall, as the public filled the galleries daily and followed every turn of the struggle with understanding and sympathy. The Clergy and Nobles did not admit outsiders.

One safe course of action was open to the Commons; they could invite the other Orders to come and verify their credentials with them, and this they did, again and again. The other Orders did not like to put themselves in the wrong with the nation by refusing outright, and they made evasive answers. Deputations passed to and fro, conferences were held between commissaries, but nothing came of them. Once the Commons had almost persuaded the Clergy to join them, when the King interfered by proposing more conferences. Then traps were laid for the Commons, first by the King and Necker and next by the Clergy, to entice them into acting as a separate Chamber; but the Commons were too wary to be caught. At length it became clear to every one that the majority of the Nobles would refuse to let their Chamber come in, while the Clergy would continue to waver, and the Commons felt that it was time to do something.

We may take a glance here at some of their leading men. Bailly, the first-elected deputy of Paris, well known as an astronomer and savant, and greatly respected for his integrity and solid worth, was one; a tall, grave, dignified man, with a long hatchet face. He was chosen as 'Dean' and led the Assembly with so much tact, wisdom, and courage that he gained all hearts. The abbe Siéyes, the last-elected deputy of Paris, had a great reputation as an original thinker, and though he was not a good speaker, his opinion was listened to with almost superstitious reverence. Siéyes was apt to be disdainful, and affected an air of mystery.

The deputy best known to the world and most talked about was a man of genius, the comte de Mirabeau, a noble who had been elected by the Tiers-état in Provence. His life had been full of adventures and scandals and quarrels with his family, especially with a harsh old father, whose chief idea of managing his rebellious son was to get the Ministers to imprison him by *lettres de cachet*. But neither persecution, nor injustice, nor well-deserved disgrace, nor the burden of debts which hung round him could ever crush the buoyant Mirabeau, or sour his warm heart and lovable nature; and such was the charm of his witty conversation, that when he met in private those who most disapproved of him, he could win them over. Mirabeau was a strange mixture of good and ill. He was one of the greatest orators the world has ever known, and yet, rather than take the trouble of getting up a difficult subject, he would often make his friends write his speeches for him in secret. He had espoused the cause of the people hotly and was a real lover of freedom, and yet he had an eye to Court favour too, because he wished to become the King's adviser. In consequence he sometimes hung back at critical moments and often acted a double part. His colleagues perceived this, and at first they distrusted him thoroughly. Mirabeau was a short, ugly man, with a large head proudly poised, and a striking face much pitted with small-pox; he used to boast laughingly of the terrifying powers of his ugliness and of his abundant crop of carefully curled and powdered hair.

Another deputy well-known already was Mounier, a young Judge from Grenoble who had been secretary to the Assemblies of Dauphine and the most prominent figure in the movement there; a delicate man with an iron will, honourable and imperious. The eloquent Le Chapelier, a spectacled Breton advocate with a somewhat mean face redeemed by a lofty forehead, was always to the front; so were two learned advocates from Paris, the red-faced Camus, honest and inflexible, and Target, whose speeches were thought too wordy and too long; so was Rabaut de Saint-Étienne, a Protestant minister from the South. Thouret, an advocate from

Rouen, high-principled, keen in face and intellect and a first-rate speaker, carried great weight, but was somewhat timid in these early days. One of the youngest deputies, Barnave, an advocate from Grenoble, fair-haired and kind-hearted, rose at once into notice for his ready eloquence, good sense, courage, and transparent honesty. The handsome Malouet, an able, upright man and a friend of Necker, annoyed his colleagues by raising objections to everything that was done, and tried to get the public excluded from the Hall. The public did not like him, and the galleries threatened him during one noisy sitting: an incident which he never forgave.

The deputies who wished to go forward, got to know each other in an institution called the Breton Club. Before the States-General opened, the numerous deputies of Brittany, fiery go-ahead men, had hired a large room to meet in. Like-minded deputies from other Provinces, especially from Dauphine and Anjou, were admitted almost from the first, and the meeting grew into a debating club where deputies talked the situation over and decided what they would do.

By June 10th the time had come, as we have said, for a decisive step and, on the motion of Siéyes, a last invitation to come and verify their credentials was sent to the other Orders, with the information that the roll-call would begin the same day. The other Orders replied, as they had replied before, that they would 'consider'. So, after waiting a certain time and sending the King a loyal address which explained the reasons of their action, the Commons began the roll-call. The names of all the deputies of the three Orders in each constituency were read out, and they were summoned to hand in their credentials. Only the Commons replied, for the other Orders were not there; but when it came to the turn of Poitiers, three bold curés answered to their names. As soon as this business was over, Siéyes made another motion; that the Assembly should now declare itself to be the Assembly of the nation and act as such. We, said the Commons, in effect, are the majority of the representatives of the nation; we have been sent here by the nation to give France a constitution, and if the privileged Orders will not join us, we will do it without them. Many deputies thought that this was too daring a step, and there was a long debate over it; but the motion passed, and on June 17th the Assembly 'constituted' itself as the National Assembly, passed its first decrees and made Bailly its first President. – At this moment arrived the King's answer to the loyal address sent him five days before; it was inscribed 'to Monsieur Bailly, Dean of the Tiers-état', and reproved the Tiers-état for calling the other Orders 'privileged'. For the King, who had left Versailles for his Palace at Marly, and was no longer close to Necker, had fallen under the influence of the Court party, headed by the comte d'Artois and the Queen, and this party had resolved to stop the career of the Commons and if necessary to get their leaders arrested.

While the courtiers were intriguing, Paris and Versailles were growing angry and excited. At Versailles the mob took to threatening the higher Clergy who would not let their Chamber join, and even to pelting them with stones. At length, on the evening of June 19th, the Clergy ceased to waver, and passed a resolution to go and verify their credentials with the Commons. On learning this, the Court party felt that something must be done at once.

A 'Royal Sitting' had been spoken of, but the date had not been announced, when early on the rainy morning of June 20th, Bailly was informed by a friend that the great Hall had been closed to the public. A note from de Brézé, which arrived soon after, explained that it was being prepared for the Royal Sitting and could not be used. Bailly wrote in answer that he should go to the Assembly as usual, summoned the secretaries, and walked to the Hall, through the rain, at the appointed time. There he found a sentinel posted at the gate, a crowd watching, and all the deputies arriving. A second note from de Brézé was now brought to him, saying that the Hall had been closed by the King's orders. The Court, in fact, had locked the National Assembly out: a simple and insulting way of preventing a meeting. But the Assembly was not to be cowed, and each member felt that the Court must be defied and a meeting held somewhere – out in the place d'Armes before the Palace, perhaps, if a shelter could not be found. A deputy suggested the tennis-court not far off, and thither the Assembly marched in a body; the sympathetic crowd followed. There was just room for all the deputies in the bare little building, and the crowd took possession of the galleries from which spectators were wont to watch the games. The owner brought in a table, a few benches, and a chair for Bailly; but Bailly would not sit while the Assembly stood. The discussion began; some of the deputies were for walking off to Paris at once, sure of welcome and support there; but Mounier proposed that they should all take an oath that the Assembly would never separate till the Constitution had been made, and the idea was received with acclamation and warmly supported by Target, Le Chapelier, and Barnave. The wording of the oath was next drawn up by Le Chapelier and Barnave; Bailly read it, so loud that the people in the street outside could hear it, and then the deputies swore it together, raising their right hands. They afterwards came up to the table one by one to sign it. One member alone, who disapproved, was bold enough to sign his name with 'opponent' after it, and raised a storm of anger which was calmed down by Bailly. The deputies did not leave the Tennis-court till six o'clock, having been on their feet since eight.

Two days after, the Hall being still closed, the Assembly met in the Cathedral, and there the majority of the Clergy, led by two Bishops, came trooping in to join it. Two of the Nobles of Dauphine came too, but the rest of the minority of the Nobles felt them-selves bound by the vote of their Chamber to stay away.

The first blow of the Court had failed, but the second, which was to put an end to the National Assembly, had been prepared; it was struck at the Royal Sitting on June 23rd. There was a rumour about, that morning, that Necker had resigned, and the deputies found their Hall surrounded by soldiers. Clergy and Nobles were let in at once at the chief entrance, but the Commons were kept waiting outside a back entrance in the rain, and Bailly knocked again and again before de Brézé admitted them. They marched in, silent and stern, and noticed that Necker was not present among the Ministers. There was a long wait before the King came in, and when he came he was smiling no longer. He issued his orders in three speeches. He promised great reforms; the abolition of the *taille* and the *corvée*, equal taxation for all the Orders, no taxes to be levied without the consent of the States-General, less use to be made of *lettres de cachet*. At the same time he declared that the steps taken on the 17th by the Tiers-état were illegal and null; he forbade the Orders to discuss together the constitution of the States-General or their own ancient rights and privileges, he forbade them to admit the public to their sittings, and he announced that if the States-General would not help him, he would do what was good for his people without them. Some of the Clergy and most of the Nobles applauded; the Commons sat in stony silence. The King then ordered the States-General to separate at once, and withdrew; the Nobles and almost all the Clergy followed him, but the Commons sat on. Workmen came in and began taking the dais down, with a clatter, and then de Brézé bustled in, and going up to Bailly asked him if he had not heard the King's orders. "I think the nation in assembly cannot receive an order," said Bailly. But Mirabeau stepped out from his place and cried to de Brézé in a voice of thunder; "Go and tell those who send you, that we are here by the will of the people, and that we will only go if we are driven out by bayonets!" The Assembly shouted; the workmen dropped their tools, and de Brézé vanished, awestruck. Camus and Barnave were on their feet at once, proposing to make a declaration that the Assembly persisted in all its previous decisions. "You are to-day what you were yesterday", said Siéyes, and a Breton deputy cried: "This is a Bed of Justice in a National Assembly!" The proposed declaration was made, and, on Mirabeau's motion, it was also declared that to arrest a deputy for anything said or done in the States-General was a crime punishable by death. After this, the Assembly rose. While it was sitting the King's Guards had invested the Hall, but the Court party was afraid of using force, and the Guards were withdrawn.

Necker was the idol of the people, and there was such a popular demonstration in his favour that the King and Queen hastened to be reconciled with him. And this was only the first-concession the King had to make, for the blow of the Court party had failed signally. The Hall was still surrounded by troops and the deputies were sitting, as it were, in the midst of an armed camp; none the less the majority of the Clergy joined the Assembly again the next day, and the minority of the Nobles followed on the day after. The eloquent young comte de Clermont-Tonnerre led them in, and the duc d'Orléans was in their ranks. The King saw that further resistance here would be useless, and wrote to the rest of the Clergy and Nobles that they must join too. They came in on June 27th, reluctantly and with many protests, and sat once more in their old places, which the Commons had carefully kept empty for them. The National Assembly was complete. There were illuminations in Paris and Versailles, and crowds cheered the King, the Queen, and Necker. From every part of France, too, addresses came daily to the National Assembly, assuring the deputies that the nation approved and ratified the great steps they had taken.

One of the Ministers who could not understand why the reforms promised by the King had not satisfied the Assembly, asked Bailly: "What does the Assembly want?" "To do things itself, and not that you should do them", answered Bailly.

The King was now gracious to the Assembly and for a short time all seemed to go well. But the Court party was preparing another blow. Their intention was to bring up enough troops to overawe Paris, and then to dissolve the Assembly and arrest the leaders. Bread was scarce in Paris and portions of the poorer classes both there and in Versailles had become dangerously disorderly; this gave the King a pretext for calling in the troops. The troops came; by July 10th there were more than seventeen regiments in and round Paris. They were encamped in the Champ-de-Mars, a large open space outside the western walls of Paris;* they guarded the road from Paris to Versailles; at Versailles they bivouacked in the huge Orangery of the Palace, where

---

* Where the Eiffel Tower now stands.

Madame de Polignac and the courtiers visited and cajoled them. They were mostly foreign troops, Swiss and Germans in the employ of France, chosen because they were unlikely to sympathize with the people; and they were helping to eat up the scanty supplies of bread. The Court party put on a triumphant air.

The Assembly did its best to get the troops withdrawn, and Mirabeau, who now took the lead, drafted a famous address to the King, which was taken to him by a deputation. Louis was warned of the dangers he was running: "Great revolutions have had less conspicuous causes," wrote Mirabeau; but the warning had no effect. On July 11th, Necker was quietly dismissed; the dismissal of the other Ministers who were favourable to the Assembly soon followed; the duc de Broglie, a veteran soldier and a Marshal, was made minister of war.

The news of Necker's dismissal reached Paris on Sunday July 12th, and Paris, already angry and alarmed at the presence of the troops, was soon in a turmoil. The Palais-Royal was, as usual, thronged with groups of people eagerly discussing the situation or listening to the orators who were ever ready to harangue them; but no one seemed to know what to do until a young black-eyed lawyer, named Camille Desmoulins, jumped up on a table under the trees and began to speak. Camille's eloquence was usually spoiled by a stammer; but he did not stammer as he urged his fellow-citizens to resist before it was too late. "To arms!" he cried; "let us all take green cockades, the colour of hope!" and he took a green ribbon and stuck it in his hat. The crowd echoed "To arms!" and followed his example, those who could not get ribbons plucking twigs from the trees. The spark was kindled and the fire spread through Paris. Some of the crowd rushed to the wax-work show of Curtius (an uncle of Mme Tussaud), seized on the wax busts of Necker and the duc d'Orléans, veiled them in crape, and carried them round the streets in procession, till they were dispersed, not without bloodshed, by a detachment of the regiment 'Royal Allemand'. This regiment, commanded by the Queen's cousin, the prince de Lambesc, was posted in the place Louis Quinze (now place de-la Concorde), a very large open square lying between the Tuileries gardens and the wooded Champs-Élysées. Here too a crowd had gathered, and, becoming aware of bloodshed, the citizens grew hostile, threatened the soldiers and began to throw stones. The General in command of all the troops, the old Swiss Baron de Besenval, a friend of the Queen's, seeing the square filling with an angry mob, ordered Lambesc to clear it, and the troopers, heedless of stones, pushed the crowd quietly back over a bridge, into the Tuileries gardens, which were full of Sunday holidaymakers. Here Lambesc found himself in a narrow space between two high terraces, from which chairs, bottles, and stones were hurled at the troopers, while the crowd began to cut off his retreat. In order to extricate his men, he charged, the soldiers hitting about them with the flat of their swords and overturning everything in their way. At the news of this charge, which did little damage, all Paris rose in fury. The tocsin* was rung, and the Gardes-françaises, a regiment of the King's Guards which had already taken the popular side, sallied forth from barracks to help the Parisians fight. There was a skirmish or two, but Besenval withdrew his troops without giving battle, and as all the authorities had vanished in the course of the evening, Paris was delivered over to anarchy. The great mass of the inhabitants was law-abiding, but, as in all large cities, there was a residue of dangerous characters, and these, reinforced by numbers of the unemployed who had flocked to Paris and, finding things no better there, had grown desperate, were ready to form a 'mob'. The mob was increased, in moments of political excitement, by steadier and more prosperous citizens. During this night of the 12th the mob burnt some of the barriers where the tolls on food-stuffs, &c., were collected, and bands of lawless men roved about searching for arms. In the morning a convent was pillaged.

* Church and other bells rung very quick with double strokes.

Paris, however, had not risen for pillage but to resist oppression, and while the mob was seizing all the arms and powder that could be found, wiser heads were beginning to organize. The 'Electors', the body which had chosen the deputies to the States-General, met in the Hôtel-de-Ville (the Town Hall) and formed themselves into a kind of municipal Council, Flesselles, the 'provost of the merchants' (the nearest approach to a mayor in old Paris), working with them. Here, sitting in the midst of surging crowds, which filled the place de Grève outside and sometimes overran the rooms of the Hôtel-de-Ville, they kept such order as they could. Under their guidance, respectable citizens of fighting age enrolled themselves by the thousand in a Guard soon known as the National Guard, and by the night of the 13th parties of these guards were patrolling the streets, protecting life and property, and quietly disarming the irresponsible mob. To distinguish them, they were all given cockades of red and blue, the old colours of Paris; the green cockades were discarded, because green was the colour of the comte d'Artois. Very shortly after, white, the old colour of France, the King's colour, was added to the red and blue.

So the Parisians armed and organized themselves and threw up barricades, expecting an attack from Besenval's troops at any moment and determined to sell their lives dearly. Arms were the chief need, and on the morning of the 14th the invading populace secured the arms in the Hôtel des Invalides, a large establishment for old soldiers. It was known that there were plenty of arms in the Bastille, and the Governor, Delaunay, had already been approached with suggestions that he should let the people have them.

The Bastille was a great oblong castle, consisting of eight prison towers, high and round, joined together by equally high walls; it was protected by a moat with drawbridges and by many outer courts and walls. It dominated the Faubourg Saint Antoine, a turbulent workmen's quarter; the cannon on its battlements could sweep all approaches, and it contained powder enough to blow the quarter to pieces. It stood, not only to Paris and to France, but to Europe as well, as a symbol of oppression and injustice.

Early in the morning of July 14th, it was seen from the streets that Delaunay was bringing the cannon on the battlements forward, as if in preparation to fire, and an angry multitude soon surrounded the fortress and penetrated into some of the outer and undefended courts. The situation was serious, and when the Electors in the Hôtel-de-Ville learnt of it, they sent a deputation to Delaunay to beg him to give his word that he would not fire on the people unless he were first attacked. The citizens of a neighbouring district also sent a deputation, and each deputation found

Delaunay reasonable; he gave his word, and seemed half inclined to surrender; his garrison was small – a handful of Invalides (veterans) and a few Swiss – and he had no food for them. But when, from his battlements, he looked down on the gathering multitudes, he lost his head in a panic. The people were still encroaching; a little later some of them forced an outer drawbridge; they took possession of a fresh court. Before there was any real necessity, Delaunay gave the order to fire, and the battle began with a desultory exchange of shots between the soldiers under cover on the battlements and the citizens in the streets. The Electors, still hopeful of preventing further slaughter, sent another deputation, with flag and drum, to summon Delaunay to a parley. The deputation was seen from the Bastille towers, and the garrison hoisted a white flag; some of the Electors moved forward, and were persuading the people to go quietly away, when Delaunay fired again. After this seemingly treacherous act, nothing would serve the citizens but the capture of the Bastille. Under the leadership of two trained soldiers, Hulin and Élie, the Gardes-françaises, the National Guard and other citizens marched on the Bastille with five cannon. They dragged them through the streets, and then on through the outer courts of the fortress raked by the fire from the towers, and planted a battery right in front of the principal drawbridge; it was a daring exploit, all the more so because Besenval's army might be expected to intervene. Delaunay gave himself up for lost; he tried to fire a powder-magazine and, when prevented by his men, he wrote a desperate note: "We will blow up the garrison and all the quarter, if you do not accept a capitulation." The note was held out to the besiegers through a hole in the gate and brought to Élie, who read it aloud and shouted: "We accept, on the word of an officer!" The multitude around only roared: "No capitulation!" but the Bastille surrendered.

It was about five o'clock. The drawbridge was lowered, the assailants rushed in. The keys of the fortress were carried in triumph to the Electors, so was Élie, borne on men's shoulders. But while the better part of the multitude hastened to spread the good news, the worse remained to take vengeance. Their leaders did all they could to get the capitulation respected, but the populace, incensed at the bloodshed and at Delaunay's treachery, was in no mood for mercy. The unhappy Governor was torn from the arms of his escort on the way to the Hôtel-de-Ville and murdered; his head was cut off, stuck on the end of a pike and carried about Paris; three or four of his officers shared his fate. Flesselles, provost of the merchants, who had sent the people to look for arms where there were none, was forced to leave the Hôtel-de-Ville, and shot outside. Two out of a party of soldiers brought to the Hôtel-de-Ville as prisoners, were carried off in spite of the efforts of Élie and of the Electors and were hanged on a lamp-iron* projecting from a house in the place de Grève. Élie persuaded the mob to pardon the rest, and there were no more murders. The Bastille itself was sacked and the prisoners were released; there were but seven, and of these two were lunatics and the rest bad characters. The demolition of the hated prison began at once. Paris rejoiced in her victory, but with no idea that the victory had been decisive and that Besenval could no longer count on the obedience of his troops; so the citizens spent another watchful, anxious night, prepared for an attack that never came.

Meanwhile at Versailles, the Assembly, in instant danger of dissolution and arrest, was sitting day and night. The common peril drew the three Orders together, and differences were forgotten as they all worked for the common good. Besides supporting the Electors of Paris in their measures, they passed a decree stating, amongst other things, that the Assembly persisted in its previous decisions, and that the King's Ministers were responsible for all that was happening. As if secure of the future, they elected a Constitutional Committee to draw up the new Constitution. They also sent deputation after deputation to the King, begging

---

* A Street lantern was drawn up to this by a chain.

him to withdraw the troops; the King answered that 'his heart was bleeding', but he did not withdraw them . . . During the night of the 14th, the duc de Liancourt, an enlightened nobleman on the popular side and much attached to the King, came to him and explained the late events in Paris. "But this is a revolt!" said Louis, "Not a revolt, Sire, but a revolution," answered Liancourt, and Louis, his eyes opened at last, hastened to surrender before it was too late. He came to the Assembly in the morning, attended only by his brothers, to make something as near an apology as a King can. He was coldly received; but when he said that he was one with the nation, that he was counting on the National Assembly to help him, that he had ordered the withdrawal of the troops – the old love for the King revived, the old faith in his good intentions. The deputies burst into rapturous cheers, and the whole Assembly accompanied him back to the Palace, as a guard of honour, to keep the happy crowds from pressing on him too closely. Then a deputation hastened to take the great news to Paris. They were received there with acclamations, even with tears of joy, and attended an important meeting of the Electors at which many speeches were made. Lafayette spoke, Clermont-Tonnerre spoke, and Lally-Tolendal, a stout, sentimental deputy of the Nobles, whose facile eloquence was much admired, gushed over the King so movingly that a crown of flowers was forced on his unwilling head. Before the meeting adjourned, Lafayette was chosen, by acclamation, to be first Commander-in-Chief of the Paris National Guard, and Bailly to be the first mayor of Paris. Every one then went off to hear a *Te Deum* in the Cathedral of Notre-Dame.

Paris was burning to see her changed and enlightened King, and to Paris the King had to go; with a sore heart, for he dreaded the humiliation, while the Queen dreaded his assassination. He made his visit on July 17th and was received at the barrier by the new Mayor, Bailly, who handed him the keys of the City, saying that they were the same keys which had been presented to Henri IV. "He", added Bailly, not too tactfully, "reconquered his people; here it is the people who have reconquered their king." The King drove slowly to and from the Hôtel-de-Ville between enormous but orderly crowds, who cheered him a little, and the nation, the deputies, and Liberty a great deal; the way was lined by the new National Guards, and a number of deputies walked round the King's carriage to protect him from danger. At the Hôtel-de-Ville, Bailly gave him a national cockade, which he stuck in his hat, and when he appeared at a window wearing it, there was immense enthusiasm. The King made a good impression and returned in safety. He had already recalled Necker and dismissed his unpopular Ministers.

The fall of the Bastille had momentous consequences, for with it the old order of things fell too. Every one could see that when a Government could be thus successfully defied, the power of that Government was broken. The princes and nobles of the Court party saw it, and many of them fled from the kingdom, the comte d'Artois, the prince de Conde, Marshal de Broglie, Lambesc, the Polignac family, and other friends of the Queen among them; this was called 'the first emigration'.

Whenever an old form of government is suddenly overturned, disorder and anarchy are sure to ensue, and this was the case now. The commotion excited by late events was increased by a rumour which spread rapidly over France, that 'the Brigands' were coming. A traveller would come rushing to a town, crying that the Brigands were plundering a neighbouring village; or news would fly round the country-side that the Brigands had been seen burning the crops hard by, and were now upon the road. No one had ever seen them himself, for the simple reason that there were no Brigands to see, but every one knew of some one who had.* Meanwhile there were riots, and sometimes murders, in many towns, and the populace when excited began to threaten anyone they suspected or disliked with 'the lantern', i.e.

* The rumour that Russian troops were passing through England, in August and September 1914, furnishes a curious parallel.

hanging from a lamp-iron. In the country the peasants plundered and burnt a large number of the nobles' chateaux, feeling dimly that it was the right thing to do. In Paris, before order could be established again, there were specially horrible murders.

Two men had long been detested: Foulon, a grasping old financier connected with the Government, who was believed to have said that he would make the people eat grass, and Bertier, his son-in-law, Intendant of Paris. The people were thirsting for their blood, and when, on July 22nd, Foulon was arrested and taken to the Hôtel-de-Ville, a howling mob surrounded the building, tore him away from the Electors and hanged him on the fatal lamp-iron. They then cut off his head, stuck it on a pike, stuffed the mouth with grass and paraded the ghastly trophy through the streets. The unfortunate Bertier, who was being escorted as a prisoner to the Hôtel-de-Ville, met and recognized the head on his way. He reached the Electors' hall, and then he too was carried off and hanged upon the lamp-iron. Lafayette, Bailly, and the Electors made effort after effort to save these men, but they were powerless in the midst of the engulfing crowd; Lafayette was so much horrified and disgusted that he resigned his command and only resumed it after much persuasion. In extenuation of all these crimes it must be remembered that the mobs who committed them were very ignorant, that they were short of bread, exasperated by the resistance of the Court, and convinced that no high-placed criminal would ever be punished in a court of law.

Side by side with disorder went a movement towards order. In the towns, men of influence formed themselves into municipal bodies and tried to set things straight, as the Electors had done in Paris. All over France, too, respectable citizens began to arm and to organize themselves for self-defence, and the National Guard sprang up as if by magic. This great force of volunteers acted in two capacities: they were the soldiers of liberty, always ready to fight oppression, and they were the keepers of order, quelling disturbances and holding the unruly in check – performing, in fact, some of the duties of the police. They were a civilian and not a military body, they were under the orders of the civil authority, and they chose their own officers. Their uniform was blue and white with red facings, the colours of the tricolour cockade, for these cockades had been adopted everywhere as the symbol of the Revolution and of patriotism. In Paris, where the Gardes-françaises were drafted into their ranks as paid companies, the National Guards were a prominent feature in daily life. Their commander, the dauntless Lafayette, pranced about the streets on a white horse, taking his hat off to the citizens' wives with a courtly grace, and all his Guards and all their women-folk adored the tall, sandy-haired young man, with awkward movements and the air of a great noble. Lafayette was a republican at heart, though perfectly loyal to the King. With many fine qualities he had a bad defect; he was excessively vain, and though his abilities were second-rate he believed that he was the one man to save France, and that it was his duty to have a finger in every pie. Yet he was so true to his trust, so true to his political convictions, that the great power he wielded, through his position and his popularity, never became a danger to the State.

In this crisis of her history France was not left without wise and bold guidance; she had the National Assembly to look to; and to the Assembly the eyes of the people turned with hope and with respect. The Assembly knew that no State can exist without order, but the majority of the deputies knew also what few bodies who care much for order have ever known; that the best way of restoring it is not merely to repress disorder, but to remove the grievances which have caused it; and they felt that they could not be severe with the populace whose arms had, after all, just freed France. Many of them felt also that the country ought to be shown at once that practical reforms were going to begin in earnest, and the Breton Club settled that the duc d'Aiguillon, a young nobleman who owned more feudal rights than any one in France except the King, should propose to establish equality of taxation, also that the Law should give all who had to pay feudal rights the power to buy them off at a low figure and so be free of them. D'Aiguillon was ready with his motion, but another young nobleman, the vicomte de Noailles, heard of it, and at the evening sitting of August 4th, he jumped up suddenly and made a similar motion himself; the Duke could only come in second. Both of them spoke words of pity and excuse for the oppressed and now revolting peasants; the Assembly was much moved by their generous speeches, and it seemed as if each man were saying to himself: 'Let us put an end at once to all these unjust privileges.' Deputy after deputy of the Nobles and Clergy rose to move the surrender of some oppressive right, vying with one another in self-sacrifice; and every sacrifice was received with shouts of joy, the cheering at one point being so prolonged that business had to be suspended for a while. The President, Le Chapelier, encouraged each renunciation and seemed to be always holding out his hands for more. After the Nobles and Clergy, the Provinces, through their deputies, renounced their ancient privileges, Dauphine and Brittany being the first; and after the Provinces came the towns and cities, Paris first and next Amiens, Abbeville, Péronne, Soissons, Rheims, and Verdun. The sitting lasted till 2 a.m., and during this 'night of the fourth of August' the Assembly decreed the abolition of all pecuniary privileges, of the sale of offices, and of the rights of hunting and keeping dovecotes; also the forfeiture of all pensions given without good reason; it made all citizens equally admissible to any employment, civil or military; it gave the payers of feudal rights and of the clerical *dimes* the power to buy them off, together with other reforms, amounting in all to an abolition of the feudal system. The deputies, thinking in the goodness of their hearts that the King would be as much pleased with their work as they were themselves, also decided that these new decrees should be taken to him in state, and that a *Te Deum* should be sung for them, and bestowed on him the title of 'Restorer of French Liberty.'

It will be best to mention here some points of the Constitution which the Assembly had already begun to make, and we must note, in passing, that the Hall had been re-arranged, with comfortable seats tier above tier in an amphitheatre, with a raised platform for the President, a large sort of pulpit, called a tribune, for the speakers, and a Bar for petitioners; that the Orders sat indiscriminately, and that most of the deputies had discarded their special dress.

Lafayette proposed to preface the Constitution with a 'Declaration of the Rights of Man', as had been done in America, and after long discussions a noble and inspiriting Declaration was drawn up. This was not intended to be a set of iron rules, but rather to be a guide to the spirit in which the laws ought to be made. 'It must be simple, and it must become the national catechism', said Barnave.

It was quickly decided that the Government must be monarchical, for every one believed that a large country like France could not hold together without a King, and no one as yet dreamed of a Republic, except a handful of enthusiasts, such as Camille Desmoulins, who were not in the Assembly. Neither did any one think of changing the King, and he was given, somewhat later, the title of 'King of the French' instead of 'King of France'.

All were agreed that the King must have a real share in the Government, and that without his assent, or sanction, a decree of the legislature could not become law; therefore he was given the power of *veto* over the laws. The hotly debated question was: whether his *veto* should be 'absolute', that is, final, or 'suspensory', that is, temporary – which meant that if, after a time, it became evident, at a general election, that the nation wished for a law which had been vetoed, the King would be obliged to consent to it. The Assembly decided in favour of a suspensory veto.

Another vexed question was: whether the future legislature should consist of one Chamber or two.

Many deputies who had come to the States-General wishing for two Chambers, had been convinced by the conduct of the privileged Orders that a second Chamber, in the present state of France, would block all reforms, and the Assembly decided the question in favour of one Chamber.

Unhappily these decisions not only caused the resignation of the Constitutional Committee, but divided the ranks of the deputies who wished for progress. Some, like Mirabeau, thought the Declaration of Rights premature and the decrees of the 4th August too sweeping, and many who had voted for these decrees repented of their enthusiasm. Mounier, who was supported by Lally-Tolendal, Clermont-Tonnerre, Malouet, and other prominent men, had intended to give France a Constitution as much like that of England as possible, with two Chambers and an absolute veto for the King. They took no heed of the changes wrought by the Revolution, and as this Constitution seemed to them the safest and the best, they were determined that France should have it, whether public opinion approved of it or no. They accused their opponents of encouraging disorder, while their opponents saw clearly that if a Constitution which public opinion did not approve was forced upon France, it would lead to fresh revolutions. The two parties seemed to be evenly balanced, yet when it came to voting,

Mourner's party was always defeated and grew both sad and sore.

These dissensions put new hope into the hearts of the King and his advisers. He was aware that if he refused to sanction the new decrees he could count on the support of a large part of the Assembly, and for a long time he delayed over the decrees of the 4th August. He had to give in here, for he feared the anger of the country, but he still deferred his sanction to the Declaration of Rights and the first articles of the Constitution. Necker was pressing for money, and the Assembly resolved not to consent to a new tax till the Declaration and the Articles had been accepted by the King. They were sent up to him again on October 2nd.

But the King had fresh plans. Paris was again in a dangerous state; bread was scarce, people were saying that if the King lived in his capital there would be plenty, and the irritated populace was taking a strong interest in politics. The *veto* caused special excitement, the name caught the fancy of the ignorant; the King and Queen were dubbed Monsieur and Madame Veto, unpopular deputies were threatened, and at meetings in the Palais-Royal resolutions were passed to send them away, and also to march on Versailles. What could be more natural than to protect the Assembly and the Court from the Paris mob by bringing fresh troops to

Versailles? And when once the Assembly felt safe, so the King thought, the majority of the deputies would vote differently and would undo their work. The courtiers intended further to carry the King off to Metz and to dissolve the Assembly – at least the public believed this. So a regiment devoted to the King, the Flanders regiment, was ordered to Versailles and arrived there. The Ministers received warnings that trouble would ensue in Paris, but they took no heed.

At this critical moment, the King's Body-Guards, a regiment composed entirely of men of noble birth, gave a splendid banquet to the new arrivals in the Opera-House of the Palace (1 Oct.). Loyal toasts were drunk, and when enthusiasm ran high the King appeared. With him was the Queen, beautiful and gracious, holding the Dauphin in her arms; they went the round of the tables while the band played a popular air: "Oh Richard! oh my King! all the world forsakes thee." The banquet became a demonstration, and after the royal pair had withdrawn, tipsy loyalty made scenes, both out of doors and in, and the national cockade was insulted. The Court encouraged these manifestations; great ladies distributed white cockades to the officers, and the Queen said openly that she had been 'enchanted' with the banquet. The news of this costly feast in a time of dearth and of the insult to the national cockade put Paris in a ferment once more.

In the early morning of Monday, October 5th, there was a disturbance at a baker's, and a small gathering of poor women suddenly made up their minds to go to the Hôtel-de-Ville and demand bread from the Authorities. They were joined by the market-women,* strong, loud-voiced and determined; their numbers swelled rapidly and they reached their destination in force. The Municipal Council was not yet sitting, so bread was not to be had from them, but the women overpowered the guard, rang the tocsin in the belfry, ransacked the building and nearly set it on fire by trying to burn official documents. By and by they began to talk of marching on Versailles to demand bread from the King and the Assembly. In the Hôtel-de-Ville they came across a young man in black, named Maillard, who had been one of the foremost at the taking of the Bastille. Maillard was a born mob-leader; he gained their confidence, managed to curb their violence, and was appointed to conduct them to Versailles.

Off they set, Maillard beating a drum to summon stragglers, and the women forcing other women, right and left, to march with them. By the time they reached the Champs-Élysées they were several thousand strong, they had two cannon, which they had seized, and they had been joined by a number of ragged men, armed

* They were called politely the 'Dames de la Halle' and vulgarly the 'Poissardes'.

with pikes, hatchets and old guns. Most of the women had come with no evil intentions, but many were very rough, and there were furies among them ready to strangle any one who thwarted them.* And as they tramped along, tired, hungry and fierce, they and the ragged men vowed vengeance on the Body-Guards who had insulted the national cockade, and talked of tearing the Queen in pieces. Terror went before them and houses were barricaded as they passed. But Maillard kept them cleverly in hand and when, in the afternoon, they reached Versailles and entered the Avenue de Paris, he persuaded them to cry *Vive le Roi*! and to sing a loyal air.

The Palace had been warned that Paris was marching on Versailles, and all was consternation. The Queen was at home, but the King was out hunting; he was hastily sent for, and the troops were called out and ranged in front of the rails which separated the courts of the Palace from the place d'Armes. The Body-Guards were in the centre, so that when the mob came up the Avenue, the women found themselves confronted by the objects of their wrath. Insults were lavished and blows were given; but while some of the women were engaged in this strife, others slipped among the ranks of the Flanders regiment, cajoling the soldiers

* The King's adherents always maintained that some of them were men dressed up as women.

and making them promise not to fire on the people. One of their leaders, in a scarlet coat, was specially active here; a pretty, insinuating woman with a soft voice, named Théroigne de Méricourt. The soldiers were patient under provocation and, to the honour of the King, they had received orders not to fire. But, to make the confusion worse, the National Guards of Versailles, who were highly incensed with the Body-Guards, were out in the place d'Armes too; more than once they exchanged shots with the Guards, and it looked as if a fight might begin at any moment.

A large number of the women, with Maillard, had halted before the Hall of the Assembly. That morning there had been a scene in the Assembly, for the King's answer had arrived at last; he accepted the articles of the Constitution, but only conditionally, and he merely criticized the Declaration of Rights. The Assembly was indignant; strong words were spoken about the 'orgy' of the Body-Guards, and it was resolved to send a deputation to the King to demand his unconditional acceptance of the articles and the Declaration. Before the sitting was ended came the news that Paris was on the march. The deputies thought it probable that the mob had come to attack the Assembly, but they sat quietly on, as was their custom in moments of crisis, and admitted a deputation of women, with Maillard as their spokesman. His rather wild account of their grievances was listened to patiently; the President, Mounier, tried to reason with the women, and the Assembly resolved to send a deputation to the King, to represent to him the sad state of Paris. This deputation started at about five o'clock, with Mounier at its head, and a number of women insisted on accompanying it and going in to see the King too. The Assembly continued to sit. By this time it was raining hard, and batch after batch of women was admitted to take shelter, till the Hall was quite full. Here the women remained all night, for the deputies treated them with great kindness, and, later on, Mounier had food distributed to them. The Assembly could see their hunger and their sufferings where the Court saw nothing but their rage. They were troublesome guests; they sat among the deputies, pulling them about, chattering, interrupting; and their disorderly conduct made continuous debate impossible. "Bread! bread! not so many long speeches!" they cried on one occasion. Mirabeau, who was very popular, silenced them once with a rebuke, but they soon began talking again.

Meanwhile, up in the Palace, the King and his Ministers were holding a Council and discussing the question whether Louis should leave Versailles at once with his family. He was pressed to do so, but refused, and the Queen, who showed great courage, refused to leave him. The deputation from the Assembly arrived;

twelve women had been let in too, and the King received them with so much sympathy that he won their hearts, and sent them away happy with a written promise that Paris should be well provisioned. Mounier, however, stayed on; he felt it to be his duty to the Assembly to make the Ministers understand that the King had better send his unconditional acceptance of the articles and the Declaration, before the demand of the Assembly reached him and, sorely against his own wishes, he insisted on this. He waited and waited but got no answer. The downpour of rain had quieted the mob, the troops had been sent to their barracks, a band of faithful followers had rallied round the royal family and the Ministers did not think the situation desperate. Then came the alarming news that the National Guard of Paris, with Lafayette at its head, was marching on Versailles. The Court was really terrified at last, and the King gave in and signed his unconditional acceptance. A little later he sent for the Assembly which he had flouted to come to him, feeling that the presence of the deputies would be his best protection in his straits.

We must now return to Paris. The march of the women had been only the first and least dangerous part of the rising, and no sooner were they gone than the National Guards began to assemble. Company after company came out and ranged itself in marching order, and the cry of every company was, that Lafayette must lead them to Versailles. What they intended to do when they got there was not clear, but their deputies told Lafayette that they were going to depose the King if he refused to listen to reason. The women were out for bread; the National Guards were out to make the King respect the will of the nation. Lafayette resisted their demands for hours; he harangued the crowds in the place de Grève, he reasoned with deputations; it was all useless, and in the end both he and the Municipal Council thought that he might prevent harm if he led the troops to Versailles, so he yielded.

Towards sunset the march began; there were about 15,000 National Guards and much the same number of other citizens armed with any weapon they could get hold of. Progress was slow in the dark and the rain, and on the way Lafayette regained his ascendancy and made his troops swear fidelity to the Nation, the Law and the King, thus turning, what might have been an attack into a demonstration, by his influence alone. The troops marched up the Avenue de Paris, and Lafayette, after stopping at the Assembly to assure the President that all was well, went on to the Palace by himself.

The courtiers murmured "Cromwell", as he stalked through the rooms; "Cromwell would not have come alone," said Lafayette. He assured the King of his own loyalty and of his army's, and undertook to guard the outside of the Palace, leaving the inside to the King's own Guards. Many of the Body-Guards were now marched quietly away from Versailles, out of reach of the people.

The long and dreadful day was over at last, and over with little bloodshed. The National Guards were in charge of the town, where all was quiet. The deputies had been up to the Palace in a body, through the rain and the mud, to be dismissed with thanks by the King, who had already seen Lafayette; the Assembly now broke up and every one sought shelter and rest. But Lafayette, with all his care, had made one mistake; he had not put a strong enough guard round the Palace.

At six o'clock the next morning some of the rougher portions of the mob, up and about already, found an unguarded entrance and began to explore curiously. They had walked into the Palace courts, right up to the innermost, the Marble Court, under the royal apartments, when some one fired, whereupon a Body-Guard, from a window, shot at the intruders and killed a young man. At once, with wild cries, the crowd rushed for the Body-Guards, seized on two of them (mere boys, who had not attended the banquet), massacred them and cut their heads off in the courtyard, while a raging band of men and women chased other Body-Guards up the Palace stairs and into the rooms which led to the Queen's apartments. Here one or two faithful Body-Guards managed to keep the door while they shouted to the Queen's women to save her, and the Queen jumped from her bed and, with a mantle thrown over her, fled by back passages to the King's apartments, just in time. A general massacre of the remaining Body-Guards seemed certain, when Lafayette and the Paris National Guards came running up and plucked them from the hands of the mob. The heads of the two victims were stuck on pikes and carried off to Paris, as a trophy, early in the morning.

The royal family, shaken but courageous, had taken refuge together in one of the rooms overlooking the Marble Court which was now filled with National Guards and the mob, when Lafayette appeared to save them a second time. He spoke to the people from the balcony, and the King spoke too, begging for the pardon of his Body-Guards, which Lafayette persuaded the people to grant. There were shouts for the Queen, and Lafayette led her and her children out on to the balcony, where she faced the people bravely and was rewarded by a flicker of popularity. But the crowd began to roar "a Paris!" and kept on roaring till the King had given his promise that he would go there; causing frantic joy thereby, for he was still beloved.

At two in the afternoon the march to Paris began; a march of triumph for the people, of bitter humiliation for the royal family, though King and Queen were often cheered on the way. Lafayette rode in front of their carriage, and a deputation from the Assembly accompanied them; they were safe enough, but they were dragged slowly along as part of a huge, disorderly procession of National Guards, Swiss Guards, Body-Guards, and the Flanders regiment, all mixed up together and wearing each others' accoutrements in sign of amity; men with pikes walked among the soldiers, and women, many of whom carried branches of trees. There were wagons of corn in the procession, and the women sang that bread would be plentiful, for they were bringing home the baker and the baker's wife and the little baker-boy.

So the royal family left Versailles for ever. The Assembly had passed a loyal resolution not to separate from the King, and the King, after a few days, decided that he must live in Paris, and summoned the Assembly to follow him. Palace and Hall remained empty and desolate, and the struggle with the King was over.

III

THE RULE OF THE CONSTITUENT ASSEMBLY 1789 – 1791

The rising of the 5th and 6th of October caused much uneasiness throughout France, and many deputies wished to fly, fearing that their lives would not be safe in Paris. Mounier retired to Grenoble in sorrow and disgust; neither argument nor entreaty could bring him back, and a few months later he left France, having become one of the bitterest enemies of the Revolution. Lally-Tolendal fled abroad and a few others withdrew. But the country was soon reassured, for Paris, now well supplied with bread, kept fairly quiet and was respectful to King and Assembly.

There had been something mysterious in the suddenness of the rising, and it began to be whispered that the duc d'Orléans had paid the mob, in the hope that the King would be deposed and he himself made Regent; Mirabeau, who was friendly with the Duke and had great influence in Paris, was also said to be concerned. Lafayette thought that Paris would be quieter if the Duke were out of the way, and persuaded the King to pack him off to England on a pretended mission, and to keep him there for the best part of a year. But when a searching inquiry into the rising was held by the Châtelet (the first law-court in Paris after the Parlement), nothing was found out which implicated either d'Orléans or Mirabeau.

For two years France was, in effect, ruled by the National Assembly, known in history by the name of the Constituent Assembly, because its mission was to make the Constitution.

Its members intended to do their work quickly and then to lay down their unlimited powers and retire, leaving their places to a new Assembly. But they were perpetually interrupted in their principal task, and circumstances, as we shall see, forced them to take on themselves duties which ought to have been performed by the Ministers and agents of the King.

The royal family settled down in the Tuileries Palace, an old royal residence with fine gardens along the Seine which were open to the public. Here they were well under the eye of Paris and guarded by the National Guards, for the King thought it wise to dismiss most

of his own Guards. The publicity of the life was
nothing new to the royal family as they had always
lived in public, but it was hard to change the reveren-
tial public of the old days for the critical and suspicious
Parisians. At first the King was very popular; this
pleased his benevolent heart, and probably, if he had
been left to himself, he would have become a real
constitutional King. But the Queen was always at his
side to remind him of what he had lost, and their
friends and advisers all belonged to the class which
had suffered through the Revolution, and considered,
one and all, that the King had been infamously treated.
Louis and the best of his advisers were genuinely sorry
for the poor and oppressed, and desirous of bettering
their lot; but it is one thing to grant as much reform
as you think fit to a grateful people, and another to
have the power of granting reforms taken away from
you, especially if you and your friends have always
believed that this power has been entrusted to you by
God. Louis and Marie-Antoinette saw that nothing
could be done at present, and they lived in hopes that
better days would come. They never understood that
the Revolution had changed their world, and expected
that the nation, led astray for a time by bad men,
would return to its old allegiance. The King's popularity encouraged them and made them think: 'After
all the heart of the people is in the right place.' And

all the while the people were thinking: 'After all our good King is really on our side.'

If the royal family had begun to lead an ordinary life at once, they might have enjoyed a great deal of freedom. But they had no desire to lead a free and comfortable life; they soon made it their aim to pose to the world as prisoners in a hostile city to which they had been dragged by force, and the King rejected Lafayette's advice to go out hunting as usual. They knew that though the peoples of Europe sympathized with the Revolution, the monarchs were beginning to be alarmed by it, and they hoped that the Queen's brother, the Emperor Leopold, might eventually be persuaded to help in restoring the King to his old position. So the Court, to put it baldly, sulked, and held as much aloof from the Assembly as possible.

The Ministers, whose business it was to carry on the government and carry out the laws, were appointed by the King; they were not and could not be members of the Assembly* and they were not dependent on the Assembly for support. Their position, therefore, was quite different from that of our own Ministers. They took their tone from the King, and, as Charles de Lameth, a witty deputy, remarked, "shammed dead." When disturbances broke out they sent no troops to

---

* In the earlier days, before 7th November 1789, three members were Ministers.

quell them; when difficulties arose in their departments they did not decide them; they either left things alone or referred them to the Assembly, as if to say: 'You have brought us to this pass; get us out if you can.' In consequence Government business of every kind was always being brought to the Assembly, and as its authority was supreme and it was universally trusted as well as respected, appeals for help and guidance came streaming in from every side. The Assembly, in fact, was called upon to decide all questions, from the form of government down to the motto on soldiers' buttons.

A great deal of this business was done by Committees whose members were appointed either for their abilities or for their special knowledge; they drew up bills which they submitted to the Assembly, and decided minor points themselves. There was a second 'Constitutional Committee', successor of the first, to draw up the Constitution; a Diplomatic Committee, small and discreet, for foreign affairs, and committees dealing with the Army, the Navy, the Colonies, Law, the national property, finance, commerce and agriculture, the discovery of plots and conspiracies,* &c., *Sec.* It was one of the principles of the Assembly that public business ought to be conducted openly, and

* This committee, a famous one, was called the 'Comité des Recherches'.

though the committees could not admit the public to their sittings, any deputies might come in, and the advice of outsiders was freely sought. The Diplomatic Committee alone was allowed to preserve some secrecy.

The debates of the Constituent Assembly offer an inspiring study to any one who cares about political ideas, and demonstrate what a lofty science politics can be. Every question, great or small, was discussed on its own merits and with reference to first principles, by men who had thought deeply on kindred subjects and took their responsibilities seriously. One of their doctrines was that each member, as he joined, became a representative of the Nation; which meant that he must consider the interests of the Nation as a whole, and must entirely subordinate the interests of his own constituents to the common good. The members were guided in their decisions by a strong sense of justice, a warm sympathy for the oppressed, a merciful pity for the erring, noble ideals of life, and an enthusiasm for liberty. Yet they were by no means mere enthusiasts, ready to sacrifice everything to a theory; on the contrary, they had plenty of common sense. They made mistakes, but they were ready to learn from experience. They swept away the old order, but they had strong conservative instincts too and were anxious to preserve what was old if it seemed to them also good. They had the greatest respect for the sanctities and pieties of human life; and a brother pleading for an offending brother, a child for a parent, a friend for a friend, was sure of a friendly hearing. There were, of course, self-seekers and intriguers among them, men who lived for ambition and not for an ideal, but they had to adopt the language of the majority of sincere and disinterested men with whom they worked. Finally, there was an unusually large number of able and talented deputies; and members who were little noticed in the Constituent Assembly became leading men in the Assemblies of later years.

In Paris the Assembly sat in the 'Manège', or riding-school of the Tuileries Palace, a long, plain, narrow building abutting on the raised terrace called the 'terrasse des Feuillants' which bounds the north side of the Tuileries gardens. The inside of the Manège had been arranged, like the Hall at Versailles, with seats in an amphitheatre, a raised platform for the President in the centre of one side, and a tribune opposite him. There were two large galleries open to the public, one at either end of the room, and smaller galleries where the seats were reserved. It is often said that the galleries, together with the crowd which gathered on the terrasse des Feuillants when anything exciting was going on, terrorized the deputies and influenced the debates. This is not true of the Constituent Assembly. The galleries applauded noisily and sometimes hissed, but they were kept in order, and their demonstrations had no effect on the deputies. The Assembly was jealous of its own dignity, and every deputy knew that he could rely on the loyalty of his colleagues for protection. Members worked hard;* there were long sittings every day, Sundays included, and thrice a week, or oftener, there were evening sittings too. Part of the sittings were taken up with the reception of deputations; envoys from corporate bodies all over France, who came with homage, congratulations, and requests. Many individuals came too, bringing 'patriotic gifts' for the Treasury, to help to pay the national debt and stave off bankruptcy. Real sacrifices were made and generous gifts offered, but certain of the donors were chiefly moved by the hope of seeing their names in the papers. All these deputations and individuals were received at the Bar, an enclosure at the foot of the tribune.

The President of the Assembly was elected every fortnight, and it was his arduous task to keep order in the debates, which were often tempestuous. He rang a little bell and waved his arms about, but if the deputies did not choose to listen to a speaker, nothing would make them, for, with all its noble ideals, the Assembly had human weaknesses. Stormy scenes were

* They were paid 18 francs a day by the State.

of frequent occurrence, and visitors who expected to find a dignified Senate debating questions in classical calm, were terribly shocked at the noise. Yet good speakers were listened to in silence, though even the best of them had to struggle for a hearing when feelings were roused. The Assembly was critical and shouted corrections of any misplaced word. The deputies loved a joke, too, and laughed when they got a chance. Target caused great amusement when he spoke one day of "Peace and concord followed by calm and tranquillity."

We must take a glance at the various parties in the Assembly; they cannot be called parties in our sense of the word, for the deputies prided themselves on their independence and would have scorned to vote at the bidding of a party. Certain sections usually acted together because they thought alike, but each man was free to break away from his friends whenever he judged proper. There were two main divisions: the party of progress, called 'the Left', because they sat on the left of the President; and the party which wished to upset things as little as possible, called 'the Right', because they sat on the right of the President. The more moderate men of each side sat nearest the President, in the centre; and the more extreme a member's opinions were, the further he sat to right or left. Hence the terms of Right, Left, and Centre, used to this day.

The Right consisted chiefly of Nobles and Clergy. A large number of this party were perfectly sincere in their opposition to reforms which they thought hasty, ill-considered, and dangerously subversive. They got the worst of it in debate, as a rule, and were always outvoted, and they took their revenge in a childish manner by systematic obstruction. They loved to make noisy scenes, and most of the tumults in the Assembly were due to them. They shouted, singly and in chorus, they interrupted rudely, they shook their fists at their foes, they even tried to squeeze the breath out of them by crowding into the tribune; they contrived to prolong debates and to make business drag. When nothing else would serve, they challenged prominent members of the Left to duels, in the hope of getting rid of them in that way. Mirabeau had the courage to refuse to fight, but other deputies, although they disapproved of duelling, could not resist a duel. Yet the deputies of the Right were not malicious; many of them were good friends with their opponents, and some of the most obstreperous would, at times, take a useful part in debate. A few who were conciliatory enjoyed a good deal of influence, for the Left always welcomed advances.

The two most conspicuous figures on the Right were two of the greatest orators of the Assembly. One was the abbe Maury, the unwearying champion of aristocracy, a man of the people by birth and an indomitable fighter, clever, and shallow. His talents and his pluck would have earned respect had he not been disliked for his bad life and his rude and vulgar behaviour in the Assembly. The other was de Cazalès, a stout, untidy young soldier, genial, careless, unselfish; a chivalrous man whom every one liked. Cazalès, a student and thinker, was a finished orator of rare and glowing eloquence. He was also remarkable for his candour, and as time went on he drew nearer and nearer to the Left.

Malouet, who still played the part of critic with sense and vigour, and Clermont-Tonnerre, eloquent and attractive, led the Right-Centre. They had taken their early disappointments bravely, and they continued to accept the decisions of the Assembly loyally and to fight on the losing side with honour and spirit.

The extreme Right possessed two thoroughly unreasonable men: d'Eprémesnil, of the Paris Parlement, who had developed a hatred of all reform; and Mirabeau's younger brother, witty and impudent, called Mirabeau-Tonneau from his barrellike shape and drinking habits. He once came into the Assembly drunk and entrenched himself in the tribune, cursing and swearing; it took an hour to remove him.

Mirabeau, who sat on the Left, towered above all the members of the Assembly. They listened with unfailing delight and admiration to the torrents of his eloquence, fiery, terrifying, scornful, or persuasive. The Assembly was frequently swayed by him, but his ambiguous behaviour still caused distrust, and his legitimate ambition to become a Minister was thwarted by an ill-judged decree (7th Nov. 1789), aimed specially at him, which forbade deputies to become Ministers while the Assembly lasted. Foiled here, he laid his plans to become the secret adviser of the Court. Yet, with all his scheming, he was often carried away by his better impulses, and casting private considerations to the winds, spoke out like a true son of the Revolution. He was the leading spirit of the Diplomatic Committee, and as time went on, he began to win trust as well as admiration.

Only a few of the distinguished men on the Left can be mentioned here. Le Chapelier and Démeuniers, a literary man of Paris, were prominent on the Constitutional Committee, and Camille Desmoulins called them 'Constitution-makers in ordinary to the Nation'. Siéyes, who was also on this committee, stood aloof and seldom spoke. The talents and characters of certain members gave them a secure position of respect and confidence. Thouret was one, an excellent debater and speaker who treated difficult subjects in a masterly manner in his reports. Fréteau, of the Paris Parlement, good, prudent, and a little fussy, was another. So was the duc de la Rochefoucault, a great noble revered by all parties for his virtues. His cousin, the duc de Liancourt, a brilliant courtier, was, besides, a philanthropist with ideas that we should consider modern.

Conspicuous among the legal lights were Tronchet, Treilhard, and Target, of the Paris Bar, and Merlin of Douai. Merlin, who afterwards held extreme opinions, started as a moderate, and this was the case with Camus, and with the abbé Grégoire, a cleric of real piety whose attitude to opponents was unchristian in violence. It was the case too with the handsome and amiable advocate Barère, a useful member and a good speaker. Barère swam with the tide, his convictions were not deep; neither were those of the clever bishop of Autun, lame, aristocratic Talleyrand, an ambitious man of doubtful morals.

The extreme Left was led by four young men who had become intimate friends: Barnave, Adrien Duport, of the Paris Parlement, and Charles and Alexandre de Lameth, two soldier brothers, nobles of an ancient house. This section wished for rather more sweeping reforms than the rest of the Left did; they believed that the great upheaval of society which the Revolution was bringing gave legislators a chance which might never occur again, and they wanted, as Duport put it, to 'plough deep' while they were about it. Adrien

Duport, a delicate, friendly man, always full of plans, was an original thinker with more than a touch of genius and a passion for humanity and for justice. It was chiefly owing to his exertions that trial by jury was established. The Lameths combined a courtly charm with an ardour for liberty and equality. Charles, amusing and warm-hearted, was a speaker of the kind we call 'breezy'; Alexandre, handsome and fascinating, was a clever parliamentary tactician and an authority on military matters. Barnave, the best orator on the Left after Mirabeau, was a first-class debater, who excelled in throwing light on difficult questions and putting things simply and clearly. Candid and conscientious, his object was to convince, and he never spoke for effect. His position in the Assembly was peculiar; he spoke late in big debates, and after he had summed up the question, the Assembly was satisfied, and would hear no one else. He often found himself in opposition to Mirabeau and vanquished the great man several times. Both Barnave and Charles Lameth were extremely popular.

A small group of men who voted with this party were more extreme; Reubell, a bluff Alsatian; Buzot, a tall, eloquent Norman, good, refined, and melancholy because life did not come up to his ideals; Pétion, an advocate of Chartres, always serene and smiling, a fine figure of a man, well-meaning and a trifle vulgar. He was a ready and useful speaker, who argued well, and he fancied himself a great orator, for his self-conceit was boundless and joyous. More extreme still than these was Robespierre, a neat, short-sighted, spectacled lawyer of Arras, a strong and devoted champion of the people, with a gift for endless outpouring of speech. He was listened to, but thought an unpractical visionary, and he was not liked. The atmosphere of the Assembly, free, fearless, and critical, did not suit the reserved, suspicious, sentimental man; but outside he found admirers and devotees amongst whom he expanded.

We will now turn from the deputies to their two years' work. One of the first tasks of the Assembly was the division of the country into the eighty-three Departments which, with a few changes, remain to this day. The idea was due to Siéyes, and the chief object was to bind the new France together by obliterating the old divisions and associations that might keep it apart. The strength of France depended on its unity, and the Assembly felt that it was of vital importance to preserve this unity, and intended to make it impossible for any Province or group of Provinces to break away from the central Government and form a federal State.

The Departments were divided into 'districts', and these again into 'cantons'. In the 'cantons' met the 'primary Assemblies', which elected the 'Electors', who in their turn chose the deputies to the National Assembly. The old system of elections in two steps was kept, but the old class distinctions were, of course, abolished. In order to become an 'active citizen' and have a vote in the 'primary Assemblies', a man had to pay some small amount in taxes; in order to become an 'Elector' he had to pay a good deal more. It was the deliberate policy of the Assembly not to grant universal suffrage, and Robespierre was thought somewhat crazy when he demanded it. The deputies were afraid of putting political power suddenly into the hands of large masses of ignorant people who knew nothing of politics and might be led by unscrupulous agitators or by rich employers hostile to the Revolution. The Assembly has been much criticized for this, but those who have seen the course of the Revolution of 1917 in Russia will hardly be inclined to think it in the wrong. Later on, for various reasons, it was decreed that only 'active citizens' should serve in the National Guard, and here again Robespierre protested.

For administrative purposes, local assemblies, or councils, all elected, were set up in each Department, and in each 'district'; the small executive committees formed in these councils were called 'directorie'. In towns and villages, or in groups of villages – all alike called *communes* – municipalities, also elected, were set up; they consisted of the municipality proper (including a mayor) and of a larger council which, together with the municipality, was called the 'General Council of the Commune', or, for short, 'the *Commune.*' Paris had a special organization of the same kind.

By the legal reforms the old judicial system was swept away. The Parlements, some of which had attempted to set up their authority against that of the Assembly, were abolished, so were the minor courts, and a new tribunal was established in each Department. There was also a Court of 'Cassation', to hear appeals, and a High Court, at Orléans, to try cases of treason. All the judges were chosen by the same 'Electors' who chose the deputies, for the Assembly could not trust the Ministers to make impartial appointments; but only properly qualified men were eligible. Magistrates, called 'juges de paix', settled minor cases and arbitrated in disputes. Criminal cases were tried by a jury but, in spite of Duport's efforts, the Assembly left civil cases to be decided by the judges. A new penal code was made with less severe punishments than the old, and the legal Committee, which proposed it, was most anxious to abolish capital punishment. Duport, who was a member of the Committee, made a famous speech on the occasion;* but the Assembly would not allow the death penalty to be done away with, and

* 31 May 1791. Robespierre, who was not on the Committee, also spoke in favour of the abolition of capital punishment.

execution by decapitation was decreed. Two deputies tried in vain to get public executions forbidden.

In the course of these changes the order of advocates was abolished, for the Assembly considered that any close corporation which restricted an employment to its members was contrary to the principle of equality. For the same reason, all the guilds and trade unions of any kind were also abolished.

The Finances had to be reorganized. New and fairer taxes were gradually substituted for the old ones – which, in the meanwhile, continued in force; but the burden of taxation could not be lightened at once and heavy sacrifices were called for. The nation, it must be remembered, was on the verge of bankruptcy, and though some old expenses were cut down, new ones were incurred. For instance, when offices were suppressed, the State had to pay the holders who had bought them a fair proportion of the money they had invested. One of Necker's expedients for raising money was a 4 patriotic contribution equivalent to an income tax of 1s. 8d. in the £1 for three years, and Mirabeau made his greatest speech, on the horrors of national bankruptcy, in support of this measure (26th Sept. 1789). Necker, however, was soon found to be a poor financier, living from hand to mouth with a tax here and a loan there, and the Assembly had to make its own plans. It was absolutely necessary to find money in abundance to pay off debts, and the simplest way to procure it was for the nation to take over the vast landed property of the Church; this was not a new expedient for, in difficult times, the Kings of France had already appropriated Church lands. Naturally there was great opposition from the Clergy; the Church property was taken over, notwithstanding, the nation making itself responsible for the payment of the Clergy and the upkeep of public worship.

Later on the monastic orders were suppressed and all monks and nuns were free to return to the world if they chose, with a pension to live on; while those who did not wish to change their condition were allowed to remain together in certain convents and monasteries (13th Feb. 1790). Besides the Church lands, the nation took over all the royal lands, except some of the palaces and parks, and in their place the King was allotted a huge Civil List of more than a million pound sterling a year, while all his outstanding debts were paid.

The nation being now in possession of much landed property, the question was, how to dispose of it. Coin had become so scarce that those who wished to purchase the land could not get enough money together to buy, and the estates did not sell. After long debates the Assembly adopted Mirabeau's idea of issuing a kind of notes, which were called *assignats* because a portion of national land of corresponding value was *assigned* to pay them off (29th Sept. 1790). Mirabeau called them 'paper-earth' instead of 'paper money'. They were made legal tender and the debts of the State were paid with them; thus they passed into circulation, and when they returned to the Treasury in payment of a purchase of land, they were burnt. The amount of notes allowed to be in circulation at the same time was strictly limited by law, and while the Constituent Assembly ruled, the assignats commanded confidence. As a result of this issue, national lands began to sell, and all who bought them felt that their fortunes were now bound up with the Revolution, since they would certainly be deprived of their property if the Revolution failed.

The Army and Navy had to be reorganized, and the Assembly began by adopting voluntary enlistment in preference to conscription. Both Services were going through a dangerous time of transition. The officers, mostly nobles, were usually attached to the old order and their men suspected them, often with justice, of disloyalty to the Revolution. On the other hand the men became so undisciplined that most officers, however good their intentions, could do nothing with them. In the autumn of 1790 there was a bad naval mutiny at Brest, and a worse mutiny in the Army at Nancy which General de Bouillé suppressed in a ruthless manner.

The Assembly, though inclined at first to sympathize entirely with the soldiers, saw later on that discipline must be maintained and the officers supported.

The tricolour had been adopted by the nation in 1789; in the autumn of 1790 it became the national flag. "The national colours", cried Mirabeau, "will win respect from all countries; not as the sign of combat and victory, but as the sign of the sacred confraternity of the friends of Liberty throughout the earth, and as the terror of tyrants and conspirators."

With regard to foreign policy, the Assembly early formulated the great principle that every nation has a right to dispose of itself. In May 1790, in consequence of a trivial dispute between Great Britain and Spain over a settlement in North America, the deputies found that France was likely to be dragged into war with England, on account of an old secret treaty with Spain. A long and celebrated debate took place on the question of whether the right of making war and peace ought to belong to the nation – i.e. to the Assembly – or to the King. All speakers on both sides were at their best, and the debate ended in a contest between Mirabeau, who took the side of the King, and Barnave, who took the side of the nation. Mirabeau won the victory, but only by throwing over his principles and adopting those of the other side, and it was decreed that while the King must propose to the Assembly to make war, war could not be declared without a decree of the Assembly, and that treaties of peace must also be ratified in the same manner. During this debate Robespierre made a fine suggestion; he wished the French nation to declare that it renounced all wars for conquest; other speakers took up the idea, and this declaration became an article of the Constitution.

The Revolution was bound to make enemies. All these changes brought losses to many and anxiety and discomfort to most, and although the bulk of the nation, uplifted by the new ideals, bore them gladly for the sake of liberty and country, there were naturally malcontents. The taking over of Church lands and, still more, the refusal of the Assembly to declare that Catholicism was the national religion (April 1790), made some of the clergy and their adherents actively hostile to the Revolution. In the South, where passions ran high, Catholics and Protestants had been living side by side in amity; they now began to quarrel, and in Toulouse, Montauban, and Nimes, serious religious riots, with bloodshed, took place in the spring of 1790. The flames of strife were fanned by the *émigrés*, over the border, where these self-exiled nobles and courtiers had rallied round the runaway princes, who were taking refuge for the moment in Turin. Rumours of plots hatched between them and the officers of the French Army flew about, and the turbulent people of Marseilles seized upon the forts of their city; troubles caused by distrust occurred in Toulon, Montpellier, and Valence.

The Assembly dealt with these disorders firmly but mercifully. Already, in October 1789, after a Paris mob, chiefly of women, had hanged an unoffending baker, a Riot Act (called 'martial law') had been passed. This act provided that the National Guard, when required to by the civil authorities, could disperse a crowd by force, if that crowd refused to disperse itself after a thrice-repeated summons and the display of a red flag.

The Revolution brought freedom of the Press, and the multitude of newspapers which sprang up helped to make the work of the Assembly known to the nation. Every one wanted to read the debates, and reports of them filled the papers; indeed some papers contained nothing else. Barère, and for a short time Mirabeau, reported them for papers of their own. The newspapers were small, cost little to run, and represented the independent opinions of their writers; they gained in interest by being obliged to put their news concisely, and they were not disfigured by advertisements. The *Moniteur* was the biggest and the best of the daily papers. A popular weekly paper, the *Revolutions de France et de Brabant*,* written by Camille Desmoulins, was a brilliant and witty essay on current political topics

* In allusion to a small revolution in Belgium, 1789–90.

of the day. Its rival the *Actes des Apôtres*, written by some deputies of the Right, ridiculed the deputies of the Left and their doings in a manner generally coarse and often obscene. There were detestable journals on both sides; one of the most bloodthirsty, called *l'Ami du Peuple,* was written by a strange, half-crazy doctor named Marat; a fierce little man with a large hooked nose and beautiful dark eyes, who wore dirty, untidy clothes and tied up his head in a handkerchief. Marat was a clever writer, with a strong sympathy for the poor, and he was entirely disinterested; but he was unscrupulous as to what he wrote, suspicious in the highest degree, and eaten up by vanity. He sometimes wrote good sense, but he had no political system, and his great idea of a remedy in any difficulties was to call for the heads of all who disagreed with him. No one paid much attention to him under the Constituent Assembly, but he was sometimes threatened with prosecution for his incendiary writings, and spent a large part of his time hiding from the law in cellars. This made him vainer than ever.

Pamphlets continued to appear in shoals, of all shades of opinion and many of them scurrilous. The Court party, strange to say, and their hired pamphleteers set the example of writing disrespectfully of the royal family; they also libelled the deputies of the Left in an outrageous fashion. The law of libel was not strong enough to stop this; yet though the deputies of the Right cried out for checks on the licence of the Press when they suffered from it themselves, the Left, daily libelled in pamphlets and cruelly attacked in newspapers, refused to endanger the freedom of the Press by fresh restrictive laws; public men, they said, must be prepared to face calumny and to live it down.

If the newspapers did much for the political education of the country, political clubs did even more. The Breton Club ended when the Assembly moved to Paris, but it was quickly revived in a slightly different form and took the name of 'Friends of the Constitution'. Its popular name was the Jacobin Club, because it sat in the convent of the Jacobins, near the Manège. At first only deputies could belong, but soon well-known and respectable citizens from outside were admitted in increasing numbers; the President was always a member of the Assembly. The motto of the club was "Vivre libre ou mourir" (live free, or die), and its object was to discuss questions which were coming before the Assembly; deputies who belonged were not bound in any way by the decisions of the Club. The Jacobins met on three evenings of the week and listened to good speeches from the best orators of the Assembly and also to dull speeches from prosy bores; in the early days the proceedings were decorous. There was nothing mysterious about the society and everything was done in a public manner; but down to May 1791, when the Club moved into a larger hall, there was little room for outsiders.

The idea of encouraging the creation of similar societies throughout France, of affiliating them to the parent society and corresponding with them, to keep them up to the mark, is attributed to Adrien Duport. It met with speedy success, and by this means the Jacobins obtained a strong influence on public opinion and became of great importance. For the first year and a half, the chief leaders of the Club were Duport, the Lameths, and Barnave; they never intended the Club to become violent, and believed that if men of unsound views but good faith were given a chance of airing them, and were argued with, they would be converted by the forces of truth and reason.

There was another side to the activities of the Jacobins. When members discovered breaches of the law, instances of tyranny, or suspicious behaviour, they used to denounce them to the Club, which took action if the matter was thought serious enough. This kind of watchfulness was useful at a time when disaffected men were always trying to evade the laws and to make trouble; but it encouraged the habit of denunciation, one of the most mischievous that human beings can fall into. In the early days, when the Club was led by generous-minded men, denunciations were not a prominent feature of its sittings, nevertheless the habit which was afterwards such a blot on the society began to be formed.

In the spring of 1790, some prominent deputies of the Left, who did not care for the Jacobin Club and wanted something safer and more select, founded another club, called 'The 1789 Society', and organized it like the Jacobins with political debates and affiliated societies. Siéyes was a founder, so was Lafayette, who, though he talked of "the sacred right of insurrection" in a speech, was in reality moderate, thought Duport's views dangerous, and was jealous of the Lameths. Thouret, Le Chapelier, and other distinguished men joined, and this division among the 'patriots' (as the Left were called) did much harm, by encouraging estrangements and making differences of opinion appear greater than they were.

The Right had clubs of their own, none of them long-lived, and there was a club of some importance to which deputies did not belong; the Cordeliers' Club. One of the districts of Paris on the south side of the river, called the 'Cordeliers' district', from a large Franciscan convent which it contained, had a local Council which championed Marat, an inhabitant of the quarter, and took a prominent and rather violent part in Parisian public affairs, under the presidency of

Danton, a rising young advocate with a mighty voice and a flow of eloquence. The district disappeared in a new division of Paris, but a club had been formed, called the Cordeliers' Club, of which advanced citizens of the quarter, such as Camille Desmoulins, were members. Danton belonged, too, but devoted his energies to the Jacobin Club, of which he was an important member.

Besides these clubs of the well-to-do, there were many Fraternal and Popular Societies, where poorer people, women as well as men, met together to hear the new laws and the Constitution explained by better-informed brethren. Political talk was not confined to the clubs; the cafés and restaurants were full of it, and in every public place there were always orators ready to jump on chairs or tubs and harangue any one who would listen, on the topics of the hour.

The most striking event of 1790 was the 'Federation', the first and greatest festival of the Revolution.

It arose in a natural and spontaneous manner. There was a general wish amongst the French people to show in some definite way their new sense of brotherhood and union, their loyalty to the Assembly and to the Constitution that was being made. An example of how to express this feeling was given by some National Guards from Dauphine and from a small neighbouring Province, who met together, in November 1789, to fraternize and to swear that they would remain united for ever in support of the laws of the National Assembly. In January a bigger meeting of the same kind took place in Dauphine, and another in Brittany, where the young men of Brittany met the young men of Anjou; and the idea began to spread.

An event in the Assembly gave fresh impetus to the desire of the citizens to bind themselves to the Revolution and to each other by an oath.

On February 4th, 1790, the King paid a surprise visit to the Manège, and declared, in a long speech, that the abolition of the Orders had been a benefit, and that he, for his part, could not regret what he had lost by the Revolution, since it was for the common good. Every one, he said, including the monarch, must henceforth work together in unity for the good of the country, and he promised to maintain constitutional liberty. The Queen, he was particular to say, shared his feelings; and they intended to bring up the Dauphin with constitutional ideas. The Queen confirmed this in a speech to a deputation sent her by the Assembly. The King's action caused great enthusiasm, and as soon as he had gone, the deputies all took an oath to be faithful to the Nation, the Law, and the King, and to maintain the Constitution. The galleries, at their own request, were allowed to swear too, and the Municipality of Paris took a similar oath the same day.

This oath was called the 'civic oath', because an oath of the kind was required of every citizen who assumed public functions.

The King had now, of his own free will, put himself at the head of the Revolution, much to the joy of his subjects, and the most loyal of them could join in the popular meetings without scruple. All over the kingdom, National Guards from different places met to federate themselves together by taking the civic oath. There were Federations large and small, and everywhere the whole population attended the joyful ceremony, while, to mark its religious character, a mass was sung and the banners of the National Guards were blessed. In May there were important big Federations at Metz and Orléans; at Lyons, at the end of the same month, there was a gigantic Federation for the whole south of France, with elaborate decorations and festivities. In June, at Strasbourg, the regular troops joined with the National Guards in another.

The Paris municipality felt that the anniversary of the Revolution ought to be celebrated by a crowning Federation in Paris; all parties in the Assembly desired it, the King gave his consent, and it was decided that the 14th July should be the day, the Champ-de-Mars the place, and that deputies should be sent by the National Guards of every Department, by every regiment in the Army, and by the Navy.

The Assembly celebrated the anniversary of the oath of the Tennis-court by a famous decree. On the evening of the 19th of June, came a deputation led by a Prussian Baron named Anacharsis Cloots, a resident in Paris and a sincere, if rather crack-brained, enthusiast for liberty. Cloots brought with him representatives of many countries, including Indians, Arabs and Chaldees, in their national costume, and in their name he congratulated the Assembly, and begged that they might join in the Federation. The Assembly saw in this testimony of sympathy from the nations of the earth a happy foretaste of the coming brotherhood of man, and no one knew that Cloots had only collected together foreigners who lived in Paris, and that Arabia and Chaldea were represented by French professors. No sooner had the deputation withdrawn, than Alexandre Lameth remarked that the sight of the chains on the statues of conquered Provinces grouped round a monument of Louis XIV, would be offensive to the National Guards from those Provinces who were coming to the Federation, and proposed to remove them. He had hardly finished when an obscure deputy, crying: "To-day is the tomb of vanity!" demanded the abolition of all titles, from Duke downwards. The nobles of the Left supported him in generous emulation; Charles Lameth first and Lafayette second. "Let us have no distinctions but those which virtue gives!" said de Noailles, and proposed to abolish liveries. Count Mathieu de Montmorency, a young member of a renowned and ancient house, proposed to abolish coats of arms and crests. Lepeletier de Saint-Fargeau, of the Paris Parlement, proposed that all citizens should be called by their family names only,* and begged leave to be known henceforth as Michel Lepeletier. It was in vain that the nobles of the Right, ably seconded by Maury, argued and protested; hereditary titles were abolished, and all the other proposals were decreed. 'How will men who serve the State be rewarded?' asked a deputy; and Lafayette answered nobly, that they would be rewarded by having served the State.

The Right were highly incensed by this decree, and not the Right only; Mirabeau did not approve and Lafayette soon began to think it impolitic. Most people, however, rejoiced at the breaking down of a barrier which separated man from man. The newspapers, interpreting the decree strictly, began to call Mirabeau, Riquetti, and Lafayette, Motier – their family names, but no one else did, and any man who wished to keep

* Before tile Revolution the Christian name was very little used in France with tile surname, and members of a family were distinguished by tacking on to the family name a 'de' with the name of an estate or piece of property belonging to the family. This was the custom among the bourgeoisie as well as among the aristocracy. The result was puzzling, especially as the family name was often dropped.

his title-name kept it, without the title. People with democratic tendencies dropped the 'de' before their names, and many lengthy names were simplified.

The time of the Federation drew near, and every preparation had been made to give the Fédérés, as the National Guards from the Departments were called, a brotherly welcome. But the Champ-de-Mars, which was being dug and levelled and heaped into terraces round a vast central space, was nothing like ready, and the workmen were taking their time over it. Some one wrote to the papers to suggest that the National Guards should help, and soon not only National Guards but citizens of all classes were thronging the Champ-de-Mars, with spades, pickaxes, and barrows. During a happy fortnight they laboured side by side in perfect friendship and perfect order. Workmen came in bands with drums and music; deputies from the Assembly lent a hand; market-women loaded barrows with earth and fine ladies wheeled them away; monks and nuns left their cloisters to help; mothers brought their families with them. There were actors and actresses, children from boarding-schools, old soldiers from the Invalides, young ones from the King's Swiss Guard, all working away, and the villages round Paris sent stout contingents of labourers, with the mayor and curé at their head. The King himself came to look on one day. There was joking and laughing and singing, the favourite song being a gay little dance-tune, set to the refrain of *Ah ça ira, ça ira, ça ira!* with any other words suitable to the occasion which came into the singers' heads. This ça *ira*! became the rage, and every one sang it.* The Champ-de-Mars was ready in time, ample and beautiful, with a gallery at one end for the King and the Assembly, and, near the Seine, a stately triumphal arch, to which a bridge of boats led. In the centre was the altar of 'la patrie', raised high on many flights of steps.

The day arrived, stormy and pouring wet. But nothing could damp the spirits of the French or chill the glow of patriotism and brotherly love in their hearts. The long route of the procession was lined with spectators, the windows were full of them, so were the roofs of the houses and the trees of the Champs-Élysées; the lucky multitude in the Champ-de-Mars sat under umbrellas, and put them down when it rained less. Every one was wet and every one was merry and ready to beguile the time with songs. The Fédérés with their banners, and the troops with the Oriflamme, the old flag of France, started their march in the north of Paris at six o'clock. All the authorities of Paris walked in the procession, which was so long that it took four hours to pass any point. The head of it reached the place

* The words used were, sometimes, "les aristocrates à la lanterne!" They were meant, on this occasion, simply as a joke.

Louis XV near noon, and the Assembly, waiting under umbrellas in the Tuileries gardens, joined it. Muddy and wet, line after line entered the Champ-de-Mars, under the arch, and took their places. Talleyrand, Bishop of Autun, and sixty white-robed chaplains of the Paris National Guard were waiting on the altar steps, and the rain poured down on them and on the Fédérés. But every one laughed at the storms, and the Fédérés began to dance, both to express their joy and to keep warm. The King and the royal family arrived and were heartily cheered, but Lafayette, in command of all the troops, was the hero of the day, and all eyes turned to him as he rode hither and thither on his white horse, ordering and directing. At length, at four o'clock, the last of the procession arrived, the rain stopped, and by and by the sun actually came out. The ceremony began; the banners and the Oriflamme were brought to the altar to be blessed, and the Bishop of Autun said mass. Then the trumpets blew, and Lafayette, grave and gallant, mounted the altar-steps alone and, touching the altar with his sword, took the oath in the name of all the National Guards of France; the troops repeated it with a clash of arms, and the guns fired. The King took his oath standing up in the gallery, and the Assembly took theirs, after their President, with more firing of cannon; every one else joined in. The Queen, present in another gallery, held up the little Dauphin, and the crowds, wild with joy, cheered King, Queen, Dauphin, Assembly, and Nation, again and again. A *Te Deum* was sung, and people and troops, cold, damp, and joyful, marched home again.

In Paris, when the guns fired, all who were left behind raised their hands and took the oath too; and all over France the municipalities called their people together, on July 14th, to join in the national festival. Perhaps the spirit of the day was best caught in two verses of a song, written for the occasion (though not used) by Joseph Chenier, which may be freely translated thus:

> God of the people and of Kings, God of the cities
>   and the fields,
> Luther and Calvin's deity, God of the ancient
>   Israelites,
> To whom the Zoroastrian in far-off lands his worship
>   yields
> When he invokes the sun 'neath mountain heights—
> Behold them, met together here, under thine all-
>   embracing glance,
> To celebrate the happiness whose rising beams begin
>   to shine,—
> From every corner of the realm, the sons and the
>   supports of France,
> All equals; in their own eyes as in thine.

IV

THE KING AND THE
CONSTITUTION JULY 1790 –
30TH SEPTEMBER 1791

The King, as we have seen, was still much beloved at the time of the Federation, and both he and the Queen laid themselves out to be gracious to the Fédérés, received with obvious pleasure the loyal addresses which many of them had brought from their Departments, and won golden opinions. Louis and Marie-Antoinette had lately taken the important step of appointing Mirabeau to be their secret counsellor. The business had been arranged by a mutual friend, the bargain being, that Mirabeau should write notes of advice for the Court and support the King's authority in the Assembly, while, in return, the King was to pay the debts which so cruelly harassed the statesman, and to give him a salary which would enable him to live in comfort. The King also set aside a large sum of money to be given to Mirabeau when the Constituent Assembly should be dissolved – provided he had given satisfaction.

All this has an ugly sound, but Mirabeau said of himself that he was "paid but not bought", and this was strictly true. He did believe that liberty could not be secured without a strong Government in which the King held much authority, and he let the King know of his determination that the monarchy must be constitutional.

Mirabeau knew that if he wished to sway the King he must win over the Queen, but the Queen had a horror and dread of him and it was difficult to persuade her to see him. She was induced to grant him an interview in strictest secrecy, and early one July morning (3rd), he came to the Palace of Saint-Cloud, near Paris, where the Court was spending the summer, and was received by the Queen in her private apartments. Each of them was delighted with the other; the Queen forgot her fears, and Mirabeau, struck with her cleverness and courage, declared afterwards that she was "the only man in her family", and built great hopes upon her sagacity. In his zeal he sent note after note of advice; the advice was graciously received, but neither King nor Queen acted on it, and Mirabeau, still hopeful, was sometimes in ecstasies over the great soul of "the daughter of Maria-Theresa", and at others was so much irritated that he talked about the obstinacy of "the royal cattle".

Some of his advice was excellent; some was detestable. It was excellent when he urged the King to change his Ministers, for they were inefficient and unpopular. Necker resigned (Sept. 1790) after a noisy Paris mob had twice demanded their dismissal; the rest stayed on, and the King did nothing. In the autumn of 1790 matters came to a crisis over the mutinies in Army and Navy, and the Ministers were so severely criticized in the Assembly that they thought it wise to resign. Only one remained, the comte de Montmorin, Minister of Foreign Affairs, an honourable but weak man, who stood well with the Assembly. Montmorin disliked the Revolution and did not care about being Minister, but he had the sense to see that the King's best course was to submit to the Assembly, and he remained in office because he had been the King's friend from boyhood and would not desert him.

The new Ministers now appointed were men loyal to the Revolution and ready to work with the Assembly. Among them was Duport-Dutertre, a plain advocate who was raised to the exalted post of Keeper of the Seals, and filled it with dignity and simplicity.

After the change of Ministers, Montmorin was put into communication with Mirabeau, to help him with his secret plans. Mirabeau had many such plans. One was that the King and Queen should leave Paris and appeal to the nation against the tyranny of the Assembly – for Mirabeau did not shrink from civil war. But most of all he wanted the royal couple to make themselves popular by pretending to be heart and soul with the Revolution, in order that they might lull the nation into security, and, when they had accomplished this, they were gradually to recover as much of their power as Mirabeau thought safe. He had, too, a gigantic scheme for influencing everybody without their being aware of it. Writers were to be paid secretly to compose pamphlets and spread them over France; spies and secret agents everywhere were to report to him; the cleverest members of the Assembly were to be made to work for his ends without suspecting it; the Queen was to have a man, entirely devoted to her, always with the King, to keep him straight in her absence. Mirabeau himself was to sit behind the scenes, pulling the strings of all his puppets. This plan was never carried out; indeed it was an impossible scheme at a time when men of all parties were sincere and open.

The chief obstacle to the King's regaining his power was the National Assembly, and the Court party was already making feeble attempts to undermine its authority. Mirabeau suggested more effective ways of doing this and undertook to carry them out. Thus, the Assembly was to be persuaded to pass bad decrees, and debates on unimportant subjects were to be prolonged, so that every one might see how badly the deputies were wasting time. But Mirabeau's better impulses sometimes ran away with him, and he only carried out his black designs fitfully. All this time he was posing in public as the loyal champion of the Assembly, and the extent of his perfidy was never known till his private papers were published some sixty years after his death.*

The King might have done well with new Ministers and Mirabeau to support him, if a measure of the Assembly which concerned the Church had not offended his conscience and made him irreconcilable. This measure was the first of the two great mistakes made by the Assembly.

Hostility had been roused by the taking over of the Church lands and the suppression of the Religious Orders, but not to the extent of making a complete breach between Catholicism and the Revolution, and, if the Assembly had let well alone, things might have settled down quietly. There was, however, among the deputies a small knot of deeply religious men, lay and clerical, who regarded themselves as good Catholics;

* Published in 1851. Carlyle's French Revolution, which takes a more favourable view of Mirabeau, was published in 1837.

Camus and Fréteau headed them, and this little band was bent on bringing the Church back to the purity of primitive times. These deputies belonged, also, to an historical party in the French Church which was hostile to the authority of the Pope and wished for a large amount of independence. The rest of the deputies of the Left, who thoroughly approved of their objects, left Church-reform to them and seldom joined in the serious and learned debates which took place.

In accordance with the views of the reformers, sweeping changes were made. All clerical salaries were fixed, the Bishops' stipends were cut down and the poorer clergy were given enough to live upon; the old bishoprics were changed for new, one in each Department, and it was decreed that both Bishops and Cures were to be elected – not by the faithful but by the 'Electors' of the Department. Bishops were to write to the Pope to announce their election, but were forbidden to ask him to confirm it. Finally, before practising their functions, the salaried clergy must take the 'civic oath', in which they promised to maintain the Constitution as decreed by the Assembly and sanctioned by the King.

These decrees, called 'the civil constitution of the Clergy', were finished in July, and the King accepted them, much against his will. Some of his advisers, and chiefly the Archbishop of Aix, a clerical deputy, tried, without success, to get the Pope to give some kind of sanction to the 'civil constitution', in the hope of ensuring peace. In the meanwhile the decrees were not carried out, and many of the higher clergy used the unpopularity of the 'civil constitution' to stir up political strife in the name of religion. Matters became so serious that something had to be done, as all parties agreed.

The Left reasoned thus: 'the State cannot continue to pay and keep in office men who are doing their utmost to oppose the will of the nation; such men must be removed from their posts.' Accordingly, at the end of November, a decree was passed ordering all the clergy who held any office paid by the State to take the oath in a specified time, on pain of being deprived of their benefices. Those who refused were allowed to continue their ministrations in an unofficial way, and, as long as they lived peaceably, were to receive a pension.

The King delayed giving his sanction to this decree and made another appeal to the Pope. The Assembly, resenting the idea of any outside interference in the affairs of France, refused to wait for the answer, and put such pressure on the King that he felt himself obliged to accept the decree. A few of the clerical deputies, with Grégoire at their head, now took the oath, but the majority did not, and the allotted time ran out. Cazalès pleaded wisely for further delay, but his colleagues, unwisely, would not grant it, and it was decreed (3rd Jan. 1791) that the oath must be taken at once. There was a great scene in the Assembly (4th Jan.) when the Bishops and Cures among the deputies were called upon to come up and take the oath and one by one refused, refusing at the same time to resign their benefices. Their example was followed by many of the most conscientious clerics throughout the kingdom, as well as by the political firebrands who hated the Revolution. In the course of time all who refused to take the oath were deprived of their benefices and replaced by elected clergy, and thus arose a schism in the Church and two kinds of priests: the constitutional clergy who had taken the oath, and the 'non-jurors' who had refused it.

A misunderstanding was at the bottom of this grievous affair. The Assembly had no intention of offending any man's conscience or of meddling with spiritual matters, and repeatedly assured the clergy of it; for the deputies could not understand why anything that regarded a temporal matter like a benefice should be considered spiritual. The clergy felt, that in limiting the authority of the Pope and in moving clerics from the posts in which the Church had placed them, the Assembly was touching spiritual matters. Down to this time large numbers of the 'lower clergy' had been friendly to the Revolution; most were now alienated, and simple country folk, in parts of the South and West, who found themselves deprived of their beloved pastors, were alienated too.

Henceforth the King had the full sanction of his conscience in trying to outwit the Assembly. He was put in a difficult position, for he did not recognize the constitutional clergy and wished to have the ministrations of non-juring priests, while the masses looked on such priests as the enemies of the Revolution. Feeling ran high, and the Paris mob made disgraceful attempts to persecute the non-jurors and their congregations. Danton, who though extreme was always kindly, one day protected a non-juring curé from an angry crowd.

In February 1791 matters were made worse by the flight of 'Mesdames', the King's aunts, who started off quietly for Rome, in order to escape from the new laws about the clergy. Rumours were already afloat that the whole royal family intended to fly, and the departure of the old ladies seemed to confirm them. There was a hubbub, with hot debates in the Assembly and prolonged disturbances in Paris.

Mirabeau was now at the height of his power and influence. He had rejoined the Jacobins, he had gained fresh lustre as President of the National Assembly, and his position with the Court appeared to be secure when, at the end of March 1791, he was suddenly taken ill. His life of strain – days filled with politics and nights with pleasure and, too often, with dissipation – had worn out his robust constitution, and his illness became critical. As soon as his danger was known, the warm heart of France forgot his faults and remembered only his greatness and his services to the Revolution. Traffic was stopped in his street, anxious crowds waited for the last bulletin and all Paris hung on the ups and downs of his sickness. The great man, though suffering terribly, was himself to the last; affectionate to his friends, fully conscious of his position, picturesque and striking in his talk. "J'emporte avec moi le deuil de la monarchie", he said once – a memorable and untranslatable phrase, signifying that the last remains of the French Monarchy were going to the grave with him. To Talleyrand, an old friend, he confided his last legacy to the Assembly, a speech he had prepared on the law of inheritance. Before dawn on April 2nd he prepared to die. The rising sun began to shine into his window; he smiled and said: "If that is not God, it is at least his first cousin," and a little later he passed away.

"Of how immense a prey has death become possessor!" said Talleyrand, and all France was shaken by the blow. In the Assembly many deputies wept, and when Talleyrand read Mirabeau's last speech it was

listened to in respectful silence, while every eye turned
to the lost leader's empty seat. And all the while the
speech had not been written by Mirabeau, but by one
of his friends, a Swiss pastor. Happily no one knew
this. It was decreed that Mirabeau should be buried in
the new church of Sainte-Genevieve – afterwards the
Pantheon – and that this church should become the
resting-place of the great men of France. The whole
Assembly, the Ministers, the Municipality, the Jacobins,
and other political clubs, walked in the funeral procession and all Paris lined the way. The weather was dry
and dusty, and an onlooker expressed surprise that the
streets had not been watered; 'the Municipality was
counting on our tears,' replied a market-woman.

Easter was close at hand, and the King decided to
spend it at Saint-Cloud, for he wished to receive his
Easter Communion from the hands of a non-juring
priest, without attracting attention. But the Parisians
guessed his reason, they also believed that he meant
to fly from Saint-Cloud, and on the 18th April, when
the royal family got into their carriage, a crowd, which
had gathered round the Tuileries, stopped it. Lafayette
and Bailly ordered the National Guards to clear the
way; the National Guards refused, and the royal family
was obliged to re-enter the Palace. The King went to
the Assembly to protest his loyalty to the Constitution,
in the hope of getting help; but, though he was received

with loyal respect, he was not encouraged to go to Saint-Cloud, and he gave up the idea. He did more, for he consented at last to take a step which the Diplomatic Committee had long been urging on him: he instructed Montmorin to send a circular letter to all his ambassadors and ministers at foreign Courts, telling them in the most unequivocal language that the King had put himself at the head of the Revolution.

Shortly after this victory, the Assembly, at the instigation of Robespierre, made its second great mistake; a fatal one.

An idea was in the air that it would be well to prevent the re-election of the members of the Constituent Assembly to the next Assembly. This idea was perhaps started by the enemies of the Revolution, who saw in it the best way of securing that the next Assembly should not have the prestige and the talents of the first. Almost all the Right were in favour of it, and it had been advocated by Mirabeau in his perfidious advice to the King. Outside the Assembly, men with pretensions who were jealous of the fame of the leading deputies thought it was high time that their own turn should come, and were eager for it; so were other men who thought the Assembly too moderate. The idea appealed to the Left as a piece of disinterested self-sacrifice, and as most people held the mistaken opinion that France could produce several more sets of men just as competent to guide the State as the first had shown themselves, the danger was not perceived. Only a small minority of enlightened deputies were strongly opposed to the popular idea; chief among them were Thouret, Le Chapelier, and the Jacobin leaders, Barnave, Duport, and the two Lameths.

It happened that at this moment the Jacobin leaders had lost much of their influence. They were too moderate to please the hot-headed extremists whom they had once delighted, for they were anxious to end the Revolution, and the extremists wanted it to go on. Their power in the Jacobins had waned, because the character of the club had altered through the admission of too many violent new members; the sittings had grown noisy and the leaders were ceasing to attend them. Further, Barnave had just flung away his popularity in opposing, vainly, a popular and dangerous piece of reform for the Colonies. This reform had been hotly advocated by a very clever journalist, Brissot, in his paper *Le Patriote français*, and by other journalists of his advanced school. These journalists were fond of praising Robespierre's inflexible principles in contrast to Barnave's love of compromise, and Robespierre's influence rose. His oratory had improved, and his telling speeches made him a power in the Jacobins and in the Assembly; it was his day, and he used it. He had already induced the Assembly to decree that no members of the Constituent Assembly should be able to become Ministers for four years after it had ended (7th April) and on the 16th May he proposed that no member of the Constituent Assembly should be eligible for re-election to the next Assembly. The motion was passed with general enthusiasm; the Right were enchanted at the folly of the Left, and Maury in his joy jumped up on his bench. Thouret, Merlin, Beaumez and Le Chapelier, who opposed, were not listened to, and Barnave and his friends were so unpopular at the moment that their opposition would have been useless.

The mischief was done, but Robespierre was too wild in his proposals to keep his ascendancy in the Assembly; before long things returned to their usual state in the Manège, and there was still hope that the decree might be repealed.

By the middle of June the work of the Assembly was drawing to a close. A Committee of Revision was helping the Constitutional Committee to separate the scattered laws of the Constitution from the laws which were not constitutional, and to put them into proper form in a Constitutional Act; the elections to the new Assembly were beginning. Suddenly, early on the morning of the 21st of June, the news spread through Paris that the King and all the royal family had vanished in the night. Louis had fled; probably to seek help from the foreigner, certainly to raise the standard of civil war, and a dark future of strife and disaster opened out to every eye. Treachery too, it was supposed, must have been at work, for the guards round the Palace had been doubled and an escape seemed impossible. Suspicion fell on Lafayette, who was responsible, and his life was in danger from the angry mob. But the Assembly was there, calm and undismayed, to act and to give the lead. The deputies had already voted several urgent measures, when Reubell rose and began to hint at Lafayette's complicity in the King's flight. Lafayette was Barnave's enemy and had lately treated him badly, but Barnave did not hesitate to risk his own reputation and safety to save the General. His warm defence of Lafayette's patriotism, and his appeal for unity, touched an Assembly which always responded to generosity. Lafayette was saved, and from that moment all parties worked together in harmony for the good of the country. Everything that could be done to reassure Paris, and France, to prevent disorder and to carry on the Government in the King's absence, was done promptly. The Ministers, abandoned by the King, were only too glad to work with the Committees, including even Montmorin, who had known nothing of the King's flight. He had been left to his fate by his royal friend, and his life had been in danger from the mob.

The wisdom and prudence of the Assembly

preserved order, and such was the respect in which it was held that France passed through this great crisis almost without bloodshed* and even without riots. The people contented themselves with tearing down royal signs over shops and other buildings; the very word 'royal' became obnoxious, and a showman who was exhibiting a 'royal tiger' altered the title to 'national tiger'.

From the first, the Assembly took the line that the King could only have been lured away from his duty by treacherous counsels, and orders were issued that the royal family must be stopped, by any one who came across them. Lafayette's aides-de-camp were already scouring the roads from Paris, and other couriers were sent on the search. The King had left behind him a long letter or manifesto, containing his reasons for flight, which was read to the Assembly. It was a somewhat querulous catalogue of his grievances, great and small, and did his cause no good.

As soon as there was a lull in the press of special business, the deputies were ready to return calmly to their usual work, and the President, Alexandre Beauharnais, said, as if nothing had happened: "Let us pass to the order of the day."

The union in the Assembly was complete, and

* One murder took place.

Robespierre had no chance of stirring up strife there; he found a different atmosphere when he went to the Jacobins in the evening. Here the Club was already talking of treachery, and Danton was demanding Lafayette's head. Robespierre poured oil upon the flames in a long, plaintive speech, of a kind that both he and his audience loved. He denounced all the Ministers and nearly all the Assembly for being concerned in the plot with the King; he dwelt on his own services and his certainty that he would be assassinated. The Jacobins, in a frenzy of enthusiasm, were shouting that they would die with him, when in trooped all the Jacobin deputies, arm in arm with the members of the 1789 Club, in token of unity and friendship, Alexandre Lameth and Lafayette, who had been the worst enemies of all, at their head. Robespierre was routed, and after the Club had been brought to see the need of union, the deputies returned to the Manège, as the Assembly was sitting day and night.

We must now turn to the royal family. The King and Queen had planned their escape some six months before, unknown to Mirabeau. They did not fly because they were in fear of their lives; their situation in Paris was highly disagreeable but not dangerous, and they knew this. They knew, too, that they might be risking their lives by flight. But they had been informed that foreign Powers would do nothing for them unless the

King got away from Paris and showed that a good number of his people were ready to support him against the Assembly. So they decided to go to the Army of General de Bouillé, whose head-quarters were at Montmédy, on the eastern frontier, and to throw themselves on the loyalty of the troops. Naturally they could not leave their young children behind, nor Madame Elisabeth, who shared all their fortunes; Monsieur and his wife were to escape separately at the same time. Only four or five persons were in the secret, one of them being de Bouillé, who arranged to post a small troop at a place a little beyond Châlons, with orders to meet and escort a consignment of money; other troops were to be posted at intervals along the way from there to Montmédy, with orders to protect it. The actual escape was managed by the comte de Fersen, a Swedish nobleman who was a devoted friend and admirer of the Queen, and a Russian Baroness procured passports for the party by a trick. If once the fugitives could get clear away past Châlons and reach the first party of soldiers, they were safe.

So far all was well contrived, but mistakes were made too. A new carriage, a 'berline', was built for the occasion, more likely to attract attention than an old one. Three former Body-Guards were chosen at haphazard to act as couriers, men of no resource, without knowledge of the road, and they were dressed in noticeable second-hand yellow liveries. Then, the duchesse de Tourzel, governess of the royal children, had to be taken, because it was her right to go with her charges, and two lady attendants had also to be taken to wait on the Princesses, which necessitated a second, smaller carriage.

On Monday, the 20th June, the royal family spent the day as usual and went to bed at the usual time. Shortly after, they got up, put on plain clothes and walked, separately, down a private staircase and through some empty apartments, of which they had the key, and so out of the Palace, unnoticed by the sentries, who were accustomed to see many people leave the Tuileries at that hour. The children were brought out first and put into a cab driven by Fersen, which waited in a square hard by until the others came. The Queen did not arrive for nearly an hour, and she had adventures on the way. First, Lafayette's carriage, in which he was leaving the Tuileries, passed so close to her that she could have touched it; then, as neither she nor the Body-Guard who was conducting her knew the way, they crossed the river, in the opposite direction, and after wandering about were finally obliged to ask it. At length a start was made, but the berline had been waiting outside a gate of the City some two hours when the cab reached it, and much time had been lost. Fersen drove the berline the first two stages and then left his charges to the ordinary postilions of the postal service, while he made his way out of France alone.

All through the day, till evening, everything seemed to be going well. The berline, drawn by six horses, went with tolerable speed, and the party did not attract attention. Their spirits rose; with every mile they were getting nearer Bouillé's soldiers and safety; but they were late, and though each moment was of importance, they did not make haste.

The movements of Bouillé's Army had already roused suspicion in the countryside, and when the small troop took up its post near Châlons and waited hour after hour for something which never came, suspicion grew, and the peasants began to be threatening. The appointed hour was long past, and the officers, who were in the secret, thinking that the King could not be coming that evening, judged it wisest to withdraw their men. And so, when the berline reached the appointed place, not only were there no soldiers, but the whole population was on the alert, expecting something, they knew not what. The berline drove on, and the troops posted along the way let it pass without doing anything, because they had received no signal. The big party of travellers now began to excite interest, and when the King imprudently put his head out of window at Sainte-Menehould, while the horses were being changed, he was recognized by the postmaster, a young man named Drouet. No sooner had the berline driven off than Drouet began to acquaint the town with his discovery, and the Municipality sent him and another man off on horseback in pursuit.

Night fell, and it was past eleven when the berline reached the little town of Varennes, in the Argonne. Here the relay of horses had been stupidly removed from the place where the couriers had been told they would find them; there was much hunting round in the dark, and the postilions refused to go farther. With difficulty they were persuaded to drive on to look for the horses at the other side of the town. Meanwhile, Drouet and his companion had galloped to Varennes by short cuts, had entered it on the other side, and were rousing the inhabitants. The toscin was rung, the bridge was barricaded, armed men stopped the two carriages under a vaulted archway, and forced the travellers to descend. They showed their passports and were told that it was too late to go on, that they must wait till the morning. Politely but firmly, the legal officer of the town, Sauce, a grocer, took them to his shop, fed them, and lodged them safely in his back bedroom. Here they were obliged to own their real names.

Yet they did not lose hope. Every one was respectful and loyal; a detachment of Bouillé's soldiers was actually in the town and might furnish an escort; their officers, devoted to the King, came to await his orders. But by this time the National Guards were up and out, they were beginning to come in from the neighbourhood; it soon appeared that the King could not get away without bloodshed, and Louis hated bloodshed. Besides, it was more than doubtful whether the soldiers would fight the National Guard. So the King and Queen tried persuasion. They did their best; after all, what law was there to forbid them travelling? They had nearly persuaded Sauce and the Municipality to let them go, when an aide-de-camp of Lafayette's arrived, bearing the order of the Assembly to stop them. All was over now. The Queen, in her anger, seized the paper as it lay on the bed where her children were sleeping, and flung it on the floor. And now began a fresh contest in Sauce's bedroom; the Municipality and the townsfolk were urgent with the King to return to Paris; the royal family tried every means of delaying their departure, in hopes that Bouillé would hear of their plight and come to their rescue. Varennes, however, was inexorable, and before eight o'clock the next morning the royal family was obliged to get into the berline and to start for Paris, escorted by a tumultuous body of National Guards. Even then there was a chance that Bouillé would come after them, and the citizens of Varennes were braving his wrath when they made the King turn back.

The return journey was full of hardships. Fresh parties of National Guards from the neighbourhood appeared at intervals to guard the King; many of them were noisy and disorderly, and the berline rolled slowly along in suffocating clouds of dust. Rough crowds gathered at each stop, and everyone was clamouring to be allowed to march with the King to Paris. The night was spent at Châlons. The second day was worse than the first; a loyal gentleman who showed his sentiments imprudently was murdered by the mob almost in sight of the tired travellers, and the berline went slower than ever. But in the evening the procession met three commissaries whom the National Assembly had sent to escort the royal family back, as soon as the news of the arrest reached Paris. Barnave, Pétion, and Latour-Maubourg (formerly a marquis), a chivalrous friend of Lafayette's, were the three, and with them was General Mathieu Dumas, a distinguished officer, to help them. The commissaries soon improved matters. Dumas took command of the National Guards, and managed by and by to get rid of the most troublesome; Barnave and Pétion got into the berline with the royal family and Madame de Tourzel; Latour-Maubourg protected the waiting-women in their carriage. Thursday night was spent at Dormans, Friday night at Meaux. National Guards from every place on or near the route still thronged to guard the King, but

Dumas and the commissaries kept them in order, and progress was quicker.

It might have been an awkward situation inside the berline, but Barnave felt nothing but pity for his prisoners in their downfall, and soon won their liking by his courtesy. Pétion was kindly too, but tactless and conceited; he tried to drive lessons home to the King, and imagined that Madame Elisabeth had fallen in love with him. The royal family bore their misfortunes with admirable fortitude and good temper; the heat and dust were trying, but the days passed in cheerful conversation. The Queen made herself charming, the little Dauphin played with the deputies and sat on Barnave's knee, Madame Elisabeth argued with Barnave, and Pétion improved the occasion.

Paris was approached on Saturday afternoon, and, after the commissaries had quelled an ugly disturbance made by a threatening mob, the capital was entered under the escort of the Paris National Guard, well-drilled and decorous. Great crowds lined the way, watching the arrival of the royal family, and receiving them in grim silence, without an insult and without a cheer, while every man kept his hat on. The three Body-Guards on the box of the berline – where the royal family, though most anxious for their safety, had foolishly insisted on keeping them – were taken by the people for three nobles, friends of the Queen, and the commissaries had some ado to protect them. But all the party entered the Tuileries safely and were handed over to the guard of Lafayette: of Lafayette, whose loyalty had saved the King in October 1789, and whom the King had left to his fate. And this time Lafayette took care that the guard should be sure, and put sentinels at every door and on every staircase.

The Assembly had 'suspended' the King until further orders, and had stopped the elections. The question now arose; what to do with the King, and whether to alter the Constitution.

By his flight the King had estranged and disgusted the mass of the nation, and there was a strong feeling that he ought to be deposed and punished. If there had been any one to put in his place, the Assembly would, no doubt, have deposed him; but there was no one. Supposing the Dauphin were to be made King, there must be a Regent, and a Regent was as hard to find as a King. The King's brothers were both hostile to the Revolution and both were abroad, as Monsieur had made his escape. The former duc d'Orléans, though revolutionary, was depraved and contemptible; his son, once duc de Chartres, a lad of promise, would presumably be under his influence. The alternative was to found a Republic, but very few people in France desired one, and the leaders of the Assembly felt that, as Pétion had bluntly told the King, "France is not ripe for a Republic." They were afraid, and with good reason, that France without a strong central Government, such as only a monarchy could supply, would fall apart into petty States and lose her grandeur. They were also afraid that if they dethroned Louis, part of the Army and of the nation would side with him, and that civil war would ensue. As it was, the mere suspension of the King had caused fresh divisions; the Right refused to take part in the debates, and a stimulus had been given to the emigration of the nobles, who began once more to leave the country and to join the Army gathered under the Princes, at Coblentz and other German towns. Cazalès, loyal to his own party though sympathizing with the Constitutionalists, was one of them, to the great regret of his colleagues. The leaders of the Assembly felt that no more Frenchmen must be alienated, that it was time to rally all who cared for France and to end the Revolution. They believed that the best way of doing this was to keep Louis on the throne, to overlook his want of good faith and to give him another chance. After all, he was well-intentioned though misguided, he had the makings of a constitutional King; the Queen was clever, and both had received a cruel lesson and had seen for themselves that the nation would not support them against the Assembly.

So the 'Constitutionalists', as the party which desired

to keep the Constitution unchanged was called, resolved to maintain the King on the throne as the best means of securing the unity, safety, and peace of France. They knew that their decision would not be popular, but they believed that the nation would come round to their opinion.

Seven Committees had been ordered to report on the affair; they decided to throw the blame for the King's flight on Bouillé and those who had helped in the escape, to impeach them, and to argue that as the King had been made inviolable by the Constitution and had not broken any law by flying, the question of guilt did not touch him. At the same time fresh laws were to be made regarding the King's duties, and further, he was to remain suspended until the Constitution had been revised and he had accepted it. He was free to refuse it, but if he did so, he was to lose his throne.

The debate lasted for three days; Pétion and Robespierre brought forward the arguments against retaining the King with much skill, Buzot spoke even better on the same side, and Grégoire put the case in a nut-shell when he said: "The King will accept; he will swear; but what confidence can you place in his oaths?" There were fine speeches on the Constitutionalist side, Duport, and Salle, a doctor, being specially eloquent, and it must be noted that none of the speakers expressed any feeling for the King; they contended, rather, that Louis would not be dangerous if kept in proper bounds, because he was neither clever nor popular. Barnave spoke last. He appealed to the Assembly to act wisely and boldly, to end the Revolution and to make France a country in which all patriotic French citizens, whatever their opinions, could live together in peace. His arguments and his fervour carried the Assembly, and even the galleries, with him, and the Committees' Bill passed on the 15th July. The continuation of the King's suspension passed separately on the 16th.

A large part of Paris was already in agitation; Robespierre was rousing the Jacobins to action, and Marat was shrieking for a Dictator to cut off prominent heads, his favourite remedy in a crisis. Neither Paris, nor the Jacobins, nor Robespierre wanted a Republic, and when the Cordeliers' Club passed a resolution in favour of one, the Jacobins expressed their disapproval. But thousands of people who were not republicans were eager for the punishment of Louis, and felt besides that the Assembly ought to consult the nation before deciding on his fate. Angry crowds surrounded the Manège and insulted the deputies when they came out, further violence being impossible because the guard had been doubled. On the 15th July the Cordeliers and the popular Societies organized a big meeting in the Champ de Mars to sign a petition against the King. On the same evening the Jacobins were discussing a petition of their own on the subject, when a large crowd from the Palais-Royal invaded the chapel which they used as a hall. The milder members decamped, and those that were left joined with the crowd in passing a resolution in favour of a new petition. Brissot drew it up, and on the morning of the 16th it was taken to the Champ de Mars for signatures. Later on, when the Jacobins learnt that the Assembly had continued the suspension of the King, they withdrew this petition. Here they acted constitutionally. None the less, at the evening meeting of the Club on the 16th, Robespierre denounced the seven Committees as traitors. He declared, further, that the Committees intended to murder him, Robespierre, the unswerving champion of truth, and worked his audience up into such a state of excitement, that the listeners in the galleries came down to mingle with the members in the hall, every one swore never to acknowledge Louis XVI as King, and many raged like maniacs.

July 17th was a Sunday. In the morning two men were found hiding under the altar in the Champ de Mars where the petitions were signed. It was reported that they had meant to blow it up while the 'patriots' were signing, and a mob hanged them. The reason why they were there was never known. Lafayette called out a force of National Guards to quell the disturbance;

some blows were exchanged and Lafayette himself was fired at. His assailant was arrested, but at once released, through Lafayette's misplaced generosity.

In the afternoon, at a fresh meeting in the Champ de Mars, a new petition against the King was drawn up by a small knot of republicans, and signed by thousands of a holiday crowd, large but orderly.

Meanwhile the Assembly had heard of the murder of the two men, and felt that these dangerous meetings in the Champ de Mars must cease. A law against inciting to sedition was discussed, and the President wrote to the Mayor, Bailly, urging him to take steps to stop disorders. Thus urged, the Municipality decided that "martial law" must be declared. The Riot Act was now read in the place de Grève, and a large body of National Guards, together with Bailly and the Municipality, set out for the Champ de Mars, carrying with them the red flag which showed that "martial law" had been proclaimed.

It was the evening of a very hot day; the National Guards, annoyed at having been called out on Sunday, were in no patient mood, and when, on the way, some of them were insulted, and even attacked, they began to retaliate. In their minds, as in the mind of the Assembly, the crowd in the Champ de Mars was supposed to be the same mob which had lynched the two men in the morning. The Municipality ought to have known better, for three members who had been sent to investigate, had reported that the meeting was orderly.* All might yet have gone well, had not Lafayette made a mistake. Instead of trying to clear the Champ de Mars scientifically, he sent his troops in by two different entrances, east and south. The crowds inside did not know that "martial law" had been proclaimed, did not see the red flag which was the signal for them to disperse, and suddenly found themselves facing the troops. Some angry men on the earthworks near an entrance were already throwing stones, the National Guards fired in the air, and then, as the rain of stones continued, accompanied by a few shots, fired, without orders, into the throng of people. The frightened multitude did not know which way to fly, and before they could disperse some of them were killed; a few National Guards also fell.

The Assembly, determined to keep order, thanked Bailly and Lafayette and commanded the prosecution of the ringleaders of the disturbances. Many arrests were made, and Danton and Camille Desmoulins, who had been active over the earlier petitions, left Paris till the affair had blown over. The firmness of the Assembly restored order, and the majority of the citizens were grateful, but in the minds of the extremists much

* The promoters had obtained leave from the Municipality to hold it; a necessary formality.

bitterness was left, and the event was always called "the Massacre of the Champ de Mars", and was spoken of as if it had been a treacherous method of putting down republicanism, though the number of the slain was certainly well below fifty, and probably about fifteen, and though the slaughter was only caused by a piece of mismanagement.

All these events had consequences. First, the Jacobins had brought themselves into disrepute, and the Jacobin deputies, disgusted at the wild doings of the Club and at the admission of the crowd to vote, broke away, and started a new club, called the Feuillants from its meeting-place in the convent of that name. Almost all the Jacobin deputies and many of the '1789 Club' joined the Feuillants, and of notable deputies only Robespierre and Pétion remained with the Jacobins. The hall of the Jacobin Club belonged to the deputies, and they might have turned the rebellious Jacobins out, but with scrupulous generosity they forbore to do so. The Jacobins, having had a lesson, did all they could to lure the deputies back, and soon the more extreme ones, who did not care to mix with the '1789' men, began to return to their old haunt. The leading Jacobins took care to keep their meetings orderly and the Club gradually regained its power, while the Feuillants' Club began to languish, because the leaders of the Assembly, too busy to attend regularly, neglected it.

Secondly, there was a new division of parties in the Assembly, for while Barnave, the Lameths, and Duport continued in close alliance with Lafayette, Thouret, and Le Chapelier, many of the men who had supported them drew away. And now was seen the mischief which the old divisions in the popular party had caused. People were accustomed to see Lafayette and the Lameths sparring and could not understand their new friendship; this made it easy for the malevolent to assert that 'the Coalition' only hung together to share the spoils of the Civil List, and to rule France through the King and Queen.

The leaders of the Constitutionalists were, in truth, trying to work on the King and Queen; they hoped to induce the King to accept the Constitution, and the Queen to use her influence with her brother, the Emperor Leopold. The situation was complicated. A league of the Powers against France, consisting of Austria, Prussia, the German Princes, and Sweden, appeared to be forming under the Emperor's auspices. Now the Constitutionalists knew that the prudent Leopold disliked the émigrés and the French Princes, and they believed that he would not care to interfere in France as long as the King was respected and the country orderly. They hoped to make him feel that an alliance with France would be to his advantage, and they persuaded the Queen to write him a letter saying that she had changed her opinions about the Revolution. The Queen wrote the letter, and sent Leopold another letter privately, telling him that her opinions were unchanged, and asking him for help; the King also wrote privately asking for help. What they wanted was a union of the Powers to coerce France by threats; they did not want an invasion, fearing the consequences. Leopold did not fall in with their views; he let them know that they had better come to terms with the leaders of the Assembly. Outwardly, however, he continued to countenance the émigrés, and in August he met the King of Prussia and the comte d'Artois at Pillnitz. Here the two monarchs signed a 'Declaration' (27th Aug.), promising to help Louis to restore the Monarchy. France naturally considered this a hostile manifestation, but politicians remarked that Leopold only promised to help Louis if all the other Powers did so too; a conjunction which he knew to be impossible. The Constitutionalists understood Leopold's manoeuvre, and saw that France had nothing to fear from him provided she settled down quietly under her new Constitution. Leopold was, in fact, waiting to see what happened, and his attitude was a great disappointment to the Queen. She continued to try for his help while she tricked the Constitutionalists by pretending to agree with their views. The Assembly had always treated her with consideration, and the

Constitutionalists were now shielding her from the anger of the people, yet she felt no gratitude; in her eyes the deputies were either upstarts or renegades.

Early in August the revision of the Constitution began in earnest, and the Assembly discussed, clause by clause, the Constitutional Act presented by the Constitutional Committee and the Revision Committee. These Committees proposed a few changes in certain laws, with the idea of making the Government more stable; the most important were, the alteration of the law which forbade the re-election of the members of one Assembly to the next, and of the law which forbade deputies to become Ministers. There was nothing in the Act which would increase the King's power in any way, but he was to be described as 'representative' of the People, to add a little to his dignity.

Nevertheless the Committees were violently attacked by all the 'patriot' journalists, with Brissot at their head, for wanting to alter the Constitution with the object of restoring the King's power, and also for wanting to revive the 'noblesse'. There was not a word of truth in this, as any one who read the Constitutional Act could see. Moreover, the Act had been signed by Pétion and Buzot, members of the Committees, whom the extremists trusted. Yet men who should have known better took up the cry, and the accusation is repeated to this day. These imaginary changes were not the real reason for the attack; they were put forward to cloak the anger of the advanced party at the attempt of the Constitutionalists to end the Revolution. Some of this party were sincere in their disapproval, others were agitators who wished the Revolution to continue because they hated order and quiet; men, as Barnave said, who "grow big and fat in public troubles, like insects in corruption".

All these attacks bred anger and suspicion, even in the Assembly, and in the heated atmosphere the wise proposal of the Committees to repeal the law forbidding the re-election of deputies had no chance of a patient hearing. The Committees had to abandon it. They issued at the same time a solemn warning, written by Thouret, that this fatal law would prevent the Constitution from working. The occurrence is an example of the harm that can be done by an unscrupulous political campaign.

The great Siéyes, though a member of the Committees, did nothing to help his colleagues, neither did another member, Talleyrand; as for Pétion and Buzot, they opposed them. Robespierre, of course, opposed too, and a stinging speech he made about the Committees is celebrated; but the Committees thought little of Robespierre. The Act was ably defended by Thouret and Le Chapelier and by Barnave, who appealed to the better self of his hearers, pleaded for union instead of division, for trust instead of suspicion, and urged all good citizens to join together and make liberty secure by establishing order. A continuation of agitation and unrest would, he warned them, lead to anarchy and thence to tyranny, because most men, in the long run, prefer "a tranquil slavery" to liberty without security and without peace. The Act was at length passed; it contained a provision for a special Assembly which might amend the Constitution, but was not to sit for thirty years.

On the 3rd of September a large deputation took the Act to the King. He was now free again, his guards were taken off, he was even allowed to leave Paris. He thought it wiser to remain, while he considered.

Should he accept the Constitution? Should he demand changes in it? Louis hesitated; he had scores of advisers, and some of them wanted him to make a kingly speech and defy the Assembly. Both he and the Queen hated the Constitution, and thought it so 'monstrous', so intolerable, that it could not last. But they saw no way out of accepting it. Leopold would not help them; Montmorin, who was still working amicably with the Committees, advised them to accept, and the leaders of the Assembly were certain that the King ought to accept without making conditions. Their advice was taken, and on the 13th September a letter from the King was read to the Assembly, in which he accepted the Constitution as the will of the Nation, and spoke of his own opinions in a candid manner which gave an air of sincerity to his words.

The relief of the Assembly at this happy ending to its labours was immense; reconciliation was the order of the day, and, at Lafayette's suggestion, a general amnesty for all offences connected with the Revolution was voted. In consequence, all who had been arrested for helping in the King's flight, or on account of the disturbances of the 17th July, were released.

The King came to the Assembly on the 14th September to swear to the Constitution. A chair was placed for him beside the President, Thouret; the Queen was in a private box with her children, and every seat was full. The Assembly rose and cheered as the King entered; Louis reached his chair and began to repeat his oath, standing. The deputies sat down, to show that they represented the sovereign Nation to whom the oath was being made. Louis looked round, and seeing every one seated, sat down too, and remained seated while he finished his oath and made a short speech. The Manège rang with loyal applause, and Thouret rose to answer the King; but as Louis continued to sit, Thouret sat down too, and spoke from his chair beside the King, with his legs crossed and his left leg waving in the air. Despite this uncourtly attitude, his speech was dignified and worthy of the occasion. After more cheering, the Assembly, in a body, escorted the King back to the Tuileries, through a joyful and applauding multitude.

The Assembly had been right in calculating that the nation would follow its lead, for now all France rejoiced at the fortunate ending of difficulties and exulted in the new Constitution. Even the 'patriot' journalists began to praise it, and the agitators were silenced for a time. Paris celebrated the occasion with fêtes and illuminations, and the King and Queen became popular once more.

The elections for the new Assembly were nearly finished, the new deputies were arriving in Paris, and the Constituent Assembly was to end with the month. Its last days were busy indeed. At the end the Constitutionalists tried to break the power of the great organization of Jacobin Clubs. Already, in the spring, an effort had been made, by passing a decree which declared it illegal for any corporate body to present a petition in its own name; all petitions were to be made only in the names of the individuals who signed them.* Now, on the 29th September, Le Chapelier brought in a bill on clubs, and prefaced it by saying that the time had come for political clubs with affiliated societies to

* A petition from MM. Dubois, Durand, Girard, Gérard, &c., would not have the same imposing effect as one from 'the Society of the Friends of the Constitution of Villefranche'.

cease. But the Constitutionalists were too scrupulous to forbid such clubs, and Le Chapelier's Bill, which passed, only provided for the punishment of the responsible members of clubs which defied the law – as some of the provincial Jacobins had been doing.

On the 30th September the King came to close the Assembly, and in a little speech, which seemed to ring true, bound himself once more to maintain the Constitution faithfully. When he had gone and the speeches and cheering were over, Thouret, still President, turned to the people in the galleries and cried in a loud voice: "The Constituent National Assembly declares that its mission is ended and now concludes its sittings."

Outside, the fickle Paris crowd was waiting to hiss the Constitutionalists, while Pétion and Robespierre were crowned with wreaths of oak and dragged home triumphantly in carriages.

So ended the great Assembly. It had given France a Constitution, it had instituted endless reforms, it had carried the country through a tremendous upheaval with very little bloodshed, it had earned the veneration and attachment of all but irreconcilables and a small party of agitators, it left France at peace and with fair prospects. If the elections had been free, most of the leaders would undoubtedly have been returned to the new Assembly, for, though Paris was fickle, they were still admired in their own Departments. With their superior talents, knowledge of public affairs, and prestige, they must have continued to guide the State, and the history of France might have been different. But the deputies' fatal mistake of cutting themselves off from the possibility of taking any share in the Government during the two years for which the next Assembly was to sit, left their work at the mercy of their successors, and France was soon plunged into fresh agitations.

PART II –
THE LEGISLATIVE ASSEMBLY

V

THE WAR 30TH SEPTEMBER
1791 – 3RD JULY 1792

The Legislative Assembly, as the new Parliament was called, was considerably smaller than the Constituent Assembly and had not the same unlimited powers, for it could not touch any of the laws embodied in the Constitution; other laws it could both make and unmake. Like the Constituent Assembly, it sat daily, Sundays and weekdays, with no intervals.

Its members were chiefly drawn from the same class as the Commons of the first Assembly, with a certain number of clergy and former nobles intermixed. Young, for the most part, they were honest, well-meaning men, loyally determined to make the Constitution work, but they were conspicuously inferior to their predecessors in judgement and stability. Men of admirable talent were not wanting, but there were no wise and politic leaders. Moreover, the large group which formed the 'Centre' and belonged to no party, did not act on fixed principles, and voted, now on one side, now on the other, on the impulse of the moment. Since their votes decided every question, it was always uncertain how the Assembly would act, and in consequence it was not much respected. The debates were dull at first, while they ran on the lines of the Constituent Assembly; it was only when the deputies ceased to discuss principles that the orators found themselves, and the sittings became lively.

The Left, a rather larger party than the Right, thought the Constituent Assembly conservative and old-fashioned, and hoped that the Revolution would go further. Condorcet, an author, philosopher, and mathematician, of European reputation, was one great ornament of this party, and was always listened to with respect. He inclined to moderation, but, though great in political theories, he was not a practical politician. The rough and honest Cambon was watch-dog over the national finances and made it his business to stop waste and squandering. Isnard, from the south, an impulsive orator whose speeches were full of sound and fury, was considered a second Mirabeau. So vivid was he that, on one occasion when he was threatening an unpopular Minister, his hearers trembled, seeing in fancy a sword suspended over that Minister's head.

Hérault de Séchelles, once a member of the Paris Parlement, and said to be the handsomest man in France, was stately, literary, pleasure-loving, and also violent. Far more violent was a trio of deputies led by Chabot, who had been a Capuchin friar. Merry, careless, and good-natured, Chabot affected dirt and untidiness in order to be like 'the people'; he imagined himself the very essence of patriotism, and others shared his delusion. He was a constant speaker, a constant denouncer, and in the Jacobins he poured forth streams of fluent rubbish, for, as he once said there: "Liberty is lost if we have not the right to talk nonsense in the tribune." At the same time he was openly immoral, and it is hard to understand how such a man should have been so popular and so powerful. His two friends were better men. Merlin de Thionville, called by the people 'Merlin moustaches', to distinguish him from Merlin of Douai, of the Constituent Assembly, though stupid, was a sincere patriot and a brave man; Basire, young and gifted with some eloquence, had a soft heart and an inclination to peace. Another violent man, less extreme, was the abbé Fauchet, a well-known preacher, with mystical ideas in religion; in politics he loved denunciation and abuse.

A shining cluster of orators came from the Department of the Gironde, and were hence called 'the Girondins.' Three of them, Gensonné, Guadet, and Vergniaud, had been advocates at the Bar of Bordeaux. Gensonné, called by his enemies 'the drake of the Gironde', from the monotonous cadence of his voice, was something of a leader; he spoke with grave authority and used plausible arguments. The impetuous Guadet, a fine and ready orator, excelled in cutting sarcasm and in patriotic outbursts; he was, like Gensonné, an estimable man in private life. Vergniaud, incomparably the greatest orator of the Assembly, was a plain, heavy-looking man who became animated and majestic in the tribune. His voice was melodious, his finished eloquence, now inspiring and now pathetic, was always classical and noble. In character he was generous and disinterested, careless of his own fame, and naturally conciliatory. His judgement often erred, though never from petty motives, and his defect was a dreamy indolence of mind; he did not care to use his great powers continuously, nor to dominate men who were his inferiors. Vergniaud's intimate friend, the charming and amusing young Ducos, a business man of Bordeaux, was an attractive speaker, clear and usually reasonable.

By ill fortune, the most prominent deputy on the Left, Brissot, was ready to beckon these gifted and generous Girondins into dangerous paths. Brissot, author and journalist, editor of an important paper, *Le Patriote français*, was a pronounced republican who now promised, in all good faith, that he would uphold the Constitution. He and the Girondins felt a mutual attraction, and together with Isnard, Condorcet, Fauchet, and other members of the less extreme Left, they gradually formed a party, called at first 'Brissotins' and later 'Girondins'. No one can be said to have led them, not even Brissot, for though they were fond of holding conferences and dining together, they were weak in concerted action. They wanted war, and beyond that it is difficult to say what their ultimate aims were; probably they themselves did not know.

Brissot, small, sallow, and serious, was a clever and ambitious man who knew a little of everything and nothing well. He had a profound belief in his own wisdom, and though he was in the habit of attacking those who disagreed with him virulently, and had, besides, in his earlier days, lived a dissipated life among blackmailing journalists, he posed as a gentle, harmless being, and often asserted that he had spent the whole of his life in doing good. His friends took him at his own estimate, but his general reputation was bad, and threw discredit on his party. It was, indeed, worse than he deserved, for he was accused of being a swindler, and in reality he had only been foolish over money transactions and always remained honourably poor. Brissot had long been eager to play a great part and knew how to exert his influence. He seldom spoke in the Assembly, and when he did, his carefully prepared and eloquent speeches, in which appeals to passion appeared under the guise of cool argument, produced a strong effect. His chief political feat hitherto had been his interference in Colonial affairs, on which a word must be said.

France possessed Colonies in the West Indies worked by slave labour, and one of them, St. Domingo, was the richest Colony in the world. The ideas of the day condemned slavery and the Constituent Assembly would fain have freed the slaves, but French commerce and industry depended largely on the trade with St. Domingo, and all parties agreed that the loss of the Colony could not be risked while France was on the verge of bankruptcy. Brissot, a strong anti-slavery man, agreed here with the rest, but he was resolved that, as the white colonials had got the franchise, the half-breeds, who were free men, should get it too. Barnave opposed this measure as premature, declaring that it would make a ferment in the Colonies, where the whites scorned the half-breeds, and that it must end in a catastrophe. Brissot set to work to destroy Barnave's influence and to assure the world that there was no possible risk in this excellent piece of reform; his friends in the Constituent Assembly believed him, and the franchise was given to the half-breeds in spite of Barnave's warnings (15th May 1791). All that Barnave had predicted came to pass, and the uproar in St. Domingo resulted in a rising of the slaves, accompanied by massacre and devastation. The Colony never quieted down again and, after some years, was finally lost to France. The news of the rising came in the early days of the Legislative Assembly, and Brissot, no whit abashed, said first that it was untrue, next that it was exaggerated, and finally that it was all Barnave's fault, as good reforms cannot produce bad results. He still claimed to be the chief authority on the Colonies, and he also claimed to be the chief authority on foreign affairs, which he understood as little as he understood the Colonies.

To return to the Assembly. The Right, whose opinions represented those of the Constitutionalists, had no orator who was a match for the orators of the Left, for though the speakers of this party often argued well, they lacked the striking phrase. Vaublanc, the most eloquent, was rather empty; Ramond and Daverhoult, a Belgian, supporters of Lafayette, were excellent speakers, and General Mathieu Dumas, who had helped to bring the King back from Varennes, was clear, temperate, and courageous – so courageous that he ventured to improvise an answer to Vergniaud's greatest speech. Theodore Lameth, a brother of the two earlier Lameths, though no speaker had much influence. The Right were too apt to fritter away their strength by opposing when opposition was not strictly necessary. Stanislas Girardin, a pupil of Rousseau's, clear-sighted and patriotic, was free from this defect, but the Left did not like him the better for it.

The majority of the Assembly often voted with the Right, and the mass of the country held constitutional opinions, nevertheless the chief political influence lay with the active, stirring Jacobin societies, where Brissot and his friends were at present predominant. This appeared when the Feuillants' Club was revived in the winter. The Jacobins could brook no rivals, and a disrespectful crowd of their adherents came to the Feuillants' meetings to annoy and interrupt. The Feuillants soon gave up holding open meetings and henceforward had no power; but the name Feuillant survived, used by the Jacobins as a term of reproach, signifying a lukewarm patriot.

Soon after the Constituent Assembly ended, Bailly and Lafayette left Paris and went into retirement, both having resigned their posts. In November, Bailly was succeeded as Mayor by Pétion. Lafayette had no successor, for, on his advice, the office of Commander-in-chief of the Paris National Guard had been abolished, and the Generals of Division took it in turns to command.

The maintenance of the Constitution depended on two things; the good faith of the King and the wisdom of the Assembly. Louis, as we have seen, was acting in bad faith; neither he nor the Queen wished the Emperor to make war on France, but they were trying to persuade him to call an armed Congress of the Powers which would, so they hoped, overawe France and make her change her Constitution. Meanwhile the King's conduct was outwardly correct, for he was trying to deceive his people into the belief that he meant to make the Constitution work. This amount of deceit he considered lawful, but he never pretended to be cordial, nor did the Queen. None the less they found it hard to convince the sovereigns of Europe that all their public actions were done under constraint, for the sovereigns did not want to be convinced, and if the Assembly had given the King no provocation, foreign sympathy would soon have failed him, and he would have been obliged, in the end, to support the Constitution in earnest.

Both sides started badly; the King delayed coming to visit the Assembly, the Assembly was piqued and decreed that when he came in future he should not have his special chair, nor be addressed as 'Your Majesty' (5th Oct.). The Funds fell at once, and there was such consternation in Paris that the decree was rescinded the next day. The deputy foremost against the King on this occasion was a young paralytic, named Couthon, whose life was a long fight with illness and who had to be carried to the tribune when he spoke.

Couthon's misfortune, his sad, gentle face and his pleasant voice, won him universal sympathy.

The Ministers were the King's agents and continued to carry out the policy of the Constitutionalists, with which the King professed to agree. Therefore the deputies of the Left set themselves to make things unpleasant for them and continually had them called to the Bar, to explain why this or that had not been done; Brissot, indeed, counted the power to summon the Ministers and to hector them, as one of the joys of a deputy's life. The Ministers cut a poor figure in the Assembly, and the Government was brought into contempt and weakened. Montmorin could hold his own, but he resigned in October; his place was hard to fill and he was finally succeeded by the Minister of the Interior, Delessart, a weak, well-meaning man.

In the early autumn terrible news came from the old papal town of Avignon. Avignon, together with a small adjoining province, formed a little foreign State, right in the middle of the south of France: a State which had been sold to the Pope by its rulers, centuries before. The Popes had once resided in Avignon during a long exile from Rome, and when they returned to Rome, had been allowed to retain possession because their rule caused France no inconvenience. But when the Revolution came, the case was altered; the little State became a refuge for the disaffected and a centre of disturbance. About half its inhabitants petitioned to be re-joined to France, while the other half wished to remain under the Pope; the two sides fought, and both committed atrocities.

This could not be allowed to go on and, after long hesitation, the Constituent Assembly decreed, in September 1791, that Avignon should be re-joined to France. Owing to the delays of the Minister, Delessart, the decree had not yet been carried out in October, but every one knew of it.

On the 16th October, Lescuyer, an unpopular member of the revolutionary party in Avignon, was lured by some opponents into a church, filled with a large gathering of men and women. He was there set upon and slowly put to death with clubs and stones and the scissors of the women. The same evening some of his friends, under the leadership of a man called Jourdan, arrived in Avignon and took vengeance for the murder. They arrested a large number of the Papal party, quite indiscriminately, both men and women, and shut them up in the Pope's old castle. In the night they brought them out one by one, slaughtered them, and flung their bodies, sometimes with life still in them, down the shaft of an open tower once used as an ice-house. Sixty-one persons perished in this manner.

The Assembly shuddered over the massacre of the

ice-tower and at first talked of bringing the murderers to justice. But there were difficulties in the way; it seemed unfair that one party should suffer for its crimes and not the other, and Brissot and the Girondins were reluctant to let good 'patriots' who had acted under provocation be punished. Arrests were made, but some months later the idea was started that the amnesty of September ought to be extended to cover the massacre. Vergniaud and Lasource, an eloquent Protestant pastor who had joined the Girondins, persuaded the Assembly to take this view (19th March 1792); the accused were released, and some of the leaders in the massacre afterwards made friends with the principal Girondins.

During the autumn the Assembly was mainly occupied with two problems: the question of the émigrés, who were gathered in arms round the Princes, at Coblentz, where their Court was, and in other German towns, waiting to invade France, and the question of the non-juring priests, many of whom were the cause of disturbances, especially in the West. In both of these questions, the views of the King ran counter to those of the Assembly.

First, as to the émigrés. The nobles were still flocking into Germany, driven by fear of persecution, or by a false sense of honour, and some, even, by the desire to be fashionable. Many of them were simply misguided, and the Right, hoping that the better disposed might return, was inclined to leniency. But the Left was determined to proceed to extremities, and a decree was at length passed, condemning all émigrés who continued in arms after the 1st of January to death as traitors, and sequestrating their property (9th Nov.). The King vetoed this decree (12th Nov.). His veto was taken quietly, as showing conclusively to the world that he was a free agent. Louis, however, did not at all approve of the émigrés; he made a proclamation ordering them to return, and wrote open letters to his brothers in the same sense. This was his genuine wish, but the Princes answered that he could not mean what he said; Monsieur, indeed, with the ex-Minister Calonne as adviser, was already claiming to be the Regent, on the ground that the King was acting under coercion. The Assembly impeached the Princes on the 1st January, 1792 and in February sequestrated the property of the émigrés.

As to the priests: it was decreed that all non-jurors must take the civic oath immediately, or forfeit the pensions awarded them during peaceable behaviour. The civic oath was easier for the clergy to take than the old oath, for it only bound a man to be loyal to Nation, Law, and King and to maintain the Constitution; and the Civil Constitution of the Clergy had not been made part of the Constitution. Nevertheless the non-jurors objected to this oath, and it was clearly tyrannical to deprive men who had done no harm of the pensions promised when the property of the clergy was taken. The King vetoed the law (19th Dec.) and the Constitutionalists were disgusted with the Assembly. In their anger, some of them, including the Lameths, began to talk privately of the necessity of altering the Constitution and introducing two Chambers; their intentions were suspected, and in future it was of little use for them to reproach the Jacobins with wishing to overthrow the Constitution.

The chief work of the Legislative Assembly was to precipitate France into a European war. In their enthusiasm for the Revolution Brissot and the Girondins proclaimed loudly that every throne in Europe was shaking; they gloried in the hatred of foreign tyrants for the Revolution; they were certain that war was inevitable – a sacred war in which France would triumph and bring liberty to every land. Brissot, in especial, bent all his craft and energy to bring about a war, and in his speeches he would enumerate, one after the other, all the monarchs of Europe, with a scoff at the feebleness of each. Isnard followed Brissot's example. In these months the European situation was critical; the monarchs were pleased to see France weakened by her long state of crisis, but they were terrified lest the ideas of the Revolution should spread to their own countries, and the speeches in the Assembly were calculated to increase their alarm.

The German Empire had two standing grievances against France: the abolition in 1789 of the feudal rights belonging to German Princes in Alsace and Lorraine, and the annexation of Avignon in 1791; and the Diet had taken up the matter of the Princes' feudal rights. But both questions, as every one knew, might well be settled by negotiating the payment of indemnities, and the Constituent Assembly had voted for such negotiations. Far more serious was the grievance of France against the Empire: the presence of armed gatherings of émigrés, near the frontier, in the States of the Electors of Trèves and Mayence, Princes of the Empire. The Emperor Leopold's attitude seemed doubtful. He and his old Chancellor, Kaunitz, still hoped that France would settle down, and did not want to go to war if they could help it. Leopold had ordered that the gatherings of émigrés in his own dominions should be disarmed, yet when asked, through the usual diplomatic channels, to use his influence with the Electors to get the armed gatherings of émigrés in their States dispersed, he made no reply. The Assembly, anxious to assert the dignity of France, requested the King to send an ultimatum to the two Electors, and on the 14th December the King himself appeared in the Manège, to announce that the ultimatum had been sent, and that he had asked the Emperor to mediate. Louis added, hoping to gain popularity, that if these measures failed, war must be declared.

At length the Emperor's answer* arrived and was read to the Assembly on the last day of 1791. It was unfriendly, even minatory, in tone, and notified that the Elector of Trèves had appealed to him for help against France, at the same time giving assurances that he had taken measures for disarming the émigrés and that he, Leopold, had given orders to his Army to support that Prince in case of an attack by France.

From this moment France was seen to be on the brink of war National pride was eager to avenge the treason of the émigrés and the slights cast on the country by the Emperor, and there was an outburst of patriotic feeling; but the state of suspense and agitation led to frequent disorders which the Ministers were powerless to put down. In Paris the mob began to arm, and quantities of pikes, 'the weapons of Liberty' as they were called, were made and sold to those who had no guns.

While dispatches passed slowly between Paris and Vienna, the Constitutionalists, maintaining that the dispute with the Emperor could yet be settled by negotiation, did everything they could to avert war.

* A note from the Emperor was called an 'office'.

They judged that France was in no condition to wage it with crippled finances, and with an army disorganized by the emigration of large numbers of officers, and by the consequent distrust and indiscipline of the soldiers – indiscipline deliberately encouraged by the Jacobins. The Girondin party, on their side, did their best to make war inevitable by appealing to passion and to patriotism, by taunting the prospective enemy, and by drawing pictures of an easy victory. Their most cogent argument was, that since war was bound to come sooner or later, it was better for France to attack before Austria was ready. The argument might have been sound if France herself had not been quite unprepared. This the Girondins did not realize; they assumed too easily that all was well. They were fortified in their optimism by a new Minister of War, Narbonne, a former noble, an agreeable, courtly soldier with advanced views, who had become a Minister through the influence of the famous Madame de Stael, Necker's daughter, and wife of the Swedish Ambassador, a woman of genius who had a political salon in Paris. Narbonne, though a Constitutionalist, pleased the Girondins by his eagerness for war, and got on well with the Assembly. He went on a tour of inspection and reported in rosy colours on the state of the Army and of the frontier defences (11th Jan.).

But the war-party met with unexpected opposition

in the Jacobins. Robespierre was once more residing in Paris, acting as public prosecutor to the new Criminal Court; he had a great following in the Club, and he was eloquent and persistent in urging that France should wait till the Emperor declared war. Not that he objected to a war, which he too believed inevitable, but he considered it madness to wage war when the King was on the side of the enemy and would betray France; the idea of war in such circumstances must, he said, be a conspiracy of the Court party. The attitude of Danton, another power in the Jacobins, was ambiguous. There were hot scenes in the Club, and though a reconciliation was patched up and Robespierre and Brissot embraced, the truce was short. The quarrel was embittered in March by a set-to between Guadet and Robespierre over a circular, written for the Jacobins by Robespierre, which Guadet thought too religious; for Guadet, with many of the Girondins, held Religion to be a mere superstition, while Robespierre sincerely believed in God and a future life. The Jacobins were nearly split in two, and henceforward Robespierre and the Girondins were deadly enemies, and the extremists denounced Brissot and his party as vehemently as they denounced Lafayette and the Feuillants.

The Emperor played into the hands of the war-party. He, or rather Kaunitz, answered the remonstrances of France by a second note, more hostile than the first.

Delessart was working hard to preserve peace, his notes to Vienna were conciliatory to the point of weakness, and when this second note arrived in mid-January he did not communicate it to the Assembly, although the suppression of the note was unconstitutional. He had an excuse, for Leopold's actions had been friendly though his words were not, and Delessart was able to report that Leopold had warned the Elector of Trèves to expect no help if invaded, unless he dispersed the gatherings of émigrés, and also that the Elector was clearing them out of his State. Delessart seized the opportunity to advise the Assembly (17th Jan.) not to push the Emperor too far; he knew, as the Assembly did not, that Prussia would come in with Austria – indeed the two Powers made a defensive alliance shortly after (7th Feb.). But neither the Emperor's friendly concession nor Delessart's advice could quench the warlike ardour of the deputies. Brissot demanded war if the Emperor did not give complete satisfaction by the 10th February; Vergniaud supported Brissot, and as Vergniaud always preserved his independence, and seemed, so it has been said, rather to come to the help of his friends than to act with them, his eloquence was doubly impressive. Finally (25th Jan.) the Assembly passed a motion of Hérault's, by which the King was requested to ask the Emperor if he meant to live in peace with France; should no satisfactory answer arrive before the 1st of March, war was to be declared. The King replied coolly; he had demanded explanations, he said, a fortnight before – as if to show the Assembly that he knew his duties without their prompting.

With the arrival of a fresh note from Austria, concealment of the actual situation became impossible, and on the 1st March Delessart was obliged to read to the Assembly several hostile dispatches, among them one from Kaunitz in which he criticized "the republican party in France", as he called the Jacobins, in the most offensive way. This insulting note would alone have made it difficult to keep peace, and on the day that it was read, the Emperor Leopold, the one man who might have averted war, died suddenly. He was succeeded, as King of Hungary and Bohemia, by his son Francis, a young man by no means reluctant to fight, and the situation changed.

Before the Emperor's death became known in Paris, Narbonne, at the height of his popularity and busy with preparations for war, was suddenly dismissed by the King on the 9th March.

Narbonne had annoyed Louis by demanding the resignation of Bertrand de Moleville, the naval Minister, whom the Assembly deemed incompetent and had nearly impeached. Bertrand was a pronounced royalist (as the partisans of the King began to be called about this time), and the only Minister whom the King liked. The King upheld Bertrand against Narbonne; Narbonne criticized the conduct of the Court sharply, and was dismissed. The next day the Girondins came to the Assembly full of wrath, determined to avenge Narbonne and to show their power. They made Delessart a scape-goat. Brissot demanded his impeachment for a long series of misdoings, including the suppressed note. Vergniaud clinched the matter by crying: "A plaintive voice calls from the terrible ice-tower of Avignon," and what the voice said was, that Delessart, by his delays in carrying out the decree of annexation, had perhaps been the real cause of the massacre. The unfortunate Minister was impeached and packed off to Orléans to await his trial by the High Court which sat there. Vergniaud did not stop at Delessart. "I see the windows of the Palace where the counterrevolution is plotting," he thundered. "Fear and terror have often gone forth from this famous Palace in the name of the despots of former days. Let them enter it to-day in the name of the Law! Let them penetrate all hearts! Let all those who dwell there know that our Constitution grants inviolability to the King alone. Let them know that the Law will reach all the guilty without distinction, that there will not be a single head criminally convicted which can escape the sword." This threat to the Queen, combined with the impeachment of Delessart, did indeed bring terror to the Court. The King and Queen gave themselves up for lost, and burnt many of their private papers; the Ministers all resigned, and the King appointed a new Ministry, composed of Jacobins who were in favour with the Girondin party.

General Dumouriez, the new Minister for Foreign Affairs, practically chief Minister, was an elderly man and an able soldier, a sort of adventurer, without convictions, who had once been employed in the secret diplomacy of Louis XV. He owed his appointment to Gensonné, who had accompanied him on a political mission and admired his powers; he also had friends at Court. A cheery, amusing man, with the ways of the old aristocrats and their loose morals, he knew how to make himself agreeable to the King. With him were two personal friends of Brissot: Clavière, a Genevese banker long resident in Paris, as Finance Minister, and Roland, an Inspector of manufactories, as Minister of the Interior. Roland, an old man, honest and able, but irritable and too conscious of virtue, was married to a very clever wife much younger than himself, who helped him in all his work, the fascinating Madame Roland, warm-hearted and injudicious, retiring in her habits and full of feminine grace. Her salon became the rendezvous for the Girondin party, and her influence among them was great.

Dumouriez set himself to be popular. He went to the Jacobins wearing the red cap of Liberty, which had lately come into fashion among 'patriots' as the head-dress of 'the people', and embraced Robespierre. Robespierre was cool, but promised him the support of the Society as long as he behaved well. Robespierre and Pétion, it may be noted, both thought the wearing of red caps foolish, and asked the Society to give it up.

In pursuance of the Girondin policy Dumouriez, on the 27th March, sent a kind of ultimatum to Austria, asking for satisfaction before the 15th April, and the Assembly hurriedly impeached the French Ambassador in Vienna one day, and rescinded the decree the next, after hearing his dispatches. No answer arrived from Austria, and on the 20th April the King came once more to the Manège, and proposed to declare war on the King of Hungary and Bohemia.* The declaration was voted the same evening, only about seven Constitutionalists voting against it.

The declaration of war was almost a relief; it created for the moment a sense of unity. Hearts were filled with patriotic enthusiasm, volunteers enlisted, and gifts flowed into the Treasury. On the night of the 25th April, the day when the declaration of war became

* In July this King was elected Emperor, as Francis II.

known at Strasbourg, the spirit of the Revolution, its ardour for liberty, its self-sacrifice, its sternness towards traitors and towards a foreign foe, was breathed into the great song which has stirred all lands; a song written by a Constitutionalist officer, Rouget de Lisle, at the request of his friend Dietrich, the Constitutionalist Mayor of Strasbourg, and called "Chant de guerre pour l'armée du Rhin." It was soon to be known as the 'Marseillaise'.

The Girondin party, once their friends were in power, were well content, and let the Court see that they meant no further harm. The new Ministers were impressed by the King's honesty. Louis might have made himself popular again if he had supported the war in a convincing manner, but he continued correct and lukewarm. As for the Queen, before war was declared, she had let Mercy, the Austrian Ambassador, now in Brussels, know where Dumouriez meant to attack, in order that Austria might be on her guard. Louis and Marie-Antoinette must not be judged too harshly; they still believed that the hearts of their people had been estranged, for a time, by wicked men. In the same way the émigrés believed that France would receive them with open arms and would welcome the chance of overturning the Revolution.

The French armies on the eastern frontier were commanded by the veteran Marshal Rochambeau and by Lafayette. As was to be expected the war began badly. Three regiments deserted to the émigrés in early days, and the first event was a double disaster. On the 28th April General Biron marched on Mons and General Dillon on Tournay. Biron found it necessary to retreat; his troops raised cries of 'Treason' and ran away in disorder. Dillon's troops fled before the enemy, murdered their General, and put their prisoners of war to death. This disgrace was keenly felt, and many Constitutionalist officers weakly resigned, Rochambeau among them; so did the Minister of War, overwhelmed by responsibility. On the 1st May Prussia declared war as Austria's ally.

The war-party in the Assembly was now thoroughly alarmed, and joined with the Right in taking measures to restore military discipline and to protect prisoners of war. The Constitutionalists might possibly have come to terms with the Girondins, if they had wished it; unfortunately many of the wiser heads of their party were dispersed or out of politics, and the active politicians on the spot were only too glad to see their opponents in difficulties, and did not care to come to the rescue. Such influence as remained to them was weakened by the ill-concealed joy of some of them at the disasters, and this want of patriotism of a few was never forgiven and laid the whole party open to unfounded suspicions.

The war went on for a time uneventfully and without fresh disasters, for the Generals took care to train their troops gradually, and only risked small encounters – a prudence which the extremists called treason. Rochambeau was succeeded by Marshal Luckner, a German veteran who had fought against France in the Seven Years' War and had afterwards taken service with her, rough and stupid, but beloved by the troops. The new Minister of War was Servan, an experienced soldier and a friend of the Girondins.

By this time the licence of the Press had become a real danger. Marat, in especial, in his paper *L'Ami du Peuple* was doing his best to instil suspicion and provoke bloodshed by perpetual cries of treason; he attributed the war to a conspiracy of the whole Assembly, he exhorted the soldiers to massacre their Generals, and his practice, now and henceforward, was to denounce each General in turn as a traitor. The Assembly impeached Marat, and with him the writer of a royalist paper, *L'Ami du Roi,* who had incited the soldiers to desert (3rd May). Marat went into hiding, but nothing happened to him and he continued to issue his paper.

Suspicion was rife enough without Marat's help. For a long time there had been talk of a supposed mysterious group of people known as 'the Austrian Committee', who met in the Tuileries and directed the conduct of affairs in the interests of Austria. The journalist Carra, a violent and credulous adherent of the Girondins, now published a statement that the ex-Ministers Montmorin and Bertrand belonged to 'the Austrian Committee'; whereupon they prosecuted him for libel. Carra informed the magistrate before whom the case came, Larivière, that he had his facts from three members of the Watch Committee of the Assembly: Chabot, Merlin and Basire. The three deputies admitted that it was so, but refused to answer questions, because the information involved had been given to the Committee under pledge of secrecy. Larivière, after trying in vain to get the papers of the Committee from the Assembly, took a daring step which exceeded his powers; he summoned the three deputies to appear before him, and sent gendarmes at daybreak to fetch them. The report of this insult to deputies roused the anger of the Assembly, and Larivière was impeached and sent to Orléans for trial (20th May). It was generally believed that he would not have been so bold unless he had been encouraged by the Court.

Gensonné and Brissot now solemnly undertook to prove the existence of 'the Austrian Committee'. Gensonné's crowning proofs were 'moral conviction' and the fact that Montmorin and Bertrand had, with the King's approval, sued Carra for saying that they belonged to it. Brissot tried to prove that the Constitutionalist party of the Constituent Assembly and all the Ministers of their time had been 'the Austrian Committee,' and moved the impeachment of Montmorin. The Assembly ordered a report on the subject, but Chabot, who made it (4th June), read such a string of wild, unsupported denunciations as proofs, that every one was disgusted and the matter was dropped.

Among the many causes of complaint against the Court was the intolerable behaviour of the King's new Constitutional Guard, given him in place of his Body-Guards, into which many known enemies of the Revolution had imprudently been admitted, and, after a denunciation by Basire and a stormy debate, it was decreed, on the 29th May, that the Guard should be disbanded and its Commander, the former duc de Brissac, impeached. A new Guard was to be formed and, for the present, the National Guard watched over the King along with his Swiss Guards, well-disciplined troops, faithful and unpolitical. The King and his friends regarded the disbanding of his household troops as a direct attack on himself, but he sanctioned the decree and it was carried out.

Another law he would not sanction, though pressed to do so by all his Ministers, for it touched his conscience. In consequence of his veto on the law which dealt with them, the non-juring priests who were causing disturbances had not been suppressed. The Assembly hardened its heart and, after long debates, gave the Directories of the Departments power to order the deportation from France of any non-juring priest who was a disturbing influence, if twenty voters of the Canton where he lived petitioned for it (25th May).

Yet another law roused the King to resistance. The Prussians were coming in and it was necessary to increase the Army.

The Constituent Assembly had done this in 1791 by instituting local battalions of volunteers, who enlisted on better terms than the regulars and elected their own officers; the Legislative Assembly had continued this policy. But the country had not yet realized the gravity of the war, and recruits were not joining in large enough numbers. Something more had to be done, and on the 4th June Servan proposed to the Assembly to form a camp, close to Paris, of 20,000 National Guards from all parts of France, who were to celebrate the Federation on the 14th July, and finally join the Army, after training. The Assembly voted for this Camp on the 8th June, but the plan was much criticized; a camp so close to Paris was seen to be a political rather than a military move, designed to overawe the Court. Robespierre disapproved. The National Guards of Paris were offended at the slight cast on their powers of keeping order in the capital; they got up a petition against the Camp, called 'the petition of the eight thousand' from the supposed number of signatures; once more Paris was in a ferment.

The King refused to sanction this decree; the Ministers represented to him that his ill-timed resistance was highly dangerous, but they argued in vain. When Louis asked for their advice in writing, Roland sent him a celebrated outspoken letter (written for him by Mme Roland) in which he told the King that it was the hostility he showed to the Constitution which prevented its working, and warned him that if he did not change his line of conduct, an explosion in France might be expected. The King turned to Dumouriez. Dumouriez did not get on with his colleagues, Roland, Clavière and Servan, respectable men who sometimes remonstrated with him on his lax morality, and he had apparently not been consulted about the Camp. He wished to be rid of them and encouraged the King to dismiss them, undertaking to remain Minister himself, in the belief, probably, that he could persuade Louis to sanction the two decrees on the non-juring priests and the Camp. Servan, Roland, and Clavière were dismissed. Their dismissal was announced on the 13th June, and the indignant Assembly voted that they carried with them the regrets of the nation, gave Dumouriez a hostile reception, and elected a Committee of twelve to examine into the state of France and propose means of saving Liberty and the Constitution (18th June).

Dumouriez had now offended his supporters, the Girondins, mortally, and as the King still refused to sanction the two decrees, his position was untenable. He resigned and went off to the Army, to take his place at the front as a General. The King, as if to irritate the Assembly, appointed a new Ministry of Feuillant opinions; with some difficulty, for no one cared to take the dangerous and unpleasant post of Minister. On the 19th June he vetoed the two decrees.

The people of the two faubourgs, Saint-Antoine and Saint-Marceau, to whom the very name of 'veto' was as a red rag to a bull, were profoundly stirred by these events and resolved to make a demonstration. Agitators were always at work among them, but agitators alone never produced the great popular movements of Paris during the Revolution. These movements were spontaneous outbursts of hot feelings, the agitators only fanned the flame, they could not kindle it, hard as they often tried.

This time the outburst took a peaceful form; the Assembly and King being at loggerheads, the people determined to see what they could do to mend matters. On the 16th June some of their leaders announced to the Council of the Commune that the citizens of the two faubourgs were coming in arms on the 20th to plant a tree of Liberty on the Feuillants' Terrace and to present petitions to the Assembly and the King. An armed gathering was illegal, and the Council refused to give permission. The want of permission made no difference, the people were resolved to march, and many of the National Guards were resolved to march with them. The perils of such a demonstration were obvious, and the Directory of the Department, the highest administrative authority in Paris, forbade the gathering and called on the Mayor to act – by the law they could take no further steps themselves. Pétion, the Mayor, good-looking, benign and never ruffled, was the idol of the people; he wished to act constitutionally, but he did not wish to lose his popularity; besides, he was a friend of Roland and Brissot and not sorry that the Court should have a lesson. He tried to persuade the Directory that it would prevent bloodshed if the National Guards were allowed to march with the people, and when he failed, he took no effectual measures to preserve order.

At early dawn on the 20th June the march began, under the leadership of the formidable Santerre, a popular brewer of the faubourg Saint-Antoine. The people were armed with pikes, sticks, knives, old swords; and the procession was bright with flags. One man carried on a pole an old pair of knee-breeches, such as were worn by the well-to-do, with an inscription, *Vivent les Sans-culottes* – a name given derisively to the poorer people who wore longer trousers. Another man carried a calf's heart, with the inscription 'aristocrat's heart'. The National Guards marched with them. When Pétion learnt that every one was well under way, he hastily called the Municipal officers together and got them to order the National Guards to escort the procession, which made the demonstration legal.

The procession moved slowly, but the hours went by, and it was at length approaching the Manège. The Assembly was in a difficulty; should 'the people' be admitted? Resistance would be difficult, and the Girondins did not want to discourage the demonstration; moreover the Assembly was in the habit of allowing armed bodies of volunteers to march through, as Vergniaud pointed out. The noise of the on-coming multitudes put an end to the debate and, in spite of plucky opposition from the Right, every one was admitted; first a deputation and then the procession. Led by Santerre and Saint-Huruge, a well-known agitator, the people marched through the hall, gay and good-natured, waving flags, dancing at intervals to the strains of the *Ça ira*, and shouting: *Vivent les sans-culottes!* *à bas le véto!* The Assembly drew the line at the calf's heart.

After leaving the Manège, the people seemed about to disperse. They marched southwards through the Tuileries gardens to the river and turned northwards again into the Carrousel, the square on the city side of the Palace. It was now well on in the afternoon. The fancy seized the mob to visit the King; they forced the gate of one of the courts in front of the Palace and, meeting no resistance, streamed in and up the stairs, still good-natured, though they battered in the door of the room where the King was. Louis, surrounded by a few faithful friends and accompanied by his devoted sister Madame Elisabeth, who refused to leave him, received them with calm, stolid courage; he stood in the embrasure of a window, while the slowly-shifting throng pressed upon him, so thickly that an evil-disposed person could easily have killed him – and there were wild, threatening figures among the crowd. Deputies from the Assembly forced their way in to share his danger, Vergniaud and Isnard among them; they harangued the people, but to no purpose. Through it all the King stood, dauntless and unwavering. A red cap was handed him, he put it on amid cheers; but though he was urged with threats to recall the popular Ministers and to sanction the two decrees, he promised nothing. The Queen, in another room, showed equal courage. She and her young daughter were also placed in a window, with a table before them on which the little Prince was set, and Santerre stood on guard over them. The crowd was not hostile, touched perhaps by the pretty boy. A red cap was given to him, and the Queen put it on his head; but Santerre, seeing that the child was hot, took it off. At last, after hours that seemed endless, came Pétion, who explained that he had not known what was happening, and harangued the people to such effect that they gradually moved away. Nothing had been stolen, hardly any damage done, no one hurt; but the Assembly had bowed before the mob, and the mob had learnt its power.

At first the King seemed to have gained by the day, for his courage was admired. A petition for the punishment of the ringleaders in the affair was circulated by two old members of the Constituent Assembly, and received so many signatures that it was known as 'the petition of the twenty-thousand.'* Indignant addresses came in also from many Directories of Departments, and from minor bodies. Pétion and the Municipality took care to prevent further disturbances, and the Assembly decreed that no more armed bodies of citizens should be admitted to the Manège in future.

When Lafayette, at the front, heard about the 20th of June, he resolved to make a political stroke for the Constitution, and leaving his army, with Luckner's

* During the Terror, to have signed this petition, or that of the eight thousand, was enough to cause a man's condemnation to death.

195

assent, he hurried to Paris, intending to overawe the Assembly, rally the National Guards, close the Jacobins' Club and save the throne. He was still admired and believed in by the nation at large, his Army was devoted to him, and he thought that he could count on the majority of the Assembly. Already he had sent the Assembly a monitory letter, complaining of Dumouriez and the Jacobins in no measured terms; and if it had not been for a taunting speech from Guadet, the Assembly would have printed this letter, meekly.

On the 28th June, Lafayette appeared at the Bar, tall and imposing, and exhorted the deputies, in the name of his Army, to punish the ringleaders of the demonstration and to uphold the Constitution. There was a good deal of applause, but again Guadet stepped forward, remarking simply that when he saw Lafayette in Paris, he supposed the Austrians must have been beaten. As this was not so, the General was himself violating the Constitution by quitting his Army. After a fierce struggle and much anger, Lafayette's friends succeeded in getting his petition referred to the Committee of twelve, and in defeating Guadet's motion for inquiries, but the effect of Lafayette's appearance had been spoiled. He went to the Tuileries, where he was coldly received by the King and Queen, who preferred running any risks to being saved by the Constitutionalists. The National Guards hailed him enthusiastically and it was decided that he should appear at a forthcoming review and harangue them. But Pétion had the review put off – it is said that the Queen sent him word of Lafayette's intention. Lafayette, finding that he could do nothing, returned to his Army the next day, having damaged his prestige by his ill-judged, if chivalrous, attempt, and having made Robespierre, Brissot and Guadet agree for once in the Jacobins on the necessity of impeaching him.

At the end of June, Pastoret, a distinguished member of the Right, reported on the state of France for the Committee of twelve. The report showed dissatisfaction with the King, both for his veto on the law about the priests and for his inaction, and proposed a remonstrance on the subject of the guilty advisers who surrounded him. Even moderate men like Pastoret were owning that the King was being grievously led astray, and a few days later (3rd July) Vergniaud shook the throne till it tottered.

'What should we do', he asked, 'if the King, while we are at war, did thus and thus?' – enumerating all the ways in which Louis might have been faithless to the spirit of the Constitution while keeping to the letter. 'If such things were possible', Vergniaud continued, 'we might say to him': "O King! you who doubtless thought as the tyrant Lysander did, that truth is no better than lies, and that men must be kept quiet by promises as children are by the game of knuckle-bones – you who feigned to love the laws, merely that you might grasp the power which would serve you to defy them; who feigned to love the Constitution, so that you might not be hurled from the throne where you needs must sit if you are to destroy it; who feigned to love the nation so that you might ensure the success of your perfidies by winning its confidence – do you think that you can still trick us by your hypocritical protestations, and deceive us as to the cause of our misfortunes by the artifice of your excuses and the audacity of your sophisms?'' 'But all this', said Vergniaud, 'is only a horrible supposition', and he professed belief in the good intentions of the King, and proposed sending him a message which might lead to a better understanding. Vergniaud did not see that when such an explanation of a King's conduct, in a time of national peril, can even be suggested, that King is doomed. The Girondins, shrinking from the uncertainties of a great upheaval, did not see it; but the Jacobins did; and so did the people of Paris, and not of Paris only. The day before Vergniaud spoke, there started from revolutionary Marseilles a band of five hundred volunteers, all picked men, raised by the city originally to go to the camp near Paris, before the veto on that camp was known. Young Barbaroux of Marseilles, now in Paris, a friend of the Rolands, had written to his Municipality to send up men who "knew how to die", and 'patriots' trusted that the fiery zeal of the southerners would rouse the cooler north. As the five hundred marched to Paris they sang Rouget de Lisle's new song, which had just reached Marseilles. They sang it through France, they brought it to the capital, and it was re-named from them 'the Marseillaise'.

VI

THE REVOLUTION OF THE
TENTH OF AUGUST JULY 3RD –
SEPTEMBER 20TH 1792

In the third quarter of 1792 France went through one of the most perilous times in her history. The war had given no great cause for alarm as long as the Austrians alone had to be faced; it became serious indeed when the Prussians began to march upon France, for the Prussian troops were reputed to be the best trained in Europe, and strong with the prestige of former victories. France had not yet grasped the change in the situation; recruiting was unsatisfactory, and the Assembly debated anxiously on the question of how the country could best be roused. Finally, on the 11th July, a solemn declaration was made: "Citizens, the country is in danger!" Immediately, as had been previously decreed, every administrative body in the land was bidden to be permanently on the alert, and every National Guard became liable to be called up, while, to begin with, each canton was ordered to select a certain number of its National Guards and to send them to the Army. The nation responded to this appeal with loyal patriotism. In Paris, the Commune proclaimed through the streets with pomp and ceremony: "The country is in danger!" Garlanded tents on platforms were set up as recruiting stations, and during several days the flower of Parisian youth flocked to them to enlist. A custom grew up, that as soon as a company was formed, the 'Section' to which the recruits belonged should present them to the Commune and to the Assembly, with martial music and speeches and cheers, in order that these authorities might encourage their ardour and speed them on their way. As the weeks went on, companies came marching from all parts of the Kingdom; raw recruits for the most part, totally undisciplined, with nothing but their zeal to recommend them. Many were well equipped, through the patriotic gifts for the war offered in generous abundance by rich and poor alike; but many were unarmed and ill-clad. France was new to the idea of a war waged by the nation itself, and these raw troops were supposed to be ready to go to the front with little or no training; for it was an axiom among the revolutionaries that a patriot could fight by the light of nature. As for the patriot who stayed at home, he was expected to fight on occasion with a pike, and a bill was passed, on the 1st August, for supplying one to every citizen capable of bearing arms, who did not own a gun – beggars, tramps, and dangerous characters excepted. This was by no means a measure for arming the mob; the pikes were to be used to defend towns and villages in case of an invasion.

As France began to realize her peril, a change came over the political attitude of her people. Immediately after the 20th June, the great mass of the nation was probably still loyal to the Constitution, in a few weeks' time the same majority was ready to see it set aside. Most men could understand the difficulties of carrying on a life and death struggle when the head of the Government was lukewarm. But the King was an integral part of the Constitution, and if Louis were deposed there was no one to put in his place, as had been perceived the year before. So that the choice lay, in effect, between Louis and a republic; and a republic was unknown ground.

There were strong forces on the side of the Constitution. There was, it must be remembered, no proof that Louis had played the nation false; it was still possible to believe, as the Constitutionalists did, that he was honest though misguided, and that he might yet be reformed. Civil war, too, might follow his overthrow, and thoughtful and responsible men, the men who had made the first Revolution, shrank from the second. The higher administrative bodies, composed of such men, had a considerable influence in the country; the Government was in the hands of Constitutionalists. Lafayette, who had become a kind of figure-head for the Constitutionalists, might have been a tower of strength, but he had somewhat shaken public faith in him by his ill-judged appearance in Paris, and the Assembly was discussing whether his petition had been blameworthy or no. He was, however, still a power.

Against the Constitution stood extremists of every kind and degree, and even among these the wiser heads hesitated, determined on a change but hoping to obtain it by legal means. Danton was still urging constitutional measures in the Jacobins on the 13th July; Robespierre was writing a journal, called, though without much reason for the name, *Le Défenseur de la Constitution*. The extremists had allies in the Assembly prepared to go to any lengths: Chabot, Merlin, and Basire. They had, too, an easy way of working up public opinion, in a new power that was springing up in Paris, the power of the Sections. In order to explain what this was, it is necessary to say a few words on the organization of Paris.

The Constituent Assembly had divided Paris into

forty-eight Sections, each of which had a Sectional Assembly in which all the 'active citizens' (voters) within its boundary had a right to sit. These Sectional Assemblies were intended to meet but seldom; their attempts to take part in politics had been repressed, and their chief business was to elect. They elected the Mayor and the legal officers of the Commune; namely a 'procureur' who gave advice on all measures submitted to the Commune, and his two assistants. They also elected representatives, three for each Section, who formed the 'General Council' of the Commune, a body which did not meet often.

From this 'General Council' were chosen a smaller 'Municipal Council', which met oftener, and 'Administrators' who, with the Mayor, carried on the ordinary business of the city. All Paris lay in the Department of Paris, which took in some outlying towns as well. The Departmental Council, called, for short, 'the Department', was superior to the Commune, and the Commune could ill brook its authority.

There was much to do and to discuss in the troublous days of the war; the 'General Council' met more frequently and the Sectional Assemblies followed suit. The taste for meeting grew, and by July there was in each Section a kind of small Parliament, eager to express its opinions on the questions of the day and to send them, in the form of resolutions or petitions, to the Commune, the Legislative Assembly, or the other Sections. The Commune encouraged these activities and helped the Sections to communicate with each other. When the country was declared in danger, the Sections, though legally they were not administrative bodies, clamoured for permission to meet daily as other administrative bodies did, and, to please Paris, the Assembly put them *en permanence*, as the term was, near the end of July. In these Sectional Assemblies numbers fluctuated, proceedings were often irregular as well as noisy, and outsiders were sometimes allowed to vote. Agitators attended assiduously and cowed moderate men, while most of the 'active citizens', and especially the industrious ones, stayed at home. Yet, on the whole, the resolutions passed did usually reflect the opinion of the Section, and if extremists dominated many of the Sectional Assemblies, it was because the majority of the voters distrusted the King profoundly and did not resist them.

A few of the Sections were moderate and constitutional, a larger number were extreme, and among these, three were prominent: the Quinze-Vingts, part of the Saint-Antoine quarter; Mauconseil, more central; and, most famous of all, the Théâtre-Français on the south side of the river,* formerly known as the Cordeliers

* The Odéon Theatre is on the site of the old Théâtre-Français.

district, and home of the Club of that name. Here lived a cluster of revolutionaries who made their mark. Danton, now assistant procureur of the Commune; his two friends, Camille Desmoulins, witty and unstable as ever, and Fabre d'Églantine, the dramatist, clever, unbalanced and shifty; the crazy Marat, who was often in hiding; Fréron, a brutal journalist approved by Marat; Chaumette, another journalist, a young man with lank, oily hair, a wild, furtive look and a persuasive tongue; Momoro, the printer, an early socialist, rough and hairy; Sergent, an engraver, who, together with Panis, from another section, was 'Administrator' of the Commune in the police department; Manuel, procureur of the Commune, an ardent republican, who had written and published a letter to the King, beginning "Sire, I do not like Kings at all." All these men and many others were working for the overthrow of the Monarchy.

A misunderstanding of the doctrine of the 'Sovereignty of the people', much in vogue, gave the Sections an undue power. 'The people is sovereign', so men argued; 'therefore its voice ought to decide every question. It is necessary to choose representatives to speak for the people; but a representative has ceased to be one of the people, by the very fact of his having been singled out. He is therefore inferior to his constituents; he ought to be nothing but their mouthpiece, and they have a right to recall him at any moment.

The Legislative Assembly, elected by "Electors", is far away from the people; the Commune, elected directly, is nearer; the Sectional Assemblies, not elected at all, are the people itself.' Even the Legislative Assembly accepted much of this doctrine, tolerating impertinent petitions from Sections and individuals, because they came from 'the people', and allowing the galleries filled with 'the people' to be noisy and insolent, with hardly an attempt to curb them. It was part of the doctrine that 'the people is always good and just'; nevertheless it was acknowledged that the said people is often led astray by bad men, and must be kept carefully informed of the truth.

Between the Constitutionalists and the extremists stood the Assembly, and to the Assembly the country, and even Paris, still looked for a lead. The Assembly, as usual, wavered and had no policy. On July 7th there was a momentary reconciliation between parties, when Lamourette, Bishop of Lyon, appealed for unity in the face of the common foe. The deputies took an oath that the Constitution should never be changed, either by the admission of the two-chamber system or of a republic. Then, by a common impulse, Right and Left mingled, enemies embracing each other and sitting down side by side. The King was sent for, and came to protest earnestly that he and the nation were one; a new era seemed to have opened. Unfortunately, that very day, the 'Department' suspended Pétion and Manuel for neglecting their duty on June 20th. The news put Paris in an angry flutter; the Commune demanded its magistrates back, the Sections petitioned in favour of "the virtuous Pétion and the courageous Manuel". It fell to the King to confirm or annul the sentence of the 'Department', and, after some hesitation, he confirmed it. But the Assembly, which had legally the last word, reinstated Pétion at once and Manuel later on. The result of the affair was that the King made himself more unpopular than ever; and the scene of the short-lived reconciliation was called derisively 'le baiser de Lamourette' (*l'amourette*).*

The designs of the extremists were forwarded by a body of men who were now beginning to arrive in Paris; the National Guards, sent up from the Departments to celebrate the fall of the Bastille by a Federation in the Champ-de-Mars, as in 1790, and hence called 'Fédérés'. They were received by the revolutionaries with open arms, and the Jacobins made them specially welcome, admitting them to the Club and listening to their violent, foolish speeches; while Robespierre, on behalf of the Club, hailed their arrival in an address which assured them that their mission was to save the State. Under the fostering care of the

* *Amourette* signifies a love-affair without depth or seriousness.

Jacobins, the Fédérés set up a 'Central Committee' which worked for a revolution; and their share in the enterprise of Paris seemed to the revolutionaries to give it the sanction of 'the people' of the Departments.

It was expected that something would happen on July 14th, but the ceremony, which was attended by the King, passed off quietly. Pétion, just reinstated, was the hero of the day, much cheered and acclaimed. The Fédérés had been ordered by a decree to proceed to a camp at Soissons after a few days in Paris, but a number of them stayed on, and throughout the month more were arriving. Twice in the last half of July (17th and 23rd) they petitioned the Assembly to suspend the King; the second time they petitioned also that a Convention might be summoned.

The Fédérés had put into words the idea which was floating in the air: that the King ought to be suspended or dethroned. Agitators began to preach it in the public places; the Sections were ready to discuss it, so were the Jacobins and the Cordeliers. A new fear made the question seem even more urgent; the King was said to be calling up his disbanded Guards secretly and filling his palace with armed men and ammunition; he intended to make a sortie and overwhelm Paris, where there were now no regular troops, all having been sent to the front on July 15th. Surely the Assembly would do something. But the Assembly did nothing decisive, for, now that the moment for action had come, the Girondins hung back. In common with the majority of the Assembly they feared a rising, and fancied that the Court was trying to provoke one, in order to have a pretext for crushing Paris. Therefore they pleaded not only for constitutional measures, but for delay, and persuaded the Assembly to make a last appeal to the King, for they too seem to have believed in his honesty. Vergniaud, Guadet, and Gensonné went so far as to give the King advice in a letter, written at the request of some of his friends.* If Louis wished to keep his throne, they wrote, he must identify himself irrevocably with the nation in the eyes of Europe. The advice was excellent, but Louis did not take it; he still imagined that if things grew bad enough, they must mend; besides, the Prussians were marching. So he continued to act in the old reckless way. His new Ministers had resigned in a body on July 10th, finding it impossible to carry on the Government, and he appointed others, as shadowy and as ephemeral. He also threw away his last chance by refusing to trust himself to the Constitutionalists, when Lafayette and other leaders were anxious to save him and his family by conveying them to Compiègne or Rouen. The Queen had much to do with this refusal.

* Vergniaud wrote another, similar letter; both were written to the Court painter Boze, for communication to Louis.

Louis, passive in his hostility, had no idea of attacking Paris, and was calling his friends round him simply to defend the Palace if he were attacked. Meanwhile, in spite of all that had happened, the Parisians still showed a certain odd respect for him. The Tuileries Gardens had been closed since May, a sad deprivation for Paris, and late in July the Assembly reopened the Feuillants' Terrace, deciding that it was in their own precincts. Guards were set at each stairway that led down from the Terrace to the garden, and affrays began between these guards and the people who once more thronged the Terrace. By a happy inspiration the guards were removed, and a tricolour ribbon was stretched across the top of each stairway. The people, packed thick on the Terrace, made no attempt to cross the ribbons into the King's domains, and contented themselves with pinning mocking inscriptions to the tiny barrier, for there was still much gaiety among the crowd.

Two important questions were before the Assembly: the suspension of the King and the censure of Lafayette, and the decision on both was anxiously awaited. Lafayette's affair had become complicated by an accusation of treason. Old Luckner, a muddle-headed veteran who knew little French, was visiting Paris, and told some deputies that Lafayette had sent him proposals to march on Paris and put down the

Jacobins. The Girondins took this up, and the Assembly weakly consented to discuss whether Lafayette, a General in command of an army in the field, was a traitor. Bureaux de Pusy, the General said to have carried Lafayette's proposals to Luckner, was called to the Bar, and proved that the story was false; Luckner himself denied having made the accusation; yet the Assembly continued to discuss Lafayette, and the Sections were never weary of petitioning for his impeachment. Lafayette had, indeed, apparently formed some designs of marching on the capital; with the consent of Luckner and the Minister of War, he moved to the northern command (Dunkerque to Montmédy) in order to be nearer Paris, exchanging commands with Luckner, who moved south (Montmédy to Besançon). Each General took his trusted troops with him, and this manoeuvre, risky in the face of the enemy, inspired fresh distrust. It is known as the *chassé croisé*.

In the last days of July came a powerful reinforcement of Fédérés; first a battalion from Brest, 300 strong, and then the terrible Marseillais themselves, who arrived on the 30th. They were conducted by Barbaroux and other leaders to a banquet prepared for them in a restaurant in the Champs-Elysées. By ill hap the Grenadiers of the Filles-Saint-Thomas battalion, the most royalist of all the National Guards, were feasting in another restaurant close by. Their shouts of *Vive le roi*! *vive Lafayette*! possibly intended to annoy the Marseillais, annoyed some 'patriot' spectators outside and led to a conflict. At the noise of the scuffle, the Marseillais came leaping and bounding out of their restaurant into the middle of the fray. Shots were exchanged and the Grenadiers got the worst of it; one was killed and the rest were driven into the Tuileries Gardens. Paris rang with the story, and the revolutionaries declared that the Grenadiers had arranged their banquet on purpose to insult the Marseillais. A few days later the Marseillais were moved from barracks in the north to others in the Théâtre-Français Section, so that they might be ready to act in concert with the 'patriots' there; for the details of the insurrection were now being arranged.

An insolent manifesto signed by the Duke of Brunswick, commander of the Prussian Army, which reached Paris at the end of July, caused deep resentment and stiffened French resistance. It had been written for Brunswick by an emigre. The Duke declared that the allies were coming to restore the King, and threatened that Paris should be given over to a military execution if the slightest harm were done to the King or his family. Louis again protested his complete loyalty to the nation, but his words carried no conviction.

By the beginning of August the Sections had lost patience with the Assembly. Twice already the rising had been put off, and now, on the invitation of the Mauconseil Section, made on July 31st, a number of Sections agreed to march to the Manège on August 5th, with the object of declaring that they no longer recognized Louis XVI as king, and of asking the Assembly whether it was going to save the country or no. The Assembly censured this impudent resolution, but did no more.

And further, the Assembly delayed answering a petition, presented by the Commune and the forty-eight Sections on August 3rd, for the dethronement of the King and the calling of a Convention, which, said the petition, would declare the will of the people, "our Sovereign, and yours". The rising on the 5th was deferred at the last moment by the persuasions of Pétion and the Commune; but, in consequence of a resolution of the Quinze-Vingts Section (Aug. 4th), it was fixed for midnight on Thursday, August 9th. At that hour, if the Assembly had not yet granted the wish of the people, the tocsin was to ring and the Sections to march. Thus every one knew beforehand the exact moment of the revolt; and yet Paris awaited events with outward gaiety.

The Sections, however, were by no means unanimous, and the irresolute Assembly still hesitated to take action. On Wednesday, August 8th, a report on Lafayette, recommending his impeachment, was presented, and after a stormy debate the impeachment was rejected by a large majority. This incensed the mob, and the deputies of the Right were savagely attacked as they left the Manège. They made their just complaints on Thursday morning, amid the jeers and hoots of the galleries. In the afternoon came Rœderer, legal officer of the 'Department', with news that a rising was certain; but Pétion assured the Assembly that adequate preparations had been made to deal with it. The Right proposed to send the Fédérés off to Soissons; the Left would not hear of it. The fatal night had come, and the Assembly had done nothing.

Mandat, the General whose turn it was to command the National Guard, a man devoted to the Constitution, was in charge of the defence of the Tuileries. He had received orders from the Mayor, a few days before, to take all needful measures and to repel force by force. So he called up large contingents of the National Guard, placing strong posts on the bridges to keep the southern Sections and the Marseillais from crossing, and a strong post near the Hôtel-de-Ville to attack the people from Saint-Antoine in the rear, when they had just passed through a narrow arcade and were still in confusion. He posted his troops in the gardens behind the Palace, in the Palace itself, and in the courts in front of the Palace which separated it from the 'place du Carrousel'. It was expected that the attack would be made on these courts, and some of the guns of the National Guard were placed there. The Palace was defended by the Horse-Gendarmerie and by about 900 of the Swiss Guards as well as by the National Guards, fresh detachments of whom arrived during the night. The numbers of the garrison were imposing, but it was doubtful whether National Guards or Gendarmerie would fire on the people.

The Sections had made preparations too. Only a portion of the National Guards, it must be remembered, had been called up by Mandat, and many remained to march to the attack; there were also the citizens without votes who did not belong to the Guard. Both National Guards on the popular side and Fédérés were well supplied with ammunition, for Panis and Sergent had given orders at the Royal Arsenal to serve it out to the Marseillais and the rest. About midnight the tocsin began to ring and the drums to beat, and slowly the National Guards gathered in their Sections.

But the Sections did not trust the Commune to go far enough, and had resolved to make a new 'General Council'. So, in the course of the night, about twenty-eight Sections elected Commissaries, most of whom were obscure men, and sent them to the Hôtel-de-Ville with full powers to save the State. The legal Commune was sitting all night, with Danton and Manuel in its midst to help on the revolution, and for some hours the Commissaries of the Sections sat in another room and both bodies took measures. Finally the Commissaries turned out the legal Commune and took its place. But they kept Pétion, Manuel, and the 'Administrators' in office. Before this happened, the legal Commune had ruined Mandat's plan of defence by ordering the withdrawal of his posts on the bridges; and when it leaked out that he had told his troops to fire on the rear of the people, he was summoned from the Tuileries to explain what was called his treason. Mandat thought himself bound to obey the summons, made by the legal Commune, and came, though reluctantly. The Commissaries examined him and deposed him on the spot, appointing Santerre, one of the leaders in the rising, Commander-in-chief of the National Guards in his stead. Mandat was then bidden to sign an order withdrawing half his troops; he refused courageously, and was arrested. A few hours later he was murdered on the steps of the Hôtel-de-Ville, as he was being taken to the Abbaye prison.

Pétion was not present at these scenes. Early in the night he had been obliged to go to the Palace to report to the King, and fearing that he would be seized as a hostage, had taken the first opportunity of going out to walk in the gardens. Here he fell in with the Grenadiers of the Filles-Saint-Thomas battalion, who threatened him and gave him a terrible fright. The Assembly, hastily called together, was sitting, and Pétion managed to make his danger known to his friends there, and to get himself summoned to the Bar to report; this gave him a good excuse for leaving the Tuileries precincts. Having thus escaped decorously, he retired to the shelter of the Mayor's house, whither, at his own request, the Commune sent a guard of 600 men to keep him a prisoner, so that he might be unable to do anything, and safe whichever side won the day.

Inside the Palace that night, no one went to bed, and the royal apartments were crowded. The Ministers were there, so was Rœderer with other members of the Department, so were the municipal officers of the legal Commune, and many gentlemen who had rallied round the King. The night was hot and through the open windows the tocsin was heard, but cheering news came that the gatherings in the Sections were small. Dawn broke, and Madame Elisabeth called the Queen to look at the red sky. Mandat left, and did not return. At about six o'clock the King was persuaded to go out and review the troops, in the hope that the sight of him would encourage their doubtful loyalty; the review was a failure, and the gunners in the Palace Courts cried: *Vive la nation!* So did other troops, and after the review they began to melt away. By this time the insurgents were marching into the Carrousel, the Marseillais, the Brest Fédérés and contingents from south Paris were the first to appear. Armed men began to knock at the gates of the Courts, and Rœderer and the other officials went round reading to the troops inside them the order to repel force by force. "Can we fire on our brothers?" asked the National Guards. The rising grew and grew; and now there were guns in the Carrousel, brought by the attacking National Guards; and now the National Guards inside were parleying with the assailants; and now Saint-Antoine, under Santerre, was coming up. Rœderer and the officials judged it impossible to hold the Courts, and returned to the Palace to persuade the King that the only chance of safety for him and his family was to seek shelter in the Assembly.

The King was reluctant to go, the Queen more reluctant still, but at length he gave his consent, and at about eight o'clock the little band left the Palace. Mme de Lamballe,* Mme de Tourzel and the Ministers accompanied the royal family, Rœderer and the officials walked with them to protect them, and they were guarded on either side by a detachment of the Swiss Guards and by the Filles-Saint-Thomas battalion. Down into the garden they came, and turned to the right opposite the entrance to the Manège. As they neared the Feuillants' Terrace the leaves were lying thick under the trees, swept into heaps by the gardeners.

* She had emigrated and had returned from safety in England to be with the Queen.

"What a number of leaves!" said the King, "they are falling early this year"; and the little Prince, holding his mother's hand, amused himself by kicking them between the feet of the grown-ups in front of him. There was a hostile crowd on the Terrace, and it was only with difficulty that Rœderer got his charges safely into the Manège. They were courteously received; "I have come here to prevent a great crime," said the King, and Vergniaud, who was presiding, replied that the Assembly was ready to die at its post. This was no idle vaunt; through all the dangers of the day the deputies stood firm and did their best to prevent bloodshed.

Since the Assembly could not legally debate in the King's presence, the royal family was conducted to a small box behind the President, prepared for the reporters of a paper called the *Logotachigraphe*. Not long after their arrival the sound of firing was heard; it continued and became a cannonade. The King, when leaving his Palace, had given no instructions to his guards; he now hastily wrote an order for the Swiss to cease firing and to abandon the Tuileries, and an officer took it off.

When the King left the Palace, the Swiss outside had been recalled within. Soon afterwards the gate of the central Court was either stormed or opened, and through it Marseillais and National Guards burst in, full of good will to their comrades and eager to convert the Swiss. There was a general embracing; the National Guards in the Court went over to the invaders, almost to a man, and moved their guns into the Carrousel. Such Swiss as were visible seemed well-disposed; some of them even threw their cartridges down from the windows in sign of peace. Defenders and assailants were mingling and the lower steps of the great staircase were crowded, when suddenly some of the Swiss officers gave the order to fire. Their well-trained soldiers obeyed; from window and staircase they swept the Courts, and the unsuspecting invaders, together with the National Guards who had gone over, were driven back, leaving their dead and wounded behind them. The Swiss sallied out and manned their guns in the Court; it seemed for a time that they would hold the Palace. But by and by there was a rally; Saint-Antoine had come up in force, and Paris and the Fédérés moved to the attack, mad with rage at what they considered the treachery of the garrison. The Gendarmerie, which had also gone over, joined them. The guns of the National Guard battered at the Palace front; the low line of buildings that ran along the boundary walls of the central court took fire, and clouds of smoke filled the air. At length the ammunition of the Swiss began to give out and their fire to slacken; at about the same time the King's order to cease fire reached them, and they abandoned the Palace and began to retreat through the gardens.* Soon after mid-day the Tuileries Palace was in the hands of the insurgents; National Guards, Fédérés, savage men armed with pikes, and fierce viragoes, filled the Courts, swarmed over the Palace, and thronged the gardens. Less than four hundred killed and wounded had fallen on the popular side, but imagination magnified the number to thousands. The Swiss, conspicuous in their red coats, found no mercy, and the armed gentlemen, when recognized, shared their fate. Some of the Swiss retreated to the Manège, and there the mob would have killed them if prominent deputies had not pleaded for their lives; but the Assembly managed to keep them safe till anger had cooled and they could be moved to a place of detention to await their trial. Some sixty were taken prisoners and massacred at the Hôtel-de-Ville by order of the President of the new Commune. Dead bodies of Swiss, stripped naked by the mob, lay all about the Tuileries, in Courts and gardens, and some of the bodies were thrown into the burning buildings, which were now blazing up till the Carrousel was like a furnace. There were murders in the streets[†] and heads carried round on pikes; it was a scene of triumph and horror. But all well-disposed persons deplored the cruel deeds of the enraged mob, and many a life was risked to help some

* It is a disputed point whether they could have held out longer.
† Clermont-Tonnerre was one of the victims.

223

unfortunate victim to escape. Even the mob showed mercy to the Queen's ladies, who expected death and found themselves unharmed. The Palace was wrecked, but there was hardly any looting, and any one caught at it was lynched; while poor, ill-clad men brought treasures from the royal apartments and handed them over to the Assembly or the Commune. One of the first cares of the populace was to tear down all the statues of kings which adorned Paris.

The Assembly accepted the revolution; the previous inaction of the deputies had left them no choice, and many of them heartily approved of it. They gave a qualified sanction to the new Commune, but would not consent to dethrone the King, judging this beyond their powers. Vergniaud, speaking for the Commission of twelve (now of twenty-one) proposed to call a Convention, in order that the nation might decide the question; to suspend the King meanwhile, and to elect a new Ministry. Pitiful to a fallen foe, he did not care to shut the door of hope on the King in his very presence, and he proposed also that a Governor should be chosen to educate the little Prince, and that the royal family should be guarded in the Luxembourg Palace. His Bill passed, and the Assembly elected new Ministers; Roland, Clavière, and Servan to their old posts, Danton as Minister of Justice. All through the long, hot day and for three days more, the royal family sat in the stuffy little box, sad and patient, listening to the debates; at night they slept in some cells of the Feuillants' Convent hard by. The new Commune, now fortified by commissaries from all the Sections, did not wish to lodge them in the Luxembourg and, after a struggle, the Assembly was forced to give in and to hand them over to the guard of the Commune. On the evening of the 13th they were taken, under strong escort, to 'the Temple', which was a large enclosure containing many buildings, and were imprisoned in one of them, the small, ancient tower of the Knights Templars. The popular triumph and the imprisonment of the King and Queen were commemorated in a famous song, sung to a rollicking dance-tune called the Carmagnole, and beginning:

> Madam' Veto avait promis
> De faire égorger tout Paris.
> with the refrain: "Dansons la carmagnole,
> Vive le son du canon!"

It was an anxious question how the Armies, especially Lafayette's troops, would take the overthrow of the Constitution, and the Assembly dispatched three commissaries to each Army, to explain matters and to remove or arrest all objecting officers. Lafayette, who was at Sedan, tried to organize a constitutional resistance;

he persuaded the local authorities to protest, and to arrest the three commissaries of the Assembly on their arrival, hoping that France would rally round him and defy Paris. But he failed to carry his Army with him; the soldiers were all for the revolution and soon began to regard their once-loved General as a traitor. Lafayette saw that his cause was lost, and because he believed that his life might be of supreme value to his country later on, he would not stay to be arrested, but crossed the frontier, in company with a number of constitutionalist officers, intending to fly to Holland or England. The party fell into the hands of the Austrians, who treated them badly and handed over Lafayette and three Generals, distinguished members of the Constituent Assembly,* to the Prussians, under whom, and afterwards under the Austrians, they spent many years in a cruel captivity. Dumouriez was given Lafayette's command and Kellermann, an Alsatian, succeeded Luckner; while all officers who did not agree to the new order were retired by the commissaries.

France, like the Assembly, accepted the revolution of the 10th August, and almost everywhere public functionaries took the new civic oath; to be faithful to the nation and to maintain liberty and equality with

---

* Alexandre Lanieth, already impeached; Latour-Maubourg, Lafayette's friend; and Bureáux de Pusy, thrice President of the Constituent Assembly.

all their power, or die at their posts. There was no great enthusiasm, but few protests were made, for there was a general determination, patriotic and instinctive, to keep the country together at any cost, and to follow where the Assembly led. The administrative bodies which protested were censured and removed, and here the Assembly showed comparative leniency. But no leniency was shown to former Ministers and to prominent Constitutionalists who fell under any suspicion, and impeachments and arrests were frequent. The air was full of suspicion, and some of the King's private papers found in the Tuileries seemed, in the heat of the moment, to justify it all. Non-juring priests were not spared; Cambon, who wanted to save their salaries for the nation, was particularly hard on them. It was decreed, towards the end of August (19th and 26th) that they must leave the kingdom within fifteen days, or be deported to the hot, unhealthy colony of Guiana – Vergniaud, to his honour, protested against sending them there. Even priests with no public functions, formerly excepted, were now obliged to choose between taking the oath and being deported if six citizens of their canton demanded it. Thus was one veto wiped out; the Assembly had already wiped out the other by ordering the formation of a camp near Paris.

It proved a costly failure. One immediate consequence of the 10th August was the disappearance of the distinction between 'active' and 'non-active' citizens. All Frenchmen of twenty-one and upwards, except domestic retainers, were given votes in the election of the Convention. But the system of electing in two steps was kept.

The conduct of the war was the most important business, both of the Assembly and of the new Ministry, and such deputies of the Right as were still sitting co-operated loyally. While Vergniaud was the voice of patriotic resistance in the Assembly, Danton was the soul of the Government, dominating the other Ministers by his strong personality and his ardour, driving his measures through the chaos in every department by sheer force of will, and proving himself a first-rate Minister, to the surprise of those who knew him only as a demagogue. A large, powerful man, with a fine head and a red face, marked by small-pox and flattened and disfigured by injuries received in childhood, he could make himself terrible in look and word and never hesitated to take the sternest measures when he thought them requisite. Yet by nature he was jovial, magnanimous, widely tolerant, sympathetic with weaker souls, incapable of personal hatred, and always ready to save a victim. His voice was extremely powerful; his eloquence, fresh and unstudied, pierced straight to the heart of a subject; he could blend the familiar with the grand in a way peculiar to himself. He had been an advocate in good practice, and was in private life a family man, happily married. He was fond of wit and gaiety, so fond that he was careless about the character of amusing friends. As a Minister he employed too often unsuitable and unworthy agents; thus, he put Camille Desmoulins and Fabre d'Églantine, neither of whom was fit for it, into positions of trust in the Ministry of Justice.

The Assembly was still the rallying point for France; but it had followed and not led the new revolution, as the Parisians were well aware, and in Paris it was powerless; the new Commune was, in fact, the only power which could at all control the mob and stem the tide of anarchy. Danton understood this and worked well with the Commune; the Assembly saw in the Commune nothing but a band of rebels, and refused to be dictated to. Pétion was standing aloof, and the lead in the Commune was taken by Robespierre, who had become a member on August 11th. Inspired by him, the Commune sent frequent deputations to the Assembly bearing orders disguised as petitions, and continued to send them, backing each petition with threats of a popular rising, until the Assembly had granted it. Thus, the Assembly had decreed that the surviving Swiss Guards should be tried by a court martial, while the Commune had decided that all the 'enemies of the revolution' should be tried by a special court. Step by step concessions were wrung from the Assembly. Two deputations came in one evening to demand a new tribunal, and the second had orders to wait for a decree. Robespierre himself headed a deputation the next day, and finally, on August 17th, after Brissot had reported against the innovation, came another deputation with an outrageous address, containing a threat that the tocsin should ring at midnight if the new tribunal were not granted. The Assembly rebuked the petitioners, but, fearing a massacre in the prisons, passed, the same day, a bill for the formation of a court to try offences connected with the 10th August. A body of special jurymen had already been elected by the Sections, who now chose the Judges, through 'Electors'. The new Court, from whose sentences there was no appeal, was known as 'the Tribunal of the 17th August' and was rapidly installed. Robespierre was chosen as President, but declined to sit, saying honourably, that as he had always denounced the enemies of his country, he was not the man to try them. The Commune ordered that prisoners condemned by this tribunal should be executed in the place du Carrousel on the scene of their crime, and that the guillotine* should be set up

---

* Called after Guillotin, a philanthropic doctor, member of the Constituent Assembly, who first proposed this mode of execution, which was already known. He did not plan the machine. Non-political executions continued to take place in the place de Grève in front of the Hôtel-de-Ville, as before.

there permanently. This instrument had been definitely adopted by the Legislative Assembly in March 1792, as the most merciful method of execution, and was first used in April.

The trials began on August 20th and were fairly lengthy, as the judges, legal men, did their best to be impartial and were reluctant to condemn. The first victim, a man said to have raised a secret band who served the King by making trouble, was executed on the evening of the 21st by torchlight, in the presence of a vast crowd. Two more executions followed, at intervals, and the populace began to murmur that justice was slow; then came two acquittals, and they murmured that justice was not sure. The second man acquitted, Montmorin, Governor of Fontainebleau, cousin of the Minister who was also in prison, was supposed by the people to be the Minister himself, and there were howls in the Court at his acquittal. The presiding judge, Osselin, only saved him from lynching by conducting him back to the Conciergerie prison* himself.

Meanwhile another battle was raging between Commune and Assembly, over the Paris 'Department'. The Commune suspended the 'Department', quite illegally, wishing to get rid of it, for, as Robespierre justly observed, the fewer the authorities which stood between

* The Conciergerie, where prisoners awaiting trial were kept, is under the Palais de Justice.

the people and the Assembly at such a time, the better. The Assembly ordered the election of a new 'Department'. As soon as it had been elected, Robespierre came with a deputation, demanding that it should be turned into a mere Commission to deal with taxes. This was too much; the Assembly knew that the Commune was becoming unpopular among the Sections, and plucked up heart enough to refuse the petition on August 29th. On the 30th the doings of the Commune were more intolerable still, and the Assembly resounded with complaints. First Roland announced that the Commune had dismissed the 'Administrators', in concert with whom he had made his arrangements for provisioning Paris. Next, it appeared that the Commune had ordered the arrest of the present editor of *Le Patriote français*, Girey Dupré, a young friend of Brissot, because he had misrepresented their intentions. Finally, Gensonné reported that the Commune was blockading the War Office and allowing no one to leave the building, because the printer of *Le Patriote français* was said to be inside. The Assembly dissolved the Commune forthwith, and ordered the election of a fresh Commune in twenty-four hours. The Commune prepared to resist; a few Sections recalled their representatives, a few others confirmed them; but the news from the seat of war became so alarming that the services of the Commune could not be dispensed with, and a truce was patched up. The Assembly continued the Commune and doubled the legal number of its members, giving the Sections the right, which they had already assumed, of recalling their representatives at any moment. The Commune, on its side, reinstated the 'Administrators' and the Municipal Council.

The Prussians had entered France on the 19th August, and had at once invested the fortress of Longwy, called 'the iron gate of France'. The fortifications were in a bad state, and Longwy surrendered on the 23rd, after a short bombardment. The news reached Paris on the 25th, and from now on each day brought some new excitement to the agitated city. On the 26th a great funeral fête in the Tuileries Gardens, commemorating the victims of the 10th August, turned men's minds afresh to thoughts of vengeance – that vengeance on the 'enemies of the people' which still delayed, though the Marseillais had stayed on in Paris expressly to see it carried out. On the 27th the Assembly voted a fresh levy of 30,000 men, armed and equipped, to be raised by Paris and the surrounding Departments. On the 28th Danton persuaded the Assembly to allow the Commune to search houses for the purpose of finding firearms, which were to be taken for the troops, and of arresting all suspected persons at one swoop; the Commune had been arresting them daily in detail, yet there were many still at large. So, on the nights of August 29th and 30th, all traffic was stopped in the streets, and an armed force went from house to house, searching. Every house had to be lighted up, and any citizen found in another man's house was liable to arrest. Many arrests of suspected persons were made, and the prisons of the Abbaye and la Force were filled with royalists and non-juring priests. On the 31st came Montmorin of Fontainebleau's acquittal. On September 1st a convict was said to have revealed a plot for arming all the prisoners secretly and organizing their simultaneous outbreak to overwhelm the patriots.

On Sunday, September 2nd, the dread news burst on Paris, that the great fortress of Verdun, besieged by the Prussians, could not hold out eight days; that Dumouriez's Army was cut off from Kellermann's; that if Verdun fell, the enemy might be in Paris in a fortnight. The Commune, always energetic over war measures, at once made a proclamation inviting all citizens to meet in the Champ-de-Mars when the tocsin sounded, and to raise, then and there, an army which would march on the morrow to the relief of Verdun. The Assembly thanked the Commune in the name of France, and Vergniaud, in a stirring speech, called for action. "You have sung about freedom," he said, "now you must defend it. The Kings that we must overthrow are no longer Kings of bronze."* And Danton, in a speech greater still, cried that the whole nation was burning to fight. "The tocsin that is about to ring is no signal of alarm; it sounds for a charge on the enemies of our country." He ended with the famous words: "Pour les vaincre, messieurs, il nous faut de l'audace, encore de l'audace, toujours de l'audace, et la France est sauvée." Danton was active in the Champ-de-Mars, where patriotic Paris was gathering.

'Shall we march to the front, leaving behind us prisons full of enemies, who may break out at any moment and slaughter our wives and our children?' It was a question which had often been asked in the last few days, and all the authorities were in constant expectation of a massacre in the prisons. A Section had even announced one to the Commune, nine days before. By September 2nd a massacre had been organized, and, though a mystery hangs over the crime, there is light enough to show that the chief guilt belongs to the Watch Committee of the Commune, a small body guided by the Police 'Administrators', Panis and Sergent, which sat in the Mayor's house, close to the Law Courts, and had control of the prisons. On the morning of September 2nd Panis and his colleagues

---

* An allusion to the statues overturned on August 10th.

co-opted six new members, three of whom did not belong to the Commune, and one of these was Marat, who had been crying out louder than ever for blood.* Two Sections (Poissonnière and Luxembourg) probably started the massacres by resolutions taken on that Sunday, but some one in authority had arranged the details and informed the jailers, for they fed their prisoners well, as was customary with condemned criminals, and offered no resistance.

Twenty-four prisoners, nearly all priests, were confined in the depôt of the Mayor's house; among them was the abbe Sicard, a well-known teacher of the deaf and dumb. At two o'clock, when the tocsin sounded, a band of Marseillais seized on them and conveyed them in cabs to the Abbaye prison, a building attached to the ancient Abbey of Saint-Germain-des-Pres, in south Paris. As the cabs reached the Abbey precincts, a mob set upon the prisoners and massacred them in one of the courts. Sicard, almost alone, was saved by the exertions of a man who recognized him. The murderers then went off to the Carmelite convent† near by, in the chapel of which some 150 non-juring

---

* The rest of the Committee were obscure men. It is noteworthy that Panis and Sergent did not show themselves cruel either before or after the massacres.

† The convent of the Carmelites (*Carmes déchaussés*) in the rue de Vaugirard still standing.

priests, including an Archbishop, two Bishops, and other distinguished ecclesiastics, were confined, awaiting deportation. Some of these were stabbed in the convent garden, others were killed, two by two, at the foot of the stairs leading to the garden; a few contrived to escape. The next place of slaughter was the Abbaye prison. Here the band of murderers was directed by Stanislas Maillard, the man who had led the women of Paris to Versailles in 1789. He presided over a sort of tribunal in the entrance of the prison. The judges sat round a table, with bottles of wine to refresh them and the prison register open before them; the prisoners were brought in one by one and questioned shortly. Murderers dripping with blood came in and out, and spectators edged their way in among them, sometimes with benevolent intentions. If a prisoner was considered innocent – and there were a good many acquittals, even among political prisoners – he was released amid shouts of delight; if guilty, the judges cried "a la Force!" and the unsuspecting victim was led to the door and pushed out, to be dispatched by the murderers outside, or to be dragged to the garden court of the Abbey, where another massacre, chiefly of priests, was going on. A tribunal of the same kind sat in the other prisons, notably in la Force, a prison of central Paris, where the death sentence was: "à l'Abbaye!" All night long the massacres went on in the

Abbaye and la Force, and two other prisons, the Châtelet and the Conciergerie, were invaded. On Monday they still went on, and were extended to a seminary where non-juring priests were confined, to a tower which held a number of convicts condemned to the galleys, and to the great prison of Bicêtre. No distinction was made between political and other prisoners; Paris, in its panic, seemed for the moment to regard every prisoner as a potential enemy of his country, ready to join with the foreign foe. The dead lay in heaps before the prisons, the streets ran with blood, the dead-carts plied to and fro between the prisons and the cemeteries, and still the massacres went on.

At the Abbaye the Minister Montmorin perished, and many Swiss officers were killed without the semblance of a trial. Two heroic daughters, Mesdemoiselles de Sombreuil and Cazotte, each saved an aged father by clinging to him when he was brought before the judges, and pleading for him till Maillard was softened.* Montmorin of Fontainebleau, just acquitted, was killed at the Conciergerie: Mme de Tourzel and several of the Queen's ladies were in la Force; all were fetched away by compassionate members of the Commune, except the harmless Mme de Lamballe. She was

---

* The story that Mlle de Sombreuil was compelled to drink a glass of blood is most probably untrue. Old Cazotte was executed shortly after by the Tribunal of the 17th August.

brought before the prison tribunal early on Monday, sentenced, and dragged out, half fainting, to be struck down on the top of a heap of corpses. Her body was cut in pieces; her head, on a pike, was paraded before the windows of the Temple Tower, in hopes that the Queen would see it. The Temple itself was not attacked. At Bicêtre forty-three boys under eighteen, who had been sent there as to a reformatory, were killed with the other convicts. On Tuesday thirty-five women were killed in the women's prison, la Salpêtrière – the only women slain except Mme de Lamballe and a murderess in the Conciergerie. Crowds watched the massacres, but a small number of murderers did the work, helped at times by Marseillais and others. The murderers had been promised wages, and the Commune saw to it that they were paid, while the Watch Committee took care that all the valuables found on the dead were brought safely in, and that the blood was washed away. On September 3rd this same Committee sent a circular to other municipalities inviting them to follow the example of Paris and, by the connivance presumably of Fabre d'Églantine, they sent it out from the Ministry of Justice.

The Assembly and the Commune made feeble attempts to stop the massacres by sending deputations to harangue the murderers, and from time to time the Commune dispatched commissaries to the prisons to see what could be done.* Some of these tried their best, others, as Billaud-Varenne, assistant procureur, looked on at the slaughter with approval. Manuel, sincerely horrified, made effort after effort to end the ghastly work, and all in vain. Pétion did nothing; he said afterwards that no one had told him what was happening. Santerre did nothing; if he had called on the National Guards to interfere, it is probable that they would not have obeyed. Danton did nothing; his whole energies were absorbed in organizing national defence. Roland, in whose department the prisons were, was powerless. On the night of September 2nd, Robespierre, in the Jacobins, had denounced Brissot and the Girondin party as traitors, at a moment when such an accusation might bring death, and the Watch Committee of the Commune had Brissot's papers searched and issued a warrant for Roland's arrest, which Danton stopped. On September 3rd Roland did try to rouse the Assembly by a strong letter on the prevailing anarchy; but he excused the massacres in words which expressed what most people in Paris were feeling: "I know that the people, though terrible in vengeance, blends with it a kind of justice." The Paris newspapers were saying much the same thing. At

---

* The Commune released all prisoners for debt when the massacres began, and before this a few fortunate prisoners had been removed through the interest of men in power.

length, when most of the prisons were empty, the Assembly sent commissaries to influence public opinion in the Sections, Santerre called out the National Guard, Pétion exhorted persuasively, and the massacres came to an end on the night of September 6th. Nearly 1,400 prisoners had perished, of whom considerably more than half were ordinary criminals, and a large number had been released. Vengeance was satisfied, and the Marseillais left Paris, not for the front, but for Marseilles.

There was a smaller massacre on the 9th September. The Commune wished the State prisoners at Orléans, fifty-three in number, to be brought to Paris, and a band of men, National Guards, Marseillais and others, led by an agitator called Fournier the American, went to Orléans to fetch them. The Assembly, anxious to save the prisoners, decreed that they should be taken from Orléans to Saumur, in the west; but, in defiance of the Assembly, Fournier and his band conducted them towards Paris, and all that the authorities could accomplish was to induce Fournier to take them to the less dangerous Versailles. In the streets of Versailles a mob fell on them and killed them while Fournier and his band looked on. The Mayor of Versailles flung himself between the assassins and their victims, in vain. The Minister Delessart, the magistrate Larivière, and the duc de Brissac were among the slain. Another victim of a mob was the revered duc de la Rochefoucauld, lynched as he was being brought, under arrest, to Paris. There were one or two other outbreaks, but France in general regarded the massacres with horror.

The elections to the Convention were in progress and the last days of the Legislative Assembly had come. The battle with the Commune continued, and the Commune was losing ground. It had sent a number of Commissaries into the Departments, chiefly in concert with the Ministers, but also on its own authority, and had given all of them commissions from itself. Their business was to help raise men for the Army, and they were so tyrannical and violent in carrying it out, that they made themselves a byword. Therefore, on the 14th September the Assembly forbade the sending of Commissaries to the Departments by municipalities. Paris continued lawless – a number of the crown jewels were stolen one night (Sept. 16-17) by a company of robbers – and the prisons were filling rapidly, for the Watch Committee was busy making more arrests. On September 16th and 17th there was talk of a fresh massacre, but when Vergniaud obtained a decree making the members of the Commune responsible with their own heads for the safety of prisoners, the danger passed over. Pétion bestirred himself, and denounced Marat to such purpose that the Commune forbade anyone who was not a member of the General Council to sign warrants for arrest.

While Paris was staining the Revolution with crime, the cheery optimist, Dumouriez, on the eastern frontier, was forming his unsteady troops into a fighting force worthy of France. Only the regulars of the old Army and the volunteers of 1791 were of any use as yet, for the new, unruly recruits were the despair of the Generals at the base camps, where they gathered, and of the Generals at the front, who kept as few of them there as they could. Dumouriez was an ideal leader for the special moment, full of resource and daring, never discouraged; he gained the confidence and affection of his men, and inspired them gradually with his own dauntless spirit. The weather was terrible, week after week of cold, incessant rain, but the French troops were well fed and cared for, while the ill-fed Prussians were ravaged by dysentery. Both sides were careless and both made bad mistakes, but Dumouriez was quick where Brunswick was slow.

Verdun, in desperate case, had capitulated on September 2nd after a short bombardment; the terms offered were favourable, and the terrified inhabitants insisted. The Commandant, Beaurepaire, was overruled, but he blew his brains out after signing the capitulation, rather than survive in dishonour, and his death made an immense impression in France.

Dumouriez prevented the Prussians from marching on Paris, by holding the passes of the Argonne, through which lay their route to the capital; and when this position became dangerous and he was compelled to evacuate it he extricated himself by a brilliant retreat at night, and encamped near Sainte-Menehould. Here, on September 19th he was joined by Kellermann, and here, on September 20th, an attack by the Prussians on Kellermann's forces resulted in the battle of Valmy: an artillery duel, during which the French stood firm on Valmy hillock, under the deadly cannonade of the Prussians, for half a day, and the French artillery, the pride and strength of the Army, showed its superior powers. It was a partial and indecisive engagement, but it saved France, for it taught the French Armies their own strength, and filled the confident Prussians, who had expected an easy victory, with forebodings.

PART III –
THE CONVENTION

VII

THE STRUGGLE BETWEEN THE GIRONDE AND THE MOUNTAIN SEPTEMBER 21ST 1792 – JUNE 2ND 1793

The Convention opened on September 21st, 1792.* A gigantic task lay before this new Assembly: to drive off and conquer the enemy, to suppress anarchy, to make a new Constitution. Unity was needed above all things, and as the great majority of the deputies were at one in their aims and did not differ widely in their political views, unity might have been expected. Yet the early days of the Convention were passed in a tragic strife of parties which brought irreparable evils upon France.

* After a formal meeting on the 20th. The number of deputies, when complete, was 780.

There had been no restrictions as to eligibility, and nearly two hundred members of the Legislative Assembly had been re-elected, including all the prominent men of the Left. More than eighty 'Constituents', as members of the Constituent Assembly were called, had likewise been elected; all from the Left. The deputies were drawn from the same classes as those of the last Assembly, and again lawyers predominated. There were sixteen Constitutional Bishops, a good many priests and ex-priests, and a few ex-nobles.

The Brissotins, or Girondins,* often called 'the Gironde', under their old leaders, became at once the Right of the Convention; their opponents were called 'the Mountain', because the extreme Left sat in the highest seats of the amphitheatre on that side.† The large number of moderate or timid men who sat between, the Centre, were known as 'the Plain', or unkindly as 'the Marsh', but never formed a party. Siéyes, whose reputation was great as ever, was one of them.

The Girondins were reinforced by many of the 'Constituents'; Buzot and Pétion, who had resigned his mayoralty to become a deputy, were already bound to

---

* The name Girondins, as applied to the whole party, came in later historians have, adopted it as a convenient term. One contemporary name was *hommes d'État* (statesmen), used derisively.

† The name dates from the Constituent Assembly, but did not come into common use till the Convention.

the leaders by ties of friendship; Lanjuinais and Rabaut joined them; Barère, good-looking, pleasant, able, and careful to be on the winning side, inclined to them – a wit said of Barère: "he always comes to the help of the strongest." Others took refuge with them because they were the less violent party. New men of mark were also in their ranks: Carra and Gorsas, reckless journalists whose papers were much read; Boyer-Fonfrède of Bordeaux, brother-in-law and bosom friend of Ducos, gifted and fairly moderate; Louvet, an eloquent orator, an ugly little man with a great heart, who wrote scandalous novels and saw life as a sensational plot; young Barbaroux of Marseilles, fluent and fiery, full of enthusiasm and 'beautiful as Adonis', but corpulent. The Gironde possessed nearly all the best orators and Girondin influence was strong in the Council of Ministers, where Roland, Clavière, and Lebrun, Minister of Foreign Affairs, were adherents. The Girondins made a sort of figurehead of Roland, whom they always spoke of as "the virtuous Roland", and many of them frequented Madame Roland's salon and dinners, and caught inspiration from her.

On the Mountain, Chabot, Basire, and Merlin de Thionville were prominent, as before; so, in staider fashion, were Cambon, Hérault de Séchelles, and, later on, Couthon. So were two members of the Legislative Assembly not yet mentioned: Thuriot, delicate and slender, supposed to have spoken in the summer as Danton's mouthpiece, and Lacroix,* huge and handsome, who joined the party later when he became Danton's friend; both undefinable men who varied from the wild to the sensible in their speeches and had no moral force. The 'Constituent', Merlin de Douai, placed his great legal knowledge at the service of the Mountain. Among new men there were Anacharsis Cloots, the Prussian Baron, who claimed to speak for the Human Race and dreamt of a universal Republic; Tallien, the youthful secretary of the Paris Commune, and another young man, quite unknown, whose talents soon brought him into the front rank, the handsome, haughty Saint-Just. But the Paris deputation was most conspicuous; here were Robespierre and his younger brother Augustin; Danton, who resigned his Ministry; his friends, Camille Desmoulins, Fabre d'Églantine and the butcher Legendre; the duc d'Orléans, now known as Égalité, a surname which had been bestowed on him by the Paris Commune; Manuel, Sergent, Panis, and the small, dark, stern-faced, hard-hearted Billaud-Varenne from the Commune; wild-looking Collot d'Herbois, a prominent Jacobin orator who had been an actor, a sentimentalist turned cruel; Fréron the journalist; David the great painter, and that name of terror – Marat.

---

* His real name was Delacroix, but he was usually called Lacroix.

Danton took the lead at the first sitting. At his suggestion the Convention allayed popular fears by putting life and property under the protection of the nation, and by decreeing that the new Constitution should be submitted to the people for ratification. It was also decreed that all laws should continue in force until repealed. Then, on the motion of Collot d'Herbois, seconded by Grégoire, Bishop of Blois, royalty was abolished. "Kings", said Grégoire, "are in the moral order what monsters are in the physical world." Four days later, on September 25th, a Republic "one and indivisible" was decreed; a Republic received and cherished with a passionate enthusiasm of loyalty.

The Convention opened under favourable circumstances, for the war, in the first months, went more than well. For one thing, the enemy was forced to leave the country. The Prussians were in a critical position, sick, starved, and discouraged, and Dumouriez, who even now dared not risk a direct attack, conceived the idea that by allowing them to withdraw he might detach them from Austria and secure an alliance for France. With the approval of the Council of Ministers he negotiated. The Prussians flattered him with false hopes and began to retreat, while the French hung on their rear without molesting them. On October 23rd they finally left France. Meanwhile the French armies were successful in south and east. Towards the end of

September, a state of hostility having existed for some time between the King of Sardinia and France, General Montesquiou entered Savoy, where he found the whole country anxious to join France, and Savoy was 'united' with the Republic on November 27th. Another General occupied Nice in September. In the east, General Custine carried the war among the sleepy Germans of the Rhineland, who made little resistance. He took Spires, he took Mayence (Oct. 21st), he seized on the neutral city of Frankfort. The coming of the French was welcome to some of the Rhinelanders, and Mayence became a republic; Custine's stay was not welcome, for he lived upon the country and exacted heavy contributions. On December 2nd he lost Frankfort to the Prussians, but maintained himself along the Rhine.

More important still, Dumouriez, having got rid of the Prussians, was able to turn his attention to the Austrians and to carry out his favourite plan of invading Belgium. The Austrians were bombarding Lille, and that city was holding out heroically, when Dumouriez's advance compelled them to raise the siege (Oct. 6th). On November 6th he attacked the Austrian position at Jemappes and won a brilliant victory; on the 14th he entered Brussels. The Belgians, who detested the Austrian yoke, received the French as deliverers, and the whole country was soon in Dumouriez's hands. If he had been able to follow up his advantage he might have dealt the Austrians a staggering blow, but his army could make no exertions, for Servan, the capable Minister of War, had resigned, and his successor, the incapable Pache (a Swiss protégé of Roland who became Roland's enemy), had filled the War Office with incompetent democrats, who disorganized all the Army services and left the troops unpaid and unclothed. Pache was the despair of the Generals; the Jacobins protected him because he was a good party man.

With success the spirits of the French rose, and the Convention no longer wished for peace. France, it was felt, was carrying out, through war, her sacred mission of bringing freedom and a republic to all countries; moreover she could not be considered really safe until her boundaries reached the line of the Rhine, and till all her neighbours were friendly republics. The Gironde and the Mountain agreed about this, and on November 19th a decree was passed promising friendship and help to all nations which were trying to recover freedom. This was a warning to Europe that France meant to stir up rebellion in every country. Another decree, on December 15th, ordered the Generals to organize the countries occupied by their armies afresh, under 'the Sovereignty of the people', and to sweep away all existing authorities and privileges. This done, the method followed was to send propagandist agents, great and small, into the occupied city or district, who worked with the local revolutionaries and cajoled or terrified a majority of the inhabitants into petitioning for union with France. The Convention then granted 'union', i.e. annexation, and acclaimed a new triumph for Liberty.

In Paris, as well as in the Armies, the situation was favourable to the Convention. The Commune was discredited, and the Legislative Assembly, as a Parthian shot, had ordered the immediate election of a new Commune (19 Sept.). The Commune, indeed, by promptly disowning the Watch Committee and by other astute moves, succeeded in evading the decree, with the help of protectors in the Convention. But its existence was precarious, as the Sections were clamouring for accounts, and the Convention refused to advance more money until they were produced. Much of the autumn was spent trying to make them up – with poor success. At the same time the Commune was pressing for the accounts of the Watch Committee, in whose hands much treasure, the spoils of many victims, had been deposited. The Watch Committee blustered and lied; its members could not, in fact, render an account, for they had kept no records, and some of the valuables known to be in their care were missing. The affair dragged on, and the next summer

Sergent and Panis were on the point of being prosecuted, when a turn in events brought their friends into power and saved them.

By the end of November the attendance at the Commune was so small that the Convention ordered the election of a new, provisional Commune. It met on December 2nd, a body slightly less extreme than its predecessor. The new Mayor was a nonentity, and Chaumette,* now chosen as procureur, kept the position of leading member, which he had already assumed. He raised the spirits and pretensions of the Commune, being always ready, like an unmannerly dog, to yap at the heels of the Convention, and, if the Convention raised a warning hand, to crawl humbly to the Bar with plausible explanations and excuses.

With Paris quiet and the war prosperous, the Convention might have increased a power and prestige already great, and the large majority of moderate men might have rendered extremists harmless. Gironde and Mountain were agreed upon foreign policy; both were ready to throw over any General on whom the slightest suspicion rested – except the indispensable Dumouriez; both were anxious to doom the enemies of the Republic to death. Thus, Buzot and Danton combined in getting a decree which condemned all the émigrés

* Chaumette had renamed himself Anaxagoras Chaumette.

to perpetual banishment, with death to any who returned (23 Oct.). But the circumstances of the late revolution had raised a barrier between the parties, and the September massacres, now seen in their true hideousness, lay heavy on the conscience of the Girondins, who had done nothing to stop them, and tried to convince themselves that this inaction had been blameless by constantly protesting their abhorrence. The abhorrence was, no doubt, sincere; but they certainly used the massacres as a handy accusation to fling at the Mountain.

Danton, who was ever for union and harboured no personal hatred, would willingly have joined forces with the Girondins, and if the party had been under the guidance of Vergniaud, Ducos, and Condorcet, who were not influenced by the Rolands, a way of conciliation might have been found. The Girondins, however, disdained guidance, and though they were in the habit of meeting together, had no idea of party discipline and were always at the mercy of the unwisest. So they rejected Danton's advances, cast September in his teeth, and accused him both of aspiring to a dictatorship and of not accounting for the secret service money he had received as Minister. Danton had, it is true, committed an unpardonable sin in their eyes; one day, in a debate, he had, with very bad taste, made a jocose reference to Madame Roland's influence over her husband.

The battle between Mountain and Gironde raged continually over several subjects all connected with each other: Roland, Robespierre, Marat, and Paris.

First Roland, "the exclusively and eternally virtuous man", as Robespierre once sarcastically called him. Roland was bellicose; with honest though mistaken zeal he deluged the country with Girondin pamphlets, stopped Jacobin literature in the post, made the most of disorders, cried out upon the iniquities of Paris, and prophesied ruin. In return, hardly a speaker in the Jacobins'* could open his mouth without denouncing Roland, and the Mountain denounced him perpetually in the Convention. Whenever the Mountain denounced Roland, the Gironde denounced Pache, and vice versa.

Next Robespierre. Even before the Republic was decreed, Robespierre had accused the Girondins of 'federalism', i.e. of wishing to split up France into a number of federated republics; and Barbaroux had accused Robespierre of wishing to make himself dictator. On October 29th Louvet made a great sensation with an eloquent denunciation of Robespierre's inordinate ambition, his tyranny in the Jacobins' and the Commune. But it was all accusation without proof, and a week later Robespierre brushed the whole thing away with a skilful answer.

---

* The Girondins had ceased to attend the Jacobins', and all their leaders were expelled during the autumn.

Next Marat. Marat was a man whom no strong Government would have left at large for a week in time of war, and at first there were few deputies who did not shrink from the sight of the livid little man with the jerky walk. Danton, whom Marat always praised, took care to dissociate himself from his admirer; Robespierre was not friendly. The first time Marat insisted on speaking, he met with a most hostile reception. "I have a great number of personal enemies in this Assembly," he began, and there was a shout of "All of us!" while Vergniaud expressed the general feeling when he spoke of his disgust at following in the tribune "a man all dripping with calumny and venom and blood". The Girondins changed all this; by insisting on the solidarity of Marat, the Mountain, and Paris, they forced the Mountain to protect him. Marat had plenty of impudence, and he continued, in speeches and journal, to defend murder and mutiny, to denounce Generals and deputies as traitors, and to call for a dictator. The Jacobins were his firm supporters.

Then Paris. Many of the 'Montagnards' (as they were called) were only too ready to defend crimes, even September massacres,* when they were the work of 'good patriots', and all felt, with some reason, that Paris, which had made the last revolution, deserved

---

* Collot d'Herbois, in the Jacobins (5 Nov.), called the massacres "the great article of the Creed of our freedom".

gratitude rather than abuse. But the Girondins made a regular campaign against Paris. They began it at once; Roland suggested and Buzot proposed (Sept. 23, 24) that the Convention should have a large paid guard, composed of men from the Departments, to keep the deputies safe in popular risings. This 6 Departmental Guard 5 was meant as a reproach to Paris, and it was deeply resented. The Guard was voted, but never raised.

Quarrel followed quarrel and scene scene. Many sittings were orgies of hatred, and though, at times, the Convention could discuss questions calmly on their own merits, too often any question was used to serve party manoeuvres. In vain Danton thundered for concord; in vain Pétion preached common sense and compromise; in vain Vergniaud lifted disputes to a higher plane. Buzot, the bitter idealist, Guadet, bitingly sarcastic, Lanjuinais, violent and sincere, Gensonné, Lasource, Isnard, Louvet, with their talents for oratory, Salle, the 'Constituent', and many others were always ready to attack. The Mountain was almost equally aggressive, and when the eloquent hatred of the great men was silent, the lesser men took up the tale, and a noisy pack of Montagnards shouted their spite and thought it patriotism. Each side believed the other to be traitors.

In their anxiety to get rid of their more violent

opponents, the Girondins tried to undermine the secure position of all members of the Convention. Thus, they sometimes proposed that the Primary Assemblies should be summoned to confirm or to reject their representatives, which would have meant a partial dissolution of the Convention. The Mountain, with better political instinct, saw that this would make for anarchy. Again, Buzot, on December 16th, proposed to expel Philippe Égalité and his sons from France. He did this simply to put the Mountain in a difficulty. No one cared much about Égalité, but he was a Montagnard and a deputy, and it was a dangerous precedent to banish a deputy; besides, the decree was unjust. Yet if the Montagnards protested, the Gironde would accuse them of favouring royalty. Barère's suggestion that Roland, Pache, and Égalité should all be banished, because they were the cause of quarrels, did not solve the difficulty, and the whole matter was finally adjourned.

The most important question over which the parties struggled was the fate of the King. Such majesty still hung about the ancient throne of France that Louis, dethroned and captive, was still a power; his influence was still feared. Every man who threatened or insulted him in a speech or a writing still felt that he was braving a tyrant, and the Commune never wearied of hearing reports on the doings of the prisoners in the Temple.

Their quarters in the Tower were narrow, and though they were fed with royal profusion, they were hemmed in with odious restrictions and watched in turn by members of the Commune, of whom there were always two in the sitting room. The royal family bore their misfortunes with cheerful resignation. The King, now called Louis Capet (a name invented by the royalists in the early Revolution), was a model of the Christian virtues; Marie-Antoinette was patient and dignified; the parents taught their children, the children played together, and Madame Elisabeth, devoted to them all, mended their clothes. Most of the members of the Commune who watched them were insolent and unfeeling; some were won over by the beauty of this simple family life. Pity smote the heart of Manuel, that hater of Kings, and he was not the only one who finally laid down his life for the captives.

There was a general feeling that the King ought to be punished; but while the Mountain, the Jacobins, and advanced opinion throughout the country demanded his execution, the Gironde, and probably the majority of the people, wished to keep him prisoner during the war and then to banish him. The Girondins, while professing scorn and detestation of Louis, used every artifice to drag out the proceedings connected with his trial; the Montagnards were brutal in their efforts to shorten them; and their point of view was put concisely by Saint-Just, when he declared that to be a King was a crime in itself, and by Robespierre, who said later: "You have not got to give a verdict for or against a man; you have got to take a measure for the public welfare." But a large number of deputies, though convinced of Louis's guilt, wished him to have a fair trial, that the world might be convinced too. The papers found in the Tuileries were not strong enough evidence to convince unbelievers, and Louis might have been saved but for a discovery of fresh papers, in a secret cupboard closed by an iron door, in a wall of the royal apartments. The King, who was a skilful locksmith, had worked at this craft for years with a man called Gamain. In May 1792, he had wanted to make a hiding-place for his private papers and had called in Gamain to help him; together they had constructed 'the iron cupboard'. Gamain betrayed the secret to Roland; Roland found the papers and took them straight to the Convention on November 20th. Mirabeau's treachery now came to light, and every one who had had secret dealings with the Court trembled. Yet though the King's hatred of the Revolution was amply shown in the papers, his attempts to corrupt revolutionaries and his anti-revolutionary propaganda had all been done in a constitutional way through his Ministers, and no actual proof was found of the treason to France of which he had, in fact, been guilty. There was, however, enough to satisfy men who did not care to distinguish presumption from proof.

On December 3rd it was decided that Louis should be tried by the Convention. An indictment was drawn up, and he was brought to the Bar, on December 11th, to hear it. The best description of the impression he produced there was given, strange to say, by Marat. The former King did not show the slightest anger or impatience when he heard himself addressed as Louis Capet, and was kept standing – "he in whose presence no man had the right to sit." Marat adds, that if Louis had not been a criminal, he should have thought him great. The proceedings were solemn, and the galleries were hushed into silence while the indictment was read over and Louis was questioned upon it. He answered with great presence of mind, and not always truthfully.

Louis was permitted to choose counsel – Manuel had pleaded that he must be allowed to defend himself. He chose Target and Tronchet, two famous advocates of the Constituent Assembly; Target refused the dangerous post, but Tronchet accepted. And Malesherbes, who had been one of Louis's best Ministers before the Revolution, wrote a beautiful letter to the Convention, offering to defend his former master, and was accepted too. It was one of several such offers, for fidelity to fallen friends and courage strong enough to face a charge of want of patriotism shone through the darkest days of the Revolution, and this is one of its glories. At the request of Malesherbes and Tronchet, who were old men, a younger advocate, Desèze, was joined with them. Only a short time was given to prepare a defence, and the Commune, which had already separated Louis from his family, tried to deny his counsel free access to him; in this, however, they were over-ruled by the Convention. On December 26th Louis appeared at the Bar again and Desèze read an eloquent and able defence; as it was based on the old principle of the Constitution, that the King was inviolable as long as he acted constitutionally, it was of no avail.

The Girondins now tried a new way to save Louis; they insisted that in a matter so important there must be an 'appeal to the people', i.e. a referendum. The Montagnards, feeling certain that the Primary Assemblies would not vote for Louis's death, argued that the Convention had been given full powers to decide every question, which was true. Both sides put forth all their strength, and the debates were summed up against the appeal by Barère. It was finally decided to vote by roll-call on three questions: (1) Is Louis guilty? He was declared guilty by an almost unanimous vote. (2) Shall the decision of the Convention be submitted to the people? The appeal to the people was rejected by a majority of 141; those who had voted for it were known afterwards as 'appealers'. By about

8 o'clock on the evening of January 16th, 1793, the third question was reached: (3) What punishment shall be inflicted? All through the night and the next day, for four and twenty hours, deputy after deputy mounted the tribune, as his name was called, and recorded his vote aloud, often with a short speech. Manuel was one of those who voted for Louis's detention till peace and subsequent banishment;* a few voted for a death-sentence and a respite; Égalité voted for death, and a shudder ran through the Convention; Danton, just back from a mission to Belgium, voted for death; some of the leaders of the Gironde, Vergniaud, Guadet, Gensonné, Ducos, Fonfrède, and Barbaroux, voted for death. Louis was condemned to death by a very narrow majority.

The struggle was not yet over, and after angry debates and a verification of votes, there was a fourth roll-call on the 19th, on the question of whether there should be a respite. In the early hours of the 20th January the respite was rejected by a majority of seventy. This meant execution within twenty-four hours.†

Louis had prepared to die and had made a will, a touching statement of religious faith, affection, gratitude,

* He resigned on the 19th; his resignation was not accepted, but he left the Convention.
† Executions were carried out within twenty-four hours, if possible, in order to spare the condemned suffering.

and pardon; he had no possessions to leave. He was allowed to choose a confessor, and sent for a non-juring priest, the Abbe Edgeworth de Firmont. The royal family met once more in the evening and said their last farewells with tears and cries, till Louis, telling them to forgive his enemies, tore himself away, to spend the night in religious duties and in sleep. He was ready when, soon after eight o'clock on the morning of January 21st, Santerre and two members of the Commune came to fetch him. Paris, outwardly quiet, was in a state of feverish agitation, an attempt at rescue was expected, and the streets through which the carriage passed were lined with troops; the place de la Révolution, formerly the place Louis XV, had been chosen for the execution. Louis was calm; he resisted when the executioner began to tie his hands, then, at a word from his Confessor, who had accompanied him, he submitted. On the scaffold he began to address the people, but the General commanding the troops in the Square, Berruyer, bade the drums beat to drown his voice; the executioners pushed him down. "Fils de Saint-Louis, montez au ciel!" cried the Abbe Edgeworth;* the King's head fell, and a great

---

* Although these famous words have been rejected by the authorities, they were commonly believed, at the time, to have been spoken, and a version appeared in a newspaper which could not have invented them.

shout of *Vive la nation*! rose from the surrounding multitude. The body was buried, in quicklime, in the cemetery belonging to the Madeleine Church, the usual burial-place of the Tuileries Section in which the place de la Révolution lay.

On the night before the execution, Lepeletier de Saint-Fargeau, a distinguished deputy, once a 'Constituent', was assassinated in a restaurant by a fanatic, simply because he had voted for the King's death, though he had been neither violent nor prominent in the debates. Every Montagnard felt that his turn might come next, and Lepeletier was exalted as a 'martyr of Liberty' and given a great public funeral. His corpse, half-naked, with the ghastly wound exposed, lay in state in the place Vendome and was carried by slow stages to the Pantheon and buried there.

After Louis's death, triumph mingled with agitation filled the breasts of the majority of the Convention, and for a brief space there was a lull in the incessant strife of parties. "You have declared war on kings," said Danton (January 31st), "you have thrown down your glove before them, and this glove is the head of a tyrant." The Convention had, indeed, been aware that the execution was likely to lead to a war with all Europe, and the Girondins had used the argument in the debates. France was already on the brink of war with Great Britain and Holland. The Republicans knew that Great Britain would not tolerate any encroachments on Holland, yet, in the interest of Belgium, the navigation of the Scheldt, the control of which was secured to Holland by treaties, had been declared free by the French Government. Further, Dumouriez was planning an invasion of Holland, with three objects: to liberate the Dutch, to make the conquest of Belgium more secure, and to strike a blow at England which had not recognized the Republic. Gironde and Mountain, having no idea of the irritation roused in other nations by the republican propaganda, imagined that the British people were ripe for revolution, and would gladly receive 'freedom' from the hands of France. Even when Parliament passed two bills aimed against France: an 'Aliens bill' containing strict regulations as to the admission and residence of aliens, and a bill forbidding the export of grain to France, they continued to believe that the nation was not behind the Government. Brissot was eager for the fray, and in reporting on January 12th for a 'General Defence Committee', which had been formed on January 1st, he encouraged the Convention by assuring them in his old style, that "the imposing Colossus of England" was hollow, and would topple over at the French onslaught. War might yet, perhaps, have been averted, for Pitt did not desire it and on both sides there were men working for peace, had not Louis's execution caused such horror in England that the French minister plenipotentiary was rudely expelled, and a conflict became inevitable. Again Brissot reported on the situation, and this time he exhorted the Convention to fight all the tyrants of Europe for the good of the world. War was declared on Great Britain and Holland on February 1st, and on March 7th war was declared on Spain, a neighbour hostile to the Revolution. Meanwhile there had been changes in the Ministry; Roland, utterly discouraged, resigned on January 23rd, and, with the extension of the war, Pache was dismissed on February 2nd, and Beurnonville, a General who had fought under Dumouriez, was elected in his place.* The Jacobins continued to extol Pache, and soon after his fall he was elected Mayor of Paris to console him. Here he made himself popular, and was known familiarly as 'Papa Pache'.

Half way through February, the Constitutional Committee, chosen in October, presented the new Constitution which they had prepared. Girondins predominated on this Committee; Condorcet explained the plan and Gensonné read it. It tended to throw all power into the hands of the Primary Assemblies; they were to elect the single Chamber annually, they were to elect the Ministers, and all by a complicated method

* Ministers were elected by the Convention.

of election which could hardly take less than six weeks. The plan was submitted to debate, but did not find favour, and another sore subject was added to the list of Girondin grievances.

Yet another may be mentioned here. The local Administrators, through whom the Government had to work, were often weak, or half-hearted, or even actively disloyal, and the Convention was in the habit of sending its own members to every place where something wanted doing urgently: to the Armies, where they both helped and controlled the Generals; to Departments and cities, where they quelled disturbances, raised troops, punished rebellion and conspiracy, and encouraged, drilled, threatened, and coerced the population into a patriotic and revolutionary spirit. The powers given these men, called 'Representatives of the People on Mission', were wide, sometimes almost unlimited, and they were responsible only to the Convention. It was the complaint of the Gironde that no Girondins were sent on missions; it was the complaint of the Mountain that they refused to go, in order that they might keep their party at full strength in the Convention.

On February 20th, a decree for a new levy of 300,000 men was passed. Citizens were asked to volunteer, but all unmarried men from eighteen to forty were liable to be requisitioned if the numbers were not made up. At the same time the Army was reorganized, old and new troops being brigaded together.

In February also, with a steady rise in the price of all the necessities of life, began the first of a series of crises which the Convention was called upon to face. The rise was chiefly caused by a fall in the value of assignats, of which too many had been issued, while coin, hoarded by its possessors, was disappearing from circulation. There was a great deal of misery in Paris, a great deal of unemployment, and though at this time there was no actual dearth, there was a scarcity of many commodities. Throughout the Revolution, indeed, defective methods of supply and transport often produced a temporary dearth; thus the people were kept in continual fear of famine, and therefore an easy prey to alarmists, while every rise in prices was put down to the operations of speculators and profiteers. The Convention had forbidden the export of grain, and in Paris the price of bread was kept down, for the Commune, whose business it was to buy supplies of wheat, was allowed (Feb. 7th) to impose a progressive income-tax big enough to cover the deficit made by selling corn to the bakers below cost price. But this was not considered enough by the extremists, and on February 12th a petition was presented in the name of the Sections, and not without threats, asking the Convention to fix a maximum price, above which wheat might not be sold, on pain of death. This petition was known to be the work of certain agitators called the *enrages* (madmen), and even Marat was angry. Jacques Roux, a constitutional priest, cruel and crafty, who espoused the cause of the poor with reckless fury, was the most important of the *enrages*; as a member of the Commune he had attended the King to the scaffold, and had unkindly refused to receive poor Louis's will. Another was Varlet, a wild young man too crazy for the Jacobins, who pushed about a portable pulpit from which he harangued the people.

On February 23rd fears of famine became acute in Paris; on the 24th a deputation of washerwomen came to the Convention to complain of the price of soap and to ask for death to profiteers and speculators; on the 25th and 26th there were riots, in which soap barges, on the river, and grocers' shops were plundered. Force had to be used to put the rioters down, and for a time things were quieter, but the idea of a 'maximum' had taken the popular fancy, and the Sections began to agitate for it. The Convention, fully alive to the danger of discouraging Commerce, was most reluctant to grant it, and when, on April 18th, a deputation from the Paris Department, backed by the Commune, came with a petition for the 'maximum', Vergniaud tried the effect of reason. Reason availed nothing against popular panic, and on May 1st came a deputation from Saint-Antoine, nine or ten thousand strong, threatening an insurrection if the 'maximum' were not granted and a special tax levied on the rich. The Convention reproved the petitioners, but granted the 'maximum' on May 2nd.

A more formidable crisis had been passed through in March. In February, Dumouriez with a small Army had invaded Holland – a daring and unsafe campaign. He had left his principal Army encamped round Aix-la-Chapelle and Liege, and one of his Generals, Miranda, was besieging Maestricht. In Dumouriez's absence, the enemy again took the offensive; Brunswick with his restored and renovated Prussians marching against Custine on the Rhine, and the Austrians, under the Prince of Cobourg, advancing to reconquer Belgium. The French positions were bad, and the ill-found army had fallen into a shocking state of indiscipline. Dumouriez's Generals were defeated in the first days of March; Aix-la-Chapelle and Liege were abandoned, the siege of Maestricht was raised, and the French had to retreat farther and farther. The position was critical, for Belgium, bullied and plundered by Commissaries and soldiers,* and profoundly shocked at the disrespect shown to religion by the French, was on the brink of

---

* The ill-treatment of Belgium was against Dumouriez's wishes.

a rebellion, and with any fresh defeat of his Army, Dumouriez might be cut off. Danton and Lacroix, Representatives on Mission in Belgium, hurried to Paris to stir the country to fresh exertions. They found the Convention still occupied in annexing Belgian conquests, and their report on March 8th was a rude awakening for their colleagues; once the situation was grasped, every measure that could forward recruiting was promptly taken. Danton spoke with all his old fire, and in urging the need for unity in this time of common danger, he used the memorable words: "Let us beat the enemy and dispute afterwards . . . What do I care if my name is blemished so long as France is free!" (March 10th).

With disaster, now as always, there came the cry 'we are betrayed!' and the desire to punish. Every defeated General was suspect, yet, with so many supposed traitors about, there was no longer a special Court to punish them, for the High Court of Orléans had been suppressed, and the Tribunal of the 10th August, after falling into inaction, had been suppressed too (Dec. 1st 1792). Therefore when, on March 9th, a request for a 'Revolutionary Tribunal' came from two Sections, the Convention was ready to listen.* An unknown member, Carrier, converted the request into a motion, and in

* The Commune was about to petition for it, also.

spite of a bold protest from Lanjuinais, the Convention voted the creation of an 'extraordinary criminal tribunal' from whose sentences there was no appeal, to try 'conspirators and anti-revolutionaries'. On Sunday, March 10th, the organization of this tribunal was settled, the Girondins making no opposition.

A plan had been drawn up, by Robert Lindet, which did away with a jury, but this raised a storm of protests, and it was decreed unanimously that a jury there should be. It was decided that the jury should be elected by the Convention; over the details the deputies grew weary, and the sitting was about to close, when Danton intervened, and forced his colleagues to finish their task, by a reminder that if such a Court had existed in September, the massacres might never have taken place. "Let us be terrible," he said, "that the people may not be. Let us organize a tribunal – not well, that is impossible – but as little ill as may be."

The 9th and 10th March were also signalized by the failure of a plot to attack the Convention and arrest the Girondins. It was the work of an obscure 'Insurrection Committee sitting in the Episcopal Palace and led by a few well-known agitators, conspicuous among whom were Varlet, and that political ruffian, Fournier the American. The rising was fixed for the night of March 9-10th, and rioters sacked the Press of Gorsas; but the tocsin did not ring, the Commune refused to join, and the insurrection fizzled out. The mere fact that such a plot had been possible, showed the danger in which the Convention stood, and Vergniaud, in the course of a great speech on March 13th, warned his hearers, prophetically, that the Revolution was becoming like Saturn, who devoured his own children one by one. Arrests were made, but very little evidence was forthcoming, and when Garat, Minister of the Interior, reported on March 19th, he pooh-poohed the whole affair and lulled the Convention into a blind security.

A noteworthy event of March was a decree, on the 21st, setting up in every Commune and in each section of a large town, a Watch Committee of twelve, to keep an eye on foreigners: to give those who were allowed to reside certificates, and to send away the rest. These Committees were to be elected, and no ecclesiastic or former noble might serve on them. They soon extended their watchfulness from foreigners to Frenchmen, and under the name of Revolutionary Committees dominated Communes and Sections.

It must also be noted that about this time Danton made another effort to reconcile opposing parties, and that negotiations were wrecked by the intractability of Guadet.

We must return to Dumouriez, who had been ordered back from Holland by the Convention just as he was on the point of success, and rejoined his Army in angry mood. He had long cherished ambitious thoughts of restoring the Monarchy, and he was disgusted with the Republic, with its stupidities over the Army, with its treatment of Belgium; he now wrote a disrespectful letter to the Convention on March 12th, saying exactly what he thought of the way that Belgium had been dealt with. The Defence Committee dared not read it to the Convention, for Dumouriez was the only man who could save the situation, and he had to be maintained at any cost. He did set to work to save it; he pacified the Belgians, he put fresh heart into the Army, and, after a preliminary success, he attacked Cobourg on March 18th in the plain of Neerwinden. The two-days' battle was lost, through the bad generalship of Miranda* and the desertion of some of the volunteer troops. When another battle was lost at Louvain (21st March), Dumouriez knew that it was all up with him; he was already suspect and his defeat would never be forgiven. He began to negotiate with the Austrians, and made an agreement to evacuate Holland and Belgium, in return for which they promised to remain inactive, while he marched on Paris with the object of dissolving the Convention and restoring the

---

* A Peruvian. He was tried and acquitted by the Revolutionary Tribunal.

Monarchy and the Constitution of 1791. Dumouriez, accordingly, retreated to Saint-Amand, near Valenciennes; but he made no secret of his designs, and on March 30th his treason was announced to the Convention by the Defence Committee. The Convention forthwith summoned him to the Bar, and sent four Commissaries, deputies, of whom Camus was one, together with Beurnonville, the Minister of War, to fetch him. These five men, taking their lives in their hands, sought out the famous General in the midst of his Army, surrounded by his devoted Staff, and delivered their message. He arrested them and handed them over to the Austrians, who clapped them into prison.

The Republic now stood in the gravest peril. Dumouriez was about to march on Paris; Custine's Army had been defeated at Bingen on March 27th, and, pressed by the Prussians, was retreating to the lines of Weissemburg; added to which, a serious rebellion had lately broken out in the Department of la Vendée in the West. In this crisis the Convention showed real greatness; strife there still was, but no fear, no despairing of the Republic. Dumouriez was outlawed, General Dampierre was appointed to succeed him, the rapid formation of an army to cover Paris was decreed, and Representatives on Mission were sent off to the Armies (4 April). Many arrests were made, including those of all the Bourbons still at liberty, Égalité among the number.*

Another measure had far-reaching consequences. The deputies felt the need of a central driving force, and the Defence Committee was too large and too public to serve the purpose. They therefore laid aside their fears of setting up a tyranny in the Convention, and created, on April 6th, a Committee of Public Welfare – the famous Comité de Salut public – with full powers to take all measures of defence, external and internal. The deliberations of this Committee were secret; it could control the Ministers but had no funds at its disposal. There were nine members elected monthly by the Convention, and bound to report frequently. No Girondin was elected; Barère, Cambon and Lacroix were prominent members, and Danton was the soul of the first Committee, which remained in power, by re-election, for three months, the numbers being finally raised to fourteen.

Even before the Committee was founded the worst danger had passed. Dumouriez had reckoned on the personal attachment of his Army, but, great as it was, his soldiers were good Frenchmen, and as soon as they perceived his treason they deserted him. He was obliged to fly, and crossed the frontier to go to the

* Égalité for relations with Dumouriez; the other Bourbons as hostages.

Austrians on April 5th, taking with him a small body of troops and a few of his Generals, including the former duc de Chartres, Égalité's son. The Army, under Dampierre, continued to guard the frontier.

But though the Convention was at one in standing undaunted for the Republic, Dumouriez's treason had bred fresh suspicion, and mutual hatred blazed up fiercer than ever. There was not a leading member, down to Marat, who had not defended Dumouriez at some time; the Girondins had introduced him into the Ministry, and Gensonné had been his friend and correspondent, while Danton had always insisted that he was indispensable. Yet now the Gironde accused the Mountain of being Dumouriez's accomplices in a plot to set Égalité on the throne, and the Mountain accused the Gironde of being his accomplices in a royalist plot – a supposed proof being, that they had tried to save Louis by an appeal to the people. The Girondins unwisely began the strife. Danton had been preaching peace and concord when, on April 1st, Lasource accused him and Lacroix of treasonable relations with Dumouriez. There was an exciting scene when Danton, goaded to fury at last, roared out defence and defiance, and shouted, amidst the cheers of the Mountain, that the Mountain had been right; there could be no truce with such adversaries. From this day the state of the Convention was such, that Danton aptly compared the tribune to an arena of gladiators. Interspersed with minor quarrels came a series of great attacks. Robespierre was foremost; one day he demanded Brissot's impeachment, another he denounced all the Gironde for consistent treachery, shown by their 'moderation'; an accusation refuted by Vergniaud in a famous speech. Even Pétion threw conciliation to the winds and denounced Marat. Insults passed; Guadet compared the reasoning of his opponents to the croaking of toads, at which Marat called out: "Hold your tongue, vile bird!" On one agitated evening the Gironde, provoked beyond endurance, made a rush at the Mountain, and a Girondin, Deperret, drew his sword. The galleries, completely out of hand, almost joined in the debates, hooted and howled at the Girondins and applauded the Mountain noisily. Every address or petition on either side (for the Girondins had supporters in the Departments and even in Paris) was 'like oil on flames', as a newspaper said, and while the Gironde lost no opportunity of provoking rebellion by taunts, the Mountain encouraged insolence and disorder. Outside in Paris anarchy was coming. An address by the Halle-au-Blé Section, calling on the Mountain to save the Republic and asking for the death of guilty deputies, was circulating in the Sections.

At this point the Gironde made the fatal mistake of attempting to get Marat executed by the Revolutionary

Tribunal. Marat himself, seconded by a Girondin, had accomplished the undermining of a deputy's position which the Girondins had begun, by obtaining, on April 1st, a decree that any deputy suspected on good grounds of treason should be impeached, regardless of his inviolability. Therefore when Marat, as President of the Jacobins, signed a circular of the Club beginning: "To arms, friends! We are-betrayed!" and asserting that the centre of the conspiracy was in the Convention, with an exhortation to exterminate conspirators, the Girondins saw their chance, and wrung from the Convention a decree for Marat's arrest (April 12th). He was ordered to the Abbaye, and on the following day, after endless scenes and a roll-call which lasted all night, he was impeached. The reply of Paris to Marat's impeachment was a deputation, on April 15th, from thirty-five out of the forty-eight Sections, with the Mayor at their head, bearing a petition for the compulsory withdrawal of twenty-two deputies, the leaders of the Gironde. The Convention was stirred by this direct attack and the petition was condemned. Nevertheless the campaign in the Sections against the Gironde went on. Marat, in due course, appeared before the Revolutionary Tribunal. The feeling that it was dangerous to meddle with the freedom of the Press was still strong, and he was acquitted on April 24th. And there was the noxious little man back again, borne into the Convention in triumph by a noisy mob, and more audacious than ever!

On May 10th the Convention moved to a hall which had been prepared in the Tuileries Palace. Here the deputies sat in an oblong amphitheatre opposite the President and the orator, and the public galleries were a long way off the deputies. There was a pause in party strife, but the galleries, despite their distance, were as disorderly as ever. Fierce viragoes took control of them and refused to let any ticket-holders enter them. And though the Convention carried on its duties notwithstanding interruptions, and the debates were sometimes fruitful, the situation was getting worse. While extremists demanded the expulsion of the Girondins, which meant the partial dissolution of the Convention, the Girondins were pitting the Departments against Paris in a way that might well lead to Civil War. To add to difficulties there were disasters in the War – to Custine's Army and on the Spanish frontier. In Paris, there were anxieties about food, and the forced recruiting for the war in la Vendée was unpopular and caused disturbances; the Commune was acting illegally, it went so far as to impose a forced loan on the rich for this war; the Sections were acting illegally; it was common talk that the Convention was to be dissolved, and the Jacobins were always speaking of an insurrection. The Convention became alarmed, and the Gironde being for the moment in the ascendant, Guadet proposed to dissolve the Commune. Barère, however, carried, as a compromise, a decree for the creation of a Commission of twelve members who were to examine the proceedings of Commune and Sections during the last month, and to take all measures to discover plots and prevent them (18th May). The Convention already had a large Committee of General Security (Comité de Sûreté générale) whose business it was to deal with plots, but this did not satisfy the Girondins, as their enemies Chabot and Basire were the leading spirits. The plot against the Girondins was real enough, but it was still misty, and Pache assured the Convention that there was no such thing, thereby giving once more a false sense of security. One circumstance which caused alarm was the meeting of Commissaries from the Sections in a hall of the Episcopal Palace. Pache explained that this gathering had been legally summoned to discuss methods of raising men and money. The gathering was legal, but incendiary motions were made there, and perhaps insurrection planned.

On the 21st May the Commission of twelve was elected; a Girondin Commission, of which Rabaut and Fonfrède were members. The twelve set to work at once with more zeal than discretion, and on the 24th they arrested Varlet and also Hébert, assistant procureur of the Commune. Now Hébert was a power; he was not only a high official, but the author of a much-read incendiary journal called *Le Père Duchesne*. He was a worthless man, clever and ambitious, of elegant appearance and polite manners, and he wrote his cruel paper with great skill, in a coarse, jocose, popular style, with plenty of vulgar oaths to attract vulgar readers. His arrest caused an outcry in Paris; it was considered at once an attack on the freedom of the Press and an attack on the Commune, and the Commune, greatly offended, sent a deputation, the next day, to ask for his release. To them the President, Isnard, made the terrible reply, that if another insurrection attempted any injury to the Convention, the whole of France would take vengeance, and soon people would be searching the banks of the Seine to discover if Paris had ever existed. Vain threats, that only hastened the catastrophe!

The Commission of twelve made more arrests; Danton attacked them vigorously; many of the Sections were petitioning for Hébert, and the Convention vacillated. After a long, angry sitting, on May 27th, Garat and Pache came to give fresh assurances that there was no plot, and many of the deputies left the hall. Hérault was in the chair, when in came a number of petitioners, with demands for Hébert's release and denunciations of the offending Commission. The

Mountain, finding itself in a majority, took heart, and on Lacroix's motion, the Commission of twelve was dissolved and the release of the men whom it had arrested was ordered. The Mountain was right here, it was the only way of quieting Paris. But on the morrow the Gironde was in force again, and the Commission was reinstated. At the same time the order for the release of its prisoners was maintained, as a concession, and the Convention refused to hear an explanatory report which Rabaut had prepared, whereupon the Commission resigned. It continued, nevertheless, to sit and to work.

On May 29th Danton, who had not persisted in his recent hostility, made a supreme effort towards reconciliation. Barère was reporting, for the Comité de Salut public, on the general situation, and Danton inserted in the report a passage begging the two parties, in striking words, to lay aside hatred and unite to save France from the enemy and from anarchy, lest they should be united perforce in a common doom and a common execration. The appeal was not without effect, but came too late; Paris was already taking the matter out of the hands of the Convention.

The methods pursued were much the same as in the August revolution, and the new Revolutionary Committee in each Section made a convenient centre for extremists. On May 30th, thirty-three Sections sent delegates to sit in the Episcopal Palace, giving them unlimited powers, and these delegates formed themselves into a 'General Revolutionary Assembly'. The new 'General Revolutionary Assembly' proceeded to decide that Paris was in insurrection, and ordered the barriers to be shut. Even Pache, who visited the meeting, was forced to own the reality of the insurrection. At the eleventh hour the Paris Authorities had made a futile attempt to avert a rising by convoking a meeting of the Sections; Chaumette, for all his daring speeches, was too timid to risk joining a rebellion openly, when it came to the point.

In the night of May 30th-31st the 'General Revolutionary Assembly' chose a small 'Central Revolutionary Committee' of nine, obscure men of whom Varlet is the best known, and in the early hours of May 31st, Varlet gave the order to ring the tocsin. It rang till four o'clock in the afternoon, with alarm guns firing part of the time. The Commune gathered at the sound of the tocsin, and was sitting, expectant and weary, when, at about six o'clock, nine men entered, and one of them, clad in slippers and a dirty dressing-gown,* took the President's chair, and announced that the powers delegated to the Commune were withdrawn. The Commune, after satisfying themselves that the

---

* Dobsent, who had been arrested by the Commission of twelve.

credentials of the delegates of the thirty-three Sections were in order, meekly left their hall. They were called back immediately and reinstated, after taking a fresh oath. The 'Central Revolutionary Committee' now installed themselves with the Commune, both bodies working, sometimes together and sometimes separately. Some seventeen more members were added to the Committee in the course of the day. The Committee's first care was to appoint a new Commander-in-Chief of the Paris National Guard, since the successor of Santerre (who had himself resigned to go to la Vendée) was nowhere to be found. They appointed Hanriot, one of the Commandants of the Guard, a rough, unbalanced man of violent opinions. They made arrests too; Roland, whom they tried to capture, escaped, Madame Roland was sent to prison.

The object of the insurrection was to force from the Convention a decree for the arrest of the twenty-two Girondins, and the Sections were under arms in their different centres, ready to support the 'Central Revolutionary Committee'. This Committee did not yet order the troops of the Sections to march, not wishing to proceed at once to extremities. The 31st May was an agitating day for the Convention. The great majority of deputies, including the Comité de Salut public, had no intention of being coerced, and refused to recognize the 'Central Revolutionary

Committee'; yet they received the delegates from the Sections who had formed that Committee. There was no disorder in Paris that day, and Vergniaud, who took the lead, attempted to separate the Sections, some of which were still loyal, from Commune and from 'Central Revolutionary Committee', by getting a vote that the Sections had deserved well of the country. Later on, when deputations from the people of Paris, as represented by the Sections, and from Department, Commune, and Sections, came denouncing Isnard and petitioning in a threatening manner for the impeach- ment of the twenty-two and of the Commission of twelve, there was a tumult, and Vergniaud walked out as a protest, hoping that the Convention would follow him. Hardly any one moved, and he returned, some- what tamely. Decrees were passed in the tumult; the various petitions were referred to the Comité de Salut public; the Commission of twelve was once more dissolved, by way of concession, and tickets for the galleries were abolished to please the mob. And when news was brought in, that the Sections, who had nearly come to blows among themselves, were fraternizing outside, Basire induced the Convention to close the sitting and join in the happy scene.

The danger seemed over, and though the 'Central Revolutionary Committee' was still sitting, and the Sections were still in arms, the 1st of June passed much as usual in the Convention, partly in disputes over an address to the nation. One read by Barère, on behalf of the Comité de Salut public, made the best of the 31st May, for it was Barère's maxim that it is no use criticizing revolutions; the thing is to adopt them and make use of them. In the evening, after the Convention had dispersed, the drums beat again; troops were seen advancing on the Tuileries, and about a hundred members hastened there to hold a sitting. To this small meeting came another deputation, representing Sections, Commune, and Department, hot from the Commune where Marat had been haranguing them, to present a still more threatening petition for the impeachment of twenty-three deputies. The Convention had the firmness to refer the petition to the Comité de Salut public, and ordered a report within three days. The troops retired to their Sections and the sitting closed.

Petitions having failed so far, in the night the 'Central Revolutionary Committee' gave Hanriot orders to surround the Tuileries with troops in the morning, and if the Convention would not yield, to put thirty deputies under arrest. Pressure was also put on the Comité de Salut public to report early and favourably on the petitions. The Convention met as usual on the morning of Sunday, June 2nd. All was quiet and there was no sign of troops. Again came addresses from 'the people of Paris' and from the Commune, demanding 'for the last time' the arrest of the deputies, threatening 'save us, or we will save ourselves!' Again the petition was referred to the Comité de Salut public. The petitioners left the hall uttering menaces, and men in the galleries cried 'To Arms!' and rushed out. Most of the leading Girondins were absent, expecting a massacre; Vergniaud, who had attended, had left at about one o'clock while all was still quiet, but Lanjuinais was there. Courageous as ever, he denounced the 'Central Revolutionary Committee' as "an usurping Assembly". A ring of angry Montagnards surrounded him, and he was nearly thrown out of the tribune by the butcher Legendre.

Then came Barère, to report for his Committee, with counsels of peace. The Committee could not advise the Convention to take measures against the deputies who had been denounced, but proposed that they should suspend themselves, voluntarily and for a time. Isnard, Fauchet, and two others complied at once, Lanjuinais and Barbaroux refused. Meanwhile any deputies who tried to leave the hall had been gradually finding out that all the entrances were blocked; first by a crowd of women, then by guards, who would allow no one to come out under any pretext. There was much indignation, especially among the members of the Comité de Salut public; Lacroix bellowed, Barère raged, Danton protested; a decree was passed that the troops must withdraw, and inquiries were made by whose orders they were there; no one could answer. Barère proposed a sortie to show that the Convention was free, and the deputies sallied forth, Hérault, who was presiding, at their head; he was the show member of the Convention with his good looks and his fine aristocratic presence. The Convention brushed aside the guards at the door and walked into the Palace Court on the Carrousel side; it was full of troops, troops with their guns trained on the Palace, and Hanriot himself was in command. Hérault walked up to him and summoned him to withdraw, in the name of the Law. Hanriot replied insolently that the deputies wanted must first be given up, and ordered his men to be ready to open fire at a signal from him. The Convention turned back and went into the Tuileries gardens. They walked round the gardens and up to every gate; still there were troops; always troops, and a crowd watching them; most were respectful, some were rude, but rude or civil they never budged, for Hanriot had chosen his battalions carefully. The Convention was trapped. Marat went skipping about, with a band of ragged children behind him, urging the deputies to return to the hall. The Convention returned to the hall, and surrendered. Couthon broke the gloomy silence to move that the twenty-two and the twelve should be put under arrest in their own houses; the decree passed, Lanjuinais and Barbaroux still protesting. Marat, Legendre, and others got Ducos, Fonfrède, and one or two more, who had not offended, removed from the list; when complete it contained thirty-one names; twenty-nine deputies and two Ministers, Clavière and Lebrun. Many deputies signed on the spot their protests against the decree.

VIII

THE REIGN OF TERROR

I. The Comité De Salut Public –
2 June 1793 – 31 December 1793

As soon as the Girondin leaders had been torn from
the Convention, Paris became once more quiet and
orderly; what the rest of France would say, remained
to be seen. The Mountain showed some compunction;
Marat suspended himself till the Girondins were tried,*
and the Comité de Salut public proposed to send
hostages to the Departments which had lost their
members. Robespierre defeated this proposal; 'Leave
things as they are,' he said, and the Convention was
willing, for now that the quarrelsome Girondins with
their overshadowing talents were gone, business went
peacefully forward. At the first signs of resistance from
the Departments, the leaders threw themselves on the

---

* He returned in a fortnight.

side of Paris; Danton acclaimed an insurrection which had freed the Convention from traitors, and declared that he had always desired it, while Couthon and Robespierre persuaded the Convention to adopt a Proclamation which said, that on May 31st and June 2nd the citizens of Paris had helped to save Liberty and the Republic. It is difficult to see what other line the Convention could have taken. France stood in such peril that it was indispensable to keep up the appearance of unity and a strong government.

The Mountain reckoned on being able to rally the Departments round a new Constitution, and rushed one forward. As late as May 30th, five new members, including Hérault, Couthon, and Saint-Just, had been put on the Comité de Salut public to propose a Constitution; on June 10th Hérault was already reading their work. A few amicable debates followed, and on June 24th the new Constitution was adopted and ready to be submitted to the Primary Assemblies for acceptance. It was short, simple, and intentionally sketchy: universal suffrage, one Chamber elected annually by the Primary Assemblies, Ministers elected by this Chamber from candidates named by the Departments. Like the Girondins' Constitution it was an attempt to give the people, through frequent elections, a direct control of the Government, and under such a scheme there could be no stability. But it found favour all over France.

An incident during the debates shows the spirit of the Mountain. The Constitution contained an article that peace must not be made with an enemy occupying French territory, and a Girondin, objecting to this as presumptuous, asked: "Have you made a compact with Victory?" Basire replied promptly: "We have made one with Death."

Meanwhile the unwise conduct of most of the arrested Girondins was helping to brand them as traitors. 'The Twenty-two'* were under arrest in their own houses, with gendarmes to guard them. Vergniaud, Gensonné, and some others stayed quietly in Paris, and Vergniaud addressed eloquent letters of protest to the Convention, which turned a deaf ear. But many of 'the Twenty-two' escaped – it was easy at first – and hurried west or south to encourage the Departments to march on Paris and free the Convention. Brissot was caught and brought back. Buzot traversed his own Department, the Eure, which was quickly in a ferment, and went to Caen, in Calvados, with Barbaroux, Salle, and some others. They were joined by Guadet, Louvet, Pétion, and Lanjuinais, and by the end of June there were seventeen deputies in Caen, living together and consulting endlessly. Madame Roland encouraged them by letters smuggled out of her prison. Her friends

* They were called so, though their number was twenty-nine.

were too scrupulous to take an active part in organizing resistance, and it was the local authorities of Calvados who arrested Representatives on Mission, raised troops, and gave the command of them to a General Wimpffen, a royalist at heart. Unfortunately for the Girondins, their cause attracted royalists, who welcomed a rebellion, hoping to use it for their own ends. A 'Central Committee of Resistance' was formed at Caen, to which several Departments sent representatives; yet even in these Departments opinion was not unanimous. Bordeaux, devoted to the Girondins, was another centre. The method followed in each centre was the same: the local authorities were welded into a 'Commission' or 'Committee', variously named; troops were raised, destined to march on Paris; and other Departments were invited to join. The South-east was soon aflame. Marseilles was already in rebellion; here Barbaroux's influence was strong, and the authorities raised an army and invited all Departments to send representatives to an Assembly at Bourges, in order that measures might be taken to protect the Convention. Lyon had lately had a rebellion of its own. Here the inhabitants were mainly Girondin, or, as it is more properly called, 'Federalist', with many secret royalists among them.* But the municipality was Jacobin, and

---

* An openly royalist rising in a southern Department, la Lozère, in May, led by a 'Constituent', Charrier, was put down quickly by local forces.

their 'procureur', Chalier, a fanatic with many noble qualities who inspired the Jacobins of Lyon, was an admirer of Marat, and emulated Marat's language, though he did not proceed from threats to deeds. The local authorities of Lyon, backed by the Representatives on Mission, resolved to raise a Revolutionary Army and to extort a forced loan from the rich. At this the Sections rose and, after a fight, seized the Town Hall on May 29th, arrested all the Jacobins, and forced the Representatives on Mission to sanction what they had done. A tribunal was appointed to try the Jacobins, and Lyon soon became a Federalist centre, with a 'Departmental Commission' to which deputies from all the smaller centres of the South flocked. Birotteau, one of the arrested deputies who had escaped, incited the Commission to take an oath not to acknowledge the Convention, and Lyon prepared to go to any lengths in defiance. It is significant that a royalist, the comte de Précy, was given command of the Army there. Chalier, against whom nothing but words could be proved, was guillotined on July 16th. The guillotine was new, and several strokes were required to sever the victim's head.

Not only were Bordeaux, Marseilles, and Lyon, three out of the four largest provincial cities in France, in the hands of the rebels; Paris itself was causing anxiety to the Comité de Salut public. On June 25th, the *enrage* priest, Jacques Roux, presented to the Convention, in the name of the Cordeliers' Club and of his Section, an anarchic petition, in which he asked the deputies, how long they meant to allow rich egoists to drink the purest blood of the people out of golden cups. Robespierre accused him of wishing to make real patriots look moderate, and he was sent away ignominiously; the Cordeliers and his Section disavowed him and Marat attacked him in his paper.* But on June 26th and 27th there was a two days' shameless pillage of soap-boats and grocers' shops, which naturally made groceries dearer and rarer.

The old anxieties continued. The War was going badly, how badly was, perhaps, hardly realized, as neither Prussians nor Austrians put forth their strength. Already, on April 9th, the Austrians had crossed the frontier and invested the border fortress of Conde; Mayence, the last remains of Custine's conquests, was invested by the Prussians soon after; on May 23rd the Prince of Cobourg, the Austrian general, drove the French from the Camp de Famars and began to besiege Valenciennes. Dumouriez's late Army (the Northern) was disorganized, ill-equipped, ill-fed, undisciplined. What could any generals do with such troops, especially bad generals who felt that they were not trusted, and

---

* Jacques Roux was afterwards imprisoned. He committed suicide rather than face the Revolutionary Tribunal.

were unable to resist the Representatives on Mission who insisted on their fighting? Dumouriez's successor, Dampierre, was, fortunately for himself, killed in battle early in May, and a little later Custine was summoned from the Rhine Army to take command and restore discipline. He did this in a short time, for, though no strategist, he could keep an army in order and was popular among the soldiers, who called him 'General Moustache'.

Equally alarming was the situation in the West, where, in la Vendée and the neighbouring Departments* (the old provinces of Anjou and Poitou), a rising had become Civil War. The Civil Constitution of the Clergy had spread disaffection among the peasants of the West, who were devoted to the Catholic Religion and deeply attached to their priests. When it came to the removal of the non-juring priests, the peasants were as ready to fight as the priests were to preach a crusade, and rebellion had long been simmering. It broke out in March, when the local authorities tried to enforce the law for the raising of 300,000 men, decreed in February. La Vendée refused to be enrolled; the peasants rose and seized towns. By the end of March there was a so-called *Grande Armée* in Anjou, and numerous smaller bands, under local leaders, elsewhere. Simultaneous risings

---

* The whole area of the war became known as 'la Vendée'.

took place in Brittany, already honeycombed with royalist plots, and along the Loire; Nantes, the capital of the West, the only one of the four great cities which stood firm, was threatened. For Church and King was a natural conjunction, and early in May the *Grande Armée Catholique Royale* issued its first proclamation in the name of Louis XVII. Never was a rising more popular and democratic. Among the early leaders were nobles, such as d'Elbée, Bon-champs and Lescure; a pedlar, Cathelineau, called 'the Saint of Anjou', a game-keeper, Stofflet; and an ex-naval Lieutenant, Charette, who worked independently near the coast, and seldom cared to combine with the others. It was not till July that a 'Generalissimo' was chosen; d'Elbée. The country, full of hills, woods, swamps, and deep, hollow lanes, was favourable to a new kind of war waged by untrained men who knew every inch of the ground; one large tract was known as 'the thicket', another as 'the marsh'. Ambushes and surprise attacks were frequent, and the republicans did not know how to get hold of their invisible foes; for 'the Brigands', as they called them, were always under cover, and dispersed to their homes after a fight. The war was cruel, disfigured by atrocities on both sides. It began with a long massacre of republican prisoners in the captured town of Machecoul, under Charette's auspices, and on March 19th the Convention decreed that every rebel taken in arms should be executed within twenty-four hours, which led to endless bloodshed.* The troops on both sides were, with a few exceptions, utterly undisciplined; they pillaged, slaughtered, and ran; for the Republican troops were of inferior quality, and the Vendéens, brave as they were, lacked staying power. Their ranks were soon swelled by deserters from the Republican Army.

On the north of 'la Vendée' part of the better disciplined Brest Army held Nantes for the Republic, while the la Rochelle Army held part of the coast on the west, and Saumur and Angers on the east; the rebels were in between. The Comité de Salut public sent a well-known General to command the la Rochelle Army; the fascinating Biron, once a Duke and a rakish ornament of Marie-Antoinette's Court. Biron wanted to march on the rebels from the coast inwards, thus preventing them from taking a sea-port and communicating with the British fleet. But his troops were too few and too undisciplined to carry out his plan; he was, besides, constantly thwarted by a 'Central Commission' at Saumur, consisting of minor Generals and Representatives on Mission. The rebels grew more formidable and on June 9th, after a fight, the *Grande Armée* took Saumur; on the 17th they occupied Angers. From Angers they could have marched on Paris, had

* The law was modified on May 10th by Danton's persuasion.

not the peasant soldiers melted away, as was their wont; their Generals could never induce them to hold a town for more than a few days. Their next attempt was a sharp attack on Nantes, in combination with Charette (June 29th). Nantes managed to repulse them; but they were nearly as strong as ever and ready to fight again. Biron was doing nothing and there were no signs that the insurrection would be suppressed. Here too, on the top of all the other difficulties and disasters, the Comité de Salut public seemed to have failed.

The Mountain lost patience. The members of the Committee were only elected for a month, but twice they had been kept in office. On July 10th, when the time came for the monthly renewal, Camille Desmoulins, though he was Danton's friend, attacked them, drawing special attention to their failure in la Vendée; the Convention elected a new Committee, and Danton was not a member.

Danton made no effort to regain power,* and his fall is a landmark in the history of the Revolution. He was an opportunist, but he had statesmanlike ideas; he saw the importance of eventual reconciliation, and he had wide human sympathies. He bellowed war in

---

* He had lost his wife, to whom he was devoted, during his mission to Belgium, and had married, shortly after, a young friend of hers who occupied a good deal of his attention. He was also weary of politics and longed for the country and his home at Arcis-sur-Aube.

his speeches; in secret he prepared the way for peace. It was known that he was naturally inclined to mercy; some people thought that he was not disinclined to royalty. His great achievement in these his months of power was, that, on April 13th, he persuaded the Convention to disavow the propaganda which had frightened Europe, by making a declaration that France would never interfere in the government of other Powers nor suffer them to interfere in hers. Robespierre at the same time procured a decree for punishing with death any one who proposed to negotiate with an enemy country which did not recognize the Republic; none the less, Danton and his Committee seized every occasion that offered, to open up, through secret agents, such communications with the enemy as might lead to an understanding. The Committee was seconded in this by the Girondin Minister, Lebrun; and though he was arrested on June 2nd, they continued to work with him till he was replaced. As to the general work of the Committee, their admirers say that they prepared the way for future victory, their detractors, that they failed.

The new Comité de Salut public entertained no ideas of possible peace and coming reconciliation. Barère floated in easily, he was too useful a man to lose; he could trim his sails to any wind, talk well on any subject, trumpet victory and gild defeat. He was the usual mouthpiece of the new Committee, as he had been of the old. Couthon, Saint-Just, and Hérault were also re-elected. Jeanbon Saint-André, a former Protestant minister, dark and dour, who devoted himself to the Navy, and Robert Lindet, an excellent organizer, soon became indispensable. The energetic Prieur de la Marne was good to send on missions. Robespierre, elected on July 27th, gave distinction, and the Committee was further strengthened in August by the addition of two soldiers; Carnot, 'the organizer of Victory', and Prieur of the Cote-d'Or.

The instruments of the Terror had already been forged for their use. There were the Revolutionary Committees in every Commune, in every Section of a city, to keep an eye upon each individual. There were the Jacobin Clubs to denounce all who did not hold Jacobin opinions, and now that the Mountain ruled it was hard to find salvation outside the Jacobins. There were the Representatives on Mission, in plumed high-hats and tricolour scarves, to imprison and send for trial all whom the Jacobins denounced, to cheer the Armies on to fight and accompany them into battle, to bring Generals who failed, major and minor, to the scaffold. And last, there was the Revolutionary Tribunal, about which it is time to say a few words.

The Terror proper had not yet begun and the Tribunal was slow at its work, for the President, Montane, was determined to give every one a fair trial, and the Public Prosecutor, that industrious lawyer, the black-haired, sinister-looking Fouquier-Tinville, liked to conduct matters formally. Acquittals were many and victims were sparse and often undistinguished. One of the earliest was an elderly cook, who had cried *Vive le roi!* in her cups, and frustrated efforts made to save her.* Three of Dumouriez's Generals were condemned and three were acquitted. The guillotine had been moved from the Carrousel when the Convention moved to the Tuileries, and now stood near the centre of the place de la Révolution. The first big execution here was on June 18th, when, after a long trial, twelve persons were guillotined for having joined in a very real royalist plot known as 'the Brittany Conspiracy'. The victims, especially three ladies, were much pitied by the watching crowd. Even more harrowing was the next execution, on July 13th, when nine prominent citizens of Orléans were guillotined for an attack on Leonard Bourdon, a Representative on Mission who was passing through the town. A good deal of indignation was felt in Paris, and Bourdon, who had shown no mercy, was henceforward known as 'Leopard' Bourdon. It is fair to add that Representatives on Mission rarely exacted full vengeance for personal injuries.

* The Tribunal acted on the principle of *in vino veritas* and was implacable to drunkards.

The next victim roused different feelings. On Thursday July 11th, a young lady arrived in Paris by the coach from her home in Caen; a quiet, reserved girl, gentle-mannered, good-looking, and well dressed, named Marie-Charlotte Corday. She was an ardent republican who believed, as the Girondins did, that Marat was the chief cause of the woes of her country, and she had come to Paris to kill him; a design which she confided to no one. She had visited the deputies in Caen and brought letters from Barbaroux to his friend the deputy Deperret; her ostensible business was connected with a friend's pension. She put up at an Hôtel not far from the Palais-Royal and saw Deperret, who was helpful about the pension; most of her time she spent in her room. Marat, she learnt, was ill, and not attending the Convention. Early on Saturday (13th) she bought a big knife in the Palais-Royal, took a cab, and drove over the river to Marat's flat in the rue des Cordeliers. She was not admitted, but she tried again in the evening, and this time Marat received her. She found him sitting in a slipper bath and writing; he suffered from a skin-disease, and would sit thus for hours, busy with his paper. Charlotte took a chair and told him about the deputies at Caen. He put their names down, remarking that they would soon be guillotined, at which she rose and stabbed him to the heart. He gave one cry for help, his household rushed in and Charlotte was seized; but Marat was dead. The news spread, and the quarter was soon in an uproar. Chabot and Hébert were quickly on the spot and astounded at Charlotte's calmness as she stood unflinching, prepared to face the dreadful consequences of her deed. Both in her preliminary examinations, and before the Revolutionary Tribunal on July 17th, she explained why she had killed Marat, insisting that it had been entirely her own idea. She was condemned. Her counsel, Chauveau-Lagarde, had acted as she wished in not putting forward the only possible defence, madness; and she thanked him nobly by asking him to pay her small debts in the prison; for the property of the condemned was confiscated. In the evening she was taken to the scaffold in the usual cart, dressed in the red shirt worn by parricides, because a deputy was considered a 'father of the people'. The heat had been intense for days and a thunderstorm was growling overhead, yet the streets and the great square were crowded as Charlotte passed slowly by, modest, beautiful, serene to the end, for she believed that she had saved France.* A young man from Mayence, Adam Lux, fell in love with her on the spot; "greater than Brutus" he called her, and henceforward

* It is well known that an assistant executioner buffeted her head, which he was holding up to the people; not so well known that his act was universally reprobated and that he was punished for it.

he raved about her till he brought himself to the same scaffold in November.

Marat's memory was loaded with honours; his Section, once Theatre-Français, now Marseille, changed its name to 'Marat',* and he was given a splendid funeral, which the Convention attended in a body. He was buried in the garden of the former Cordeliers' Convent, and the Cordeliers' Club kept his heart and raised an altar to it in their hall. 'The friend of the People' was worshipped as a saint by those who had given up other worship; hymns and litanies were sung to him, and his bust was put up alongside that of Brutus in every public place. Joined with him in worship were the two other 'martyrs of Liberty', Lepeletier and Chalier, but Marat was greatest of the three. His name became a touchstone of political orthodoxy; thus, one poor victim of the Revolutionary Tribunal tried to save herself by declaring that she 'regretted him with all her heart'. Neither Danton nor Robespierre cared for Marat, as we have seen, but for political reasons they encouraged this cult.

Marat's death had only bad results. For one thing it made the Girondins' position worse, as their enemies refused to believe that they had not instigated Charlotte to the murder. The unfortunate Deperret was arrested

* Most Sections changed their names during the Revolution, many more than once.

at once, so was Fauchet, and, shortly after, all the
deputies under arrest in their houses were sent to
prison. For another thing, it made way for a wickeder
man: Hébert. Marat, as it was pointed out at the time,
had been a kind of boundary mark of patriotic fury
beyond which no one might safely go. Hébert did go
beyond it, and his paper, *Le Pere Duchesne*, was far
cleverer and more brutal than Marat's; he too
denounced, and called for heads, added to which he
gloated over executions and used, if he did not invent,
horrible facetious synonyms for being guillotined, such
as 'looking through the little window' and 'sneezing
into the sack'. Marat had at least been disinterested,
Hébert had private ends in view. Outside the Convention
he had great influence; he ruled the Cordeliers' Club
and, in conjunction with Chaumette, he swayed the
Commune. In August he ventured to attack Danton,
by September he was disputing the supremacy of the
Jacobins with Robespierre. He had powerful friends
in the War Office: Vincent, the general secretary, who
is often, and justly, described as 'a young tiger', and
Ronsin, assistant to the Minister, an odious and imperious man, who went on missions to the seats of war,
chiefly to Saumur, and got himself made a General.
These two, with their friend Momoro, the printer, were
the chief 'Hébertists', as they were afterwards called; a
party of terrorists always crying for extreme measures,

always working up the public to demand them. What distinguishes them from other terrorists is their jealousy of the Comité de Salut public and their anxiety to overthrow it. Yet they had a link with the Committee in the person of the Minister of War, Bouchotte, a prime favourite with the Committee, who was much under Vincent's influence.

Committee, Hébertists, Jacobins, and much of the public were agreed upon one thing: that ex-nobles ought to be turned out of any public functions, and especially out of the Army, for they saw in each noble "the beginning of a traitor", as Barère put it. Unluckily almost all the experienced officers were ex-nobles, and the Committee understood that exceptions must be made, particularly as the Representatives on Mission with the Armies sent constant remonstrances. Yet such was the popular clamour for this measure, that many good officers were sacrificed and the Armies were yet further disorganized. The policy was carried out with gusto by Bouchotte. As soon as the new Committee came into power, Biron was sent for from la Vendée and imprisoned. There had long been a campaign against Custine, led by Hébert and Marat, and Bouchotte's agents had distributed their journals in Custine's Army. Custine was now sent for to Paris. Boastful and quarrelsome, he made a bad impression on the Committee, and his fate was sealed when Mayence, after a long and heroic resistance, capitulated to the Austrians on July 23rd, and Valenciennes to a composite force of the Allies on July 28th; Conde was already lost. Custine was sent before the Revolutionary Tribunal, and his trial, which lasted thirteen days, was one of the excitements of August. Montane had been succeeded as President by Herman, a friend of Robespierre, but the Tribunal was still slow, for there were many witnesses to hear. 'How useless to hear witnesses when Custine is obviously guilty', complained the Jacobins, and Robespierre demanded a reform of the Tribunal. Custine was condemned at last, and executed on August 28th.

On the whole, the new Committee had started prosperously. First came the collapse of the Federalist insurrection in l'Eure and Calvados. Wimpffen's troops were routed by the Republicans near Vernon on July 13th; it is said that both sides ran and the Federalists ran furthest. Wimpffen disbanded his lukewarm Army, and by the end of the month all was over. There were no proscriptions, thanks to Robert Lindet, but the Girondin deputies had to fly, and entered on a period of weary wanderings and disguises, in which the sorest trial to generous men was the knowledge that they were imperilling the lives of the friends who sheltered them. Bordeaux submitted also; food was short there, and the Representatives on Mission were able to hold up supplies. The Constitution was accepted, the 'Popular

Commission' dissolved itself on August 2nd. But the city was known to be still federalist at heart, and the Convention outlawed the Commission and every one who had joined in its acts. As the whole Department was practically implicated, this did not make for loyalty. There was, however, no more open rebellion, and terror and punishment could take their course. On October 16th the Representatives on Mission entered the city as conquerors, through a breach in the wall.

The triumph of the new Constitution was another success for the Committee. The Paris Sections accepted it with rapture, and trooped to the Convention with songs, flags, flowers, speeches, and girls in white. The great majority of the Primary Assemblies accepted; even in la Vendée there were acceptances; it might be called unanimity. To celebrate the occasion, a Federation in Paris was fixed for the 10th August; the Primary Assemblies were invited to send envoys, and David, the painter, arranged an elaborate programme. The 10th was a wonderful day, long remembered; a day of enthusiasm and brotherly goodwill. Every one joined in a great procession; eight members of the Convention carried an ark containing the tables of the Rights of Man, and all members carried bunches of corn and fruit; the envoys from the Primary Assemblies carried pikes and olive-branches, and were tied together with tricolour ribbon; the 'heroines of the 5th and 6th

October' rode on cannons; foundling babies were carried in white bassinettes; no one was left out. The procession marched slowly round to five stations, and at each of them Hérault, the imposing President of the Convention, made a speech. At three of the stations colossal plaster statues had been erected. On the ruins of the Bastille sat Nature, mostly naked; from her breasts gushed streams of water. Hérault, after a prayer to Nature, caught the water in an agate cup, poured libations on the ground, drank himself, and handed the cup in turn to eighty-eight of the oldest envoys, one from each Department, who came up to him to receive it. Further on, in the middle of the place de la Révolution sat Liberty, in an improvised grove of poplars; 'emblems of royalty' were burnt before her as a sacrifice. In the place des Invalides, on an artificial mountain, stood the French Nation, in the semblance of a giant about to club the monster Federalism, who was crawling out of "a muddy marsh" at his feet. The ugly statues remained till they crumbled away in wind and weather; sad emblems of the hopes raised by 'the Constitution of 1793'. There could be no question for the present of dissolving the Convention in order to put the Constitution in force, as every one might see.

After this triumph came another crisis, with humiliation for Committee and Convention; it was brought about by the combination of several causes.

First, the adoption of compulsory service. The levy in the Spring had not produced enough men, and in August the envoys of the Primary Assemblies joined with the Paris Sections in petitioning the Convention to invite the whole nation to rise in arms and overwhelm the enemy. The idea appealed to patriotic enthusiasm, it was voted at once (Aug. 16th), and Barère presented a vague plan for carrying out this levy 'en masse'. But Danton talked common sense, and therefore, when on August 23rd a decree put all Frenchmen under requisition, only the 'first requisition': unmarried men from eighteen to twenty-five, was called up for the present. When it came to joining, there was discontent in Paris, and agitators told the people that 'the rich' would evade the law.

Secondly, the chief cause of the crisis was the scarcity of bread. The fixing of a maximum price for corn when there was no means of controlling commerce, had proved a failure. By the terms of the law each Department fixed its own 'maximum'; chaos in the corn trade resulted and consequent dearth. The price of bread in Paris was kept down by a subsidy, in consequence bread was cheaper than in the surrounding districts, and the country folk came in troops to buy it. This was forbidden, but bread was still smuggled out. A dry summer had stopped river transport, and though Paris never actually ran short of flour, alarm was constant. Long queues at the bakers' waited half the night through, and when the precious bread was served out in the morning, it was nasty; and if people complained, food controllers called them 'agents of Pitt'. The Commune* made regulation after regulation, with small results. The Convention was solicitous and two remedies were proposed. The one which the deputies would probably have preferred was, the repeal of the Maximum law; this, it was thought, would be too unpopular, and the other was adopted, on September 3rd, in the shape of a decree for an uniform 'maximum' for the whole Republic, and the forbidding of the free sale of corn. Did not 'agents of Pitt' buy it?

Thirdly, panic helped to bring on the crisis. Very slowly the Army of the Republic, under Carteaux, had closed in on Marseilles. Marseilles showed fight, but the Federalist Army was beaten, the Sections revolted, and Carteaux entered the city on August 25th. He was just in time; the British fleet, under Hood, was in the neighbourhood, and the royalists among the rebellious authorities had begun negotiating with him. Portions of the Marseilles Army escaped to Toulon. Toulon, one of the three great naval ports of France, was already in rebellion; a 'General Committee' had been formed and the Representatives on Mission had been imprisoned.

---

* A new Commune met on August 7th; the officials were the same.

The rebellion was federalist, but here, as in Marseilles and Lyon, the royalists stepped in. Food was scarce, and on August 25th the 'General Committee' made a compact with Hood to deliver up Toulon to the Allies, in return for provisions and a promise to restore it to France when peace was made. On August 29th the British and Spanish fleets entered the Roads, and the Arsenal was handed over. So was the fleet, which made little resistance, for bad officers and insubordinate crews had brought it to a sorry state.

The news of this great disaster reached Paris on September 2nd. Agitators below and Hébertists above had for some time been playing on the public's fears, pointing out traitors everywhere, 'agents of Pitt', paid with Pitt's gold; and already the popular fancy imagined that suspects were at large in thousands, permeating society, and every one of them conspiring, or wishing to conspire, with a foreign foe. Already the Convention had been compelled to decree the principle that all suspects should be arrested (12th Aug.), having previously decreed that Pitt was 'the enemy of the human race'. Already the Jacobin Club, inspired by Hébert, had grown frantic. Danton and Robespierre had endeavoured to lead the Club in violence, doubtless with the view of keeping it in some bounds; Danton promising a third revolution, Robespierre demanding twelve tribunals with swift procedure, for Paris. But they could not touch Hébert, who demanded a revolutionary tribunal with a guillotine in every town. The Club had voted a great petition to the Convention, and various Jacobin demands were being inserted. The news of the treacherous surrender of Toulon seemed, in that moment of excitement, to confirm the wildest fears and suspicions.

Early on September 4th agitators fetched the workmen from their shops, and by the afternoon there was a great crowd in the place de Grève, clamouring for bread and occupied in drawing up a petition to the Commune. The Commune let a number of them in, and they stayed on, joining in the discussions and the votes. Pache tried to calm them, but they asked to be shown plenty of flour and he could not show it. Chaumette was more successful; he proposed a petition to the Convention for the creation of a revolutionary army, with a guillotine in its train, to go forth into the Departments, with the mission of securing corn for Paris and of cutting off the heads of the 'rich egoists' who held it up. He laid all the blame for the dearth at the door of these same 'rich egoists': "they have eaten our shirts and drunk our sweat, and now they want to bathe in our blood!" Hébert seconded Chaumette, and exhorted the people to surround the Convention, as they had done in May, and not to go away until their petition had been made law. The Sections sent deputations to the meeting, and Leonard

Bourdon came on behalf of the Jacobins, to promise that the Mountain would make the Convention vote any measures which the meeting chose to ask.

On the next morning, September 5th, the Convention had voted a new organization of the Revolutionary Tribunal, when citizens and Commune came pouring in, all quite orderly, with Pache at their head, appealing to the Mountain, through the mouth of their orator, Chaumette, to be "the Sinai of the French". The Comité de Salut public was preparing measures, but grim Billaud-Varenne took the lead out of their hands, insisting that something must be done at once; he would not admit of one half-hour's delay. Danton supported him with all his old fire, and at Danton's bidding the Convention voted the creation of a revolutionary army – the guillotine in its wake was dropped – and also that members of Sections should be paid for attendance at their meetings. Billaud next got the law forbidding domiciliary visits by night repealed, observing that the day and the night would be all too short for the task of arresting suspects. Then came the Jacobin deputation with their petition, one of their demands being; "Legislators, put Terror on the order of the day." Barère, reporting later, hailed "this great phrase, which we owe to the Commune of Paris". It would take too long to mention all the cruel demands (such as the instant trial of the Queen and the

Girondins) which were made and not adopted. When the deputy Drouet* proposed to massacre suspects if Liberty were ever in danger, Thuriot protested that the Revolution must not be stained by crime, and the Convention cheered loud and long.

Barère's enthusiastic adoption of extreme measures saved the Committee, and, by way of extra security, Billaud-Varenne and Collot d'Herbois, another terrorist and inconvenient critic, were put on it (Sept. 6th). Danton, popular once more, was also put on, by a special decree, but refused to serve, stating that he would belong to no Committee but would be a spur to all. Shortly afterwards he fell seriously ill, and in mid-October got leave to retire for change of air to Arcis-sur-Aube, his native place.

After September there were no more changes in the Committee, and the same twelve men whom we have named† were continued from month to month. It was a strong Committee, all the members were zealous, all were incorruptible – no breath of suspicion touched them; all were determined to win the war and to crush ruthlessly any person or thing which seemed to them to hinder that aim. They had neither the time nor the

---

* The man who stopped the King at Varennes.

† Robespierre, Couthon, Saint-Just, Barère, R. Lindet, Hérault, Saint André, Carnot, Prieur de la Côte-d'Or, Prieur de la Marne, Billaud-Varenne, Collot d'Herbois.

temper to sift charges, they cared nothing for justice. 'Ingratitude is a virtue in a Republic', was a common maxim of the day, and they were guided by it.

There had been no decree to put Terror on the order of the day, but it was so placed. The Revolutionary Army was organized, an army, not to fight but to spread terror, and Ronsin was aptly made Commander-in-Chief. On September 17th, Merlin de Douai presented one of the most terrible laws that the Convention ever voted, the law defining suspects.* All who had ever shown themselves partisans of tyranny and federalism; all former nobles, together with relatives and agents of émigrés, who had not shown constant attachment to the Revolution; all who had emigrated and returned; all who had been refused certificates of good citizenship by local authorities, were suspect, and there were others as well. The Revolutionary Committees were ordered to arrest and imprison them all. Chaumette, who liked to enlarge on new ideas, presented to the Commune (Oct. 10th) a list of further signs by which suspects might be known, including "those who having done nothing against Liberty, have done nothing for it".

But penal laws seemed to the revolutionaries an incident in the organization of national defence, and the Committee, in which that defence was embodied,

---

* Merlin was called afterwards 'Merlin suspect'.

riding on the top of the wave of terror, gained in prestige and power. The Comité de Sûreté générale, whose business it was to arrest, was a thorn in its side, for the leading members, Chabot and Basire, were considered too lenient to prisoners and to fair ladies who pleaded for them. So the offending Committee was swept aside. On September 13th a decree ordained that all Committees except the Comité de Salut public should be renewed, and that this Committee should present lists for each, which meant that henceforward the great Committee appointed the others. On October 10th, after a report by Saint-Just, a decree was passed that the Government should be 'revolutionary' (i.e. provisional and exceptional) till peace. Billaud afterwards proposed a code of revolutionary laws for this provisional Government which was finally adopted on December 4th. The Comité de Salut public was made supreme, under the Convention, in all matters which concerned government and public welfare; the Comité de Sûreté générale was similarly made supreme in all police and personal matters. The orders of the Comité de Salut public had the force of laws.*

---

* The two Committees, Salut public and Sûreté générale were often called 'the Government Committees', and worked much together. In future when 'the Committee' is mentioned, I will refer to the Comité de Salut public, unless it is clear from the context that it does not.

Let us turn to the war and the insurrections, remembering always that these were the cause of the Terror and the chief care of the Comité de Salut public, and that, whatever its errors, that Committee succeeded in keeping eleven armies going, well or ill, in supplying them with reinforcements, munitions, plans of campaign, and pay.

All through the summer and well into the autumn, the situation continued critical. On several occasions the Allies might have annihilated part of the French Armies, and might have marched on Paris, had they acted together and swiftly. But there was jealousy between Austria and Prussia, and neither cared to help the other to conquest.* Prussia, too, had cooled and was anxious to get out of the war; her King was intent on securing his slice of Poland, which the Powers were cutting up. Added to this, Cobourg was, like Brunswick, a cautious General, resolved to safeguard his communications before advancing into France; so he spent much of his time besieging fortresses. Meanwhile the French Armies were learning how to fight in numerous actions, small and great. None but a nation with a genius for fighting could have learned in such a school; muddle of every kind, indiscipline, lack of clothes and food, perpetual removal of officers, reinforcement by untrained

* The Allies were fighting nominally to restore the Bourbons; their real object was to dismember France for their own benefit.

levies who ran or deserted. Some of the Representatives on Mission took the levy 'en masse' literally, and called up the whole male population; but even the Representatives on Mission soon saw that this would not do.

After Custine's departure, the Northern Army was compelled to retreat behind the Scarpe, and fell into indiscipline. Early in August the command was taken over by Houchard, an Alsatian General, rough, brave, honest, and ignorant. He had seen much service and was covered with scars, but though he understood discipline, he did not possess the qualifications of a great leader. He knew it, and was forced into the post against his will. The situation shortly after he took charge was this: Britain had come into the war by land as well as by sea, and the Duke of York, at the head of a mixed body of allied troops was besieging Dunkerque, while a second army of Hanoverians, Austrians, and Hessians was supporting him. Houchard's business was to relieve Dunkerque; he had a great superiority in numbers, but the Allies had better troops. He marched into Flanders and, after a three days' stubborn battle in very difficult country, defeated the supporting Army at Hondschoote, on September 8th. The Duke of York raised the siege of Dunkerque the same day. Had Houchard pursued his advantage, he might have penned the Duke's Army between his own Army and the sea; but this would have involved risks, he thought he had done enough, and allowed the Duke to bring his troops off unmolested. There was great rejoicing in France over Houchard's victory, the first big battle won since Jemappes. Another victory followed at Menin (Sept. 13th) when Houchard's Generals crushed the Dutch Army. But Houchard did not know how to use victory, and two days later a disgraceful rout took place, also at Menin. Houchard retired behind the Scarpe to reorganize his Army, and hesitated to attack, knowing well that defeat meant a traitor's death. His incapability caused disappointment, which bred suspicion, and a Representative on Mission went to Paris to denounce him. He was arrested on September 23rd, by order of the Comité de Salut public, and imprisoned. Barère and Robespierre denounced him and popular feeling was roused against him. He was accused, among other things, of corresponding with the enemy, because he had exchanged polite letters about prisoners with enemy Generals; and these letters he had not even written himself, as he was unable to write correct French. On November 15th he appeared before the Revolutionary Tribunal, where he was called a coward. He was too stupid to defend himself well, though he did his best, and on the 16th he was executed. As was always the case when a Commander-in-Chief was disgraced, many officers shared his fall, and when the Armies heard of Houchard's fate, every General realized that he stood in peril of the guillotine, all the greater that no allowance was made for the indiscipline of the troops; the soldier could do no wrong.

Houchard was succeeded by a rising young General of his Army, Jourdan, a man of fine character, who kept a haberdasher's shop in peace time. The Austrians were besieging Maubeuge, and the Comité de Salut public ordered an attempt to relieve it. This entailed a battle, and Jourdan prepared for one, making Guise his head-quarters. On October 16th, with greatly inferior forces, he defeated the Armies of Cobourg and Clerfayt at Wattignies, and forced them to retreat across the Sambre. But he could not follow up his victory, for his Army was in such a state of destitution that he had to retire to the positions he had occupied before the battle. The enemy recrossed the Sambre and indecisive fights were frequent. The Committee wanted a big attack, Jourdan judged it impossible at the moment, and they resolved, early in January, to dismiss and arrest him. But his patriotism proved so much above suspicion that he was retired, without disgrace, early in February, he went back to his shop.

The Rhine and Moselle Armies fared ill; General after General was appointed and discarded, often unjustly. Beauharnais,* who succeeded Custine in command of

* The Constituent, first husband of Josephine.

327

the Rhine Army, resigned, completely disheartened. At the end of August this army retired to the lines of Weissemburg. These lines were considered almost impregnable, and yet, on the 13th October, the French were compelled by the Austrians, under Wurmser, to abandon them, and by the 18th they had retired in disorder under the guns of Strasbourg. The Moselle Army, defeated by Brunswick at Pirmasens (14th Sept.), withdrew behind the Sarre. Lower Alsace was overrun by the Austrians and by Conde's émigrés, who served with them, and the Prussians had been blockading the Alsatian border fortress of Landau since August.

But the tide began to turn. Towards the end of October, Saint-Just and Lebas, a member of the Comité de Sûreté générale, arrived at Strasbourg on a special mission. Saint-Just was born to command, and amazingly efficient; the kindlier Lebas mitigated his rigours. Unlike many Representatives on Mission who gave cause for scandal and accusations of favouritism, they lived simply and held themselves rigidly aloof, and though they were misled, to some extent, by the local Jacobins, though they arrested ruthlessly and packed prisoners off to Paris, they shed no blood in Strasbourg. They raised much-needed funds by a forced loan; they requisitioned beds for military hospitals, and all the cloaks in Strasbourg for the Army. Ten thousand pair of shoes were wanted; they said that the shoes must be there the next day – and they got them. Saint-Just set himself to restore discipline. The Mission was a brilliant success.

Two young and rival Generals who had just been made Commanders-in-Chief, Pichegru of the Rhine Army, Hoche of the Moselle Army, were also engaged in restoring discipline. Both these Generals were genuine sans-culottes, sprung from the people; both had risen from the ranks by sheer superiority; both were ambitious. Hoche had distinguished himself in the defence of Dunkerque and had much experience. Impulsive, impatient, magnificent to look at, he shone with military genius, yet he had a touch of vulgarity. His heart was generous, and he had already been before the Revolutionary Tribunal of Douai for defending too warmly an arrested ex-noble General, who had been his benefactor. Pichegru, supple, calculating, able, had no experience and was guided by one of his Generals, the admirable and lovable Desaix.

The object of the two Armies was to raise the siege of Landau and to prevent the enemy from wintering on French soil. Pichegru hammered at the Austrians, driving them slowly back; Hoche struck smashing blows. He was defeated in his first battle, an attack on Brunswick at Kaiserslautern (28~30th Nov.), but he brought his Army off in excellent order and his defeat was forgiven him. At Froeschwiller (Dec. 22nd) he gained a victory over Wurmser and the Austrians, after which two Representatives on Mission put the Rhine Army with its General, the unwilling Pichegru, under him. Forthwith he defeated Wurmser at the Geisberg, December 26th, and on the 28th Brunswick raised the siege of Landau and his Army left French soil. On December 30th Wurmser crossed the Rhine; Alsace was reconquered. Hoche now invaded the Palatinate and took Spires and Worms, but he soon fell out with his Government. Carnot ordered him to march on Trèves; it was icy winter weather and the troops had no shoes; he obeyed with reluctance. The march had to be abandoned and the Army was allowed to go into winter quarters, but the Committee imputed the failure to Hoche. Again, the Palatinate was to be plundered, and a host of agents of the Republic were soon stripping it bare. Hoche, though by no means squeamish, was touched with pity for the wretched inhabitants; he feared a revolt and refused to strip them further to fit out his Army. Again, the rivalry between him and Pichegru had grown into an unseemly quarrel. Pichegru was boastful, and he made Saint-Just, his protector, believe that the victories were all due to him. Saint-Just brought the Committee over to Pichegru's side; Pichegru was sent to succeed Jourdan in the Northern Army (Feb. 5th, 1794) and the Committee resolved to get rid of Hoche, who *was* troublesome and dangerously popular with the soldiers. Early in March 1794 they sent him to command the Italian Army, had him arrested just after his arrival, transferred him to Paris and clapped him into prison. His successor with the Moselle Army was Jourdan, recalled from his shop.

The two Armies in the Pyrenees saw much fighting and met with little success. The war was carried on chiefly on the French side of the border, but the Spaniards did not press home their advantages. The Italian and Alpine Armies were employed, partly in suppressing the insurrection in the South and chiefly in keeping the Piedmontese from invading.

Much chivalry was shown on both sides in the foreign wars; chivalry was unfortunately rare in the civil wars, insurrections which the foreign war had made doubly dangerous. It is small wonder that patriotic Frenchmen should thirst for the punishment of brethren who were trying to upset the Government at such a moment; the rebels deserved punishment. But a wiser Government would have seen to it that the guilty few were distinguished from the many who were merely misled, or even, perhaps, innocent.

Dubois-Crancé and another Representative on Mission gathered an army together, and summoned Lyon to surrender on August 8th; Lyon refusing, the siege began. On August 24th Kellermann, who was in command, started bombarding; Lyon still held out.

Kellermann was superseded, and battered Lyon still held out. Couthon arrived on a mission; he pressed for an attack, but Dubois-Crancé, an old soldier, who hoped to reduce the place by famine, would not consent. The impatient Comité de Salut public recalled Dubois-Crancé,* and three days later, on October 9th, the army with the Representatives on Mission entered Lyon. Vengeance began at once. On the proposal of the Committee, the Convention decreed (Oct. 12th) the destruction of Lyon. All the houses of the well-to-do were to be pulled down and a monument was to be erected among the ruins; the very name was to be effaced from the map, and such houses of the poor as remained were to be known as 'Ville (or Commune) Affranchie'. Couthon and the other Representatives were in no hurry to carry out this mad decree and, though they started the work of destruction ostentatiously, very few houses were pulled down. They set up two tribunals to try rebels, but Couthon was determined that only ringleaders should fall. Couthon was Robespierre's friend and was, no doubt, carrying out his ideas, but this policy did not suit the majority of the Committee and they sent to Lyon (Oct. 30th) Collot d'Herbois and Fouché of Nantes, a renegade priest. Collot and Fouché resolved to punish wholesale.

* Dubois-Crancé was arrested; he found little difficulty in defending himself, and was released.

They established a Commission of five, so-called, judges, who settled the fate of prisoners as quickly as possible, without any legal formalities. The guillotine could hardly keep pace with the number of the condemned, and Collot and Fouché thought of a quicker method of execution. Batches of fifty or sixty victims were tied together and taken to an open space called the Brotteaux, where trenches had been dug for graves; at the side of these they were shot down by soldiers, many of whom hated the task and did not aim well. Survivors were finished off by hand. There were four of these *mitraillades* and in one of them over two hundred perished. Collot's letters to the Convention might fitly be described as fiendish; and probably made deputies uneasy. When he returned and reported on December 21st, the Convention had been listening to a petition for mercy from Lyon, and he found, to his indignant surprise, that he had gone too far. He was actually obliged to defend his measures, and told the sympathetic Jacobins, the same evening, that public spirit had subsided singularly during his absence.

Toulon took longer to subdue than Lyon; its natural position, protected by mountains, was very strong, and it bristled with forts. But the garrison was not large enough for its task, and Pitt sent no reinforcements. A good general, Dugommier, was finally in command of the besiegers, and Napoleon Bonaparte, the young officer in charge of the artillery, distinguished himself greatly; it is, however, a mistake to say that he directed the siege. Step by step the besiegers gained ground, and at the end of three and a half months, by a tremendous effort, they took the forts which dominated the harbour (17th Dec.). Toulon was now untenable and the British left the port on December 19th, taking with them the guilty French leaders and abandoning the wretched populace to their fate. Sir Sydney Smith set fire to the Arsenal, the docks, and the fleet, and the convicts of Toulon joined with the inhabitants to prevent the conflagration spreading.* Barras and Fréron, Representatives on Mission, who had rendered great services in the South, proceeded to punish the traitor city. A number of the inhabitants who had helped to put out the flames went to meet the soldiers on their entry; two hundred of them were shot on the spot. Patriots who had been imprisoned were set to make lists of their enemies, and to try them; the guillotine was hard at work and, as at Lyon, there were wholesale shootings, called here *fusillades*. The Convention changed the name of the city to Port-de-la-Montagne, and ordered the destruction of all houses not connected with the naval establishment.†

* The destruction was not complete, and some of the ships were saved.
† Dugommier, powerless to prevent these atrocities, was on the point of resigning when he was ordered to take command in the Pyrenees.

Barras and Fréron also carried out the work of terror and destruction in Marseilles. They even made an order that until a new name was bestowed by the Convention, Marseilles should be nameless, and for five weeks Marseilles was known as 'the city without a name'. But strong remonstrances were made, the Committee felt that Barras and Fréron had gone too far, and Marseilles was allowed by decree (Feb. 12th, 1794) to keep its name.

In la Vendée the Committee managed matters ill. Here Ronsin's influence was paramount, and they chose to be guided by Choudieu, a Representative on Mission who supported Ronsin, rather than by other Representatives. They were on the look-out for sans-culotte generals, and Ronsin put forward his boon companion Rossignol, then commanding a regiment in la Vendée, lately a Parisian goldsmith, formerly a soldier, who had risen from the ranks which he ought never to have left, and was given to drinking and pillaging. Rossignol had been arrested in la Vendée for insubordination and was called to Paris to explain. Rough, ignorant, stupid, and personally brave, he seemed to the Committee, and to Danton as well, the very essence of a sans-culotte; they sent him back as a General and on July 24th gave him the command of the la Rochelle Army, under the popular delusion that patriotism would supply the want of brains.

Rossignol was a by-word in the Army and his appointment was ill received. A month later, two Representatives on Mission suspended him for theft; he had appropriated Biron's horses among other things. He went off to Paris, and returned triumphant at the end of August, with a decree recalling the two Representatives. During his absence arrived the brave and well-disciplined garrison of Mayence, under Dubayet and Kléber, sent by the Committee to fight the rebels, since the terms of their capitulation forbade their serving against the Allies. They joined the Brest Army under Canclaux, and the insurrection might now have been quickly put down.

On September 2nd a Council of Representatives on Mission and Generals was held at Saumur, to decide between two plans of campaign. One, supported by Choudieu and Rossignol, was an attack from Saumur, roughly, westwards; the other, supported by another Representative, Philippeaux, and by the best Generals, was an attack from Nantes and the coast, roughly, eastwards. This second scheme was adopted, plans were concerted with Rossignol and a junction of forces fixed for a certain date. Canclaux and Dubayet carried out their part of the plan, so did Rossignol's three Generals on the coast. But Rossignol, after meeting with a slight reverse, decided in a small Council of War, which Ronsin attended, that his Army must stay on the defensive for the present, and, without informing the Brest Army, he sent orders to his three Generals to retire. The consequences of this withdrawal were the defeat of Kléber at Torfou (Sept. 19th), and that, after a series of defeats to Rossignol's Army, Canclaux was obliged to retire to Nantes. Canclaux and Dubayet then resolved to act without Rossignol, and they had won a victory on October 6th when, immediately afterwards, both Generals, together with Grouchy,* Canclaux's right-hand man, were recalled and dismissed as ex-nobles.

On August 1st the Convention, at Barère's bidding, had passed a decree for the devastation of la Vendée and the deportation of the non-combatant inhabitants. On October 1st, again at his bidding, it was decreed that the war in la Vendée must be over by the 20th, and that all the troops engaged against the rebels should form one army, known as 'the Western Army'. The command was given to Léchelle, a conceited and incompetent protégé of Ronsin, whose idea of a campaign was marching "in a mass and majestically". Rossignol was given a command farther north, at Rennes.

Throughout the campaign fights had been continual, and reputations were forming. The Alsatian Kléber excelled all the rest in talent, as he did in stature. He

* Afterwards Napoleon's Marshal.

formed a friendship with the chivalrous and heroic Marceau, a rising young General of the la Rochelle Army, who, like himself, combined humanity with courage. The two friends passed through this terrible war unstained by cruelty, ready always to pity and to save. A man of another stamp, prominent among Rossignol's Generals, was Westermann, an adventurer who had distinguished himself at the assault on the Tuileries, daring, rash, cruel; often defeated but uncrushable.

On October 17th Kléber and Marceau defeated the Vendéens at Cholet. In this fierce battle three of the rebel leaders, d'Elbée, Lescure, and Bonchamps were mortally wounded. Bonchamps, especially, was an irreparable loss; a fine and gallant officer, he too was never stained by cruelty, and his last act was to insist upon his followers sending over to the Republican Army four or five thousand prisoners who would probably have been executed when he was dead. After the defeat at Cholet the entire *Grande Armée* crossed the Loire (17-18 Oct.) taking with them their old men, women, children and priests: a whole population. This exodus of some 100,000 people was quite against the wish of their leaders, and instigated chiefly by the young prince de Talmond, ambitious and giddy, who promised a rising on his estates at Laval. The dying Lescure was able to persuade the Vendéens to elect as d'Elbée's successor, not Talmond, but Henri de la Rochejaquelein, a valiant, generous youth, who, though barely twenty-one, possessed the confidence of the Army. He was assisted by Stofflet.

The Western Army crossed the Loire in pursuit of the Vendéens, and Barère announced to the Convention that la Vendée had ceased to exist. The next news was the rout of the Republicans at Entrammes (27 Oct.), owing to Léchelle's obstinate imprudence. La Vendée was still there. Léchelle resigned, and though his resignation was not accepted, he retired; the Army was reorganized at Angers, and the new Commander-in-Chief was none other than Rossignol! It must not be supposed that the Committee did not know what Rossignol was like; they had ample information and refused to believe it, for, as Prieur de la Marne, on Mission to la Vendée, told Kléber, Rossignol was "the eldest son of the Comité de Salut public".

Meanwhile the Vendéens marched north unmolested, occupying town after town. The leaders were already negotiating with England for help, and at Fougères, in north Brittany, they received an official answer; that if they took a sea-port, the British would effect a landing. Accordingly, on November 14th and 15th, they attacked the port of Granville on the Norman coast. It was touch and go, but Granville succeeded in keeping them out. Hopes of foreign help were now at an end, and the *Grande Armée* insisted on returning to la Vendée, against its leaders' wishes.

It was now the task of the Western Army to catch and destroy the rebels before they could cross the Loire, but, through Rossignol's incompetence, La Rochejaquelein routed the Republicans once again, at Antrain (22nd Nov.). They were obliged to retreat to Rennes, and this time Rossignol resigned. His resignation was not accepted, but he was ready to stand aside, and the Representatives on Mission, at Kléber's suggestion, appointed Marceau as temporary Commander-in-Chief. Kléber himself had refused; it was his peculiarity that he would never accept supreme command; he knew, however, that Marceau would be guided by him. The consent of the Committee was obtained, and on December 5th Marceau took command and Rossignol, still with a command, was sent to Brest. The same day arrived orders from Bouchotte to dismiss Kléber and two other distinguished Generals, one of whom had just been killed in battle; these orders were not carried out. Prieur de la Marne had already threatened Kléber with the guillotine, and neither Kléber nor Marceau was looked on with an eye of favour by the Government; they were too independent, too much inclined to leniency, too popular in the Army. "We will be guillotined together," said Kléber to Marceau, and in three weeks they had finished the campaign. The *Grande Armée*, hoping to cross the Loire south of Angers, had already attacked that city (3 and 4 Dec.) and had been defeated; they were defeated again at le Mans (12th and 13th Dec.), with horrible and indiscriminate slaughter which the Generals were powerless to prevent. The unhappy Vendéens then tried to cross the Loire farther west, at Ancenis; Westermann fell upon them. On December 23rd, Marceau defeated them once more, in the last and decisive battle of Savenay, and the *Grande Armée* ceased to exist. La Rochejaquelein was not at Savenay, nor was Stofflet. They had crossed the Loire at Ancenis to reconnoitre, and were unable to rejoin their Army. On December 30th Marceau handed over the command to the new chief, Turreau, a bad General from the Pyrenees Army, and both Marceau and Kléber were soon shelved in unimportant posts. Death for the unsuccessful general – unless he had friends in the War Office – disgrace or the cold shoulder for the too successful general who might become dangerous; this was, in effect, the policy of the Comité de Salut public. Yet the patriotism of the best officers of the Revolution was so strong, that they were always ready to sacrifice themselves, undaunted and undismayed.

A terrible vengeance was taken at Nantes on the rebels of la Vendée, men, women and children who escaped the sword. Carrier, the Representative on Mission, a gloomy and ferocious tyrant, saw to that.

He was helped by the Revolutionary Committee of Nantes and by a local band of hired ruffians called the 'Compagnie de Marat.'

The prisons, overcrowded with rebels, were ravaged by disease – it has been calculated that about 3,000 prisoners died – and the citizens trembled lest this great influx of 'Brigands' should bring to Nantes not only pestilence but famine. The prisons must be cleared, and the trials and executions which were proceeding rapidly could not clear them fast enough. Carrier allowed a new method, devised, probably, by some of his agents. A number of untried prisoners were put on a sort of lighter and battened down under hatches. The lighter was taken down the Loire and scuttled, by a special contrivance, at a convenient spot; the prisoners were drowned, and their conductors escaped in small boats. These wholesale murders, called *noyades*, were done at night.

The number of them is uncertain, and though authentic proofs of only three *noyades* exist, the best authorities agree that there were more, possibly one, possibly four. Women and children were drowned, and in one *noyade*, at least, the prisoners were tied together two and two.* Large fusillades also took place, after

* There is hardly any evidence for the so-called 'republican marriages' in which a man and a woman were tied together and drowned, and the charge was dropped at Carrier's trial. If any ever did take place, it was quite an exceptional occurrence.

which the bodies of the victims were thrown into the Loire, and the great river often washed up corpses. Some mystery surrounded the *noyades*, and though, after the second, early in December, Carrier wrote to the Convention that fifty-eight refractory priests had been put on a boat and swallowed up by the Loire, adding: "What a revolutionary torrent the Loire is!" the Convention did not grasp what was happening. Carrier himself lived in luxury and debauchery, violent and inaccessible, but he satisfied the Committee by his energy in carrying on the war.

Thus the year 1793 ended with victories: the insurrections in West and South crushed, Toulon retaken, the enemy almost entirely driven out of France. A Victory Fête was celebrated for Toulon on December 30th, and the position of the Committee was stronger than ever.

IX

THE REIGN OF TERROR

II. Robespierre August 1793 – 13 April 1794

We must now return to Paris in the autumn of 1793. The scarcity of food continued, making life hard for town-dwellers, and in Paris the Authorities whose business it was to provision the city were often at their wits' end. Ronsin's 'Revolutionary Army' did not succeed in making things easier, and a large detachment, under that General, soon went off to spread terror in Lyon. Maximum prices for all the necessaries of life had been fixed at the end of September; this naturally tended to make commodities rarer, and daily complaints of the malpractices of butchers, bakers, grocers, greengrocers, wine and wood merchants, were bitter as ever, and discouraged trade yet more. Only the rich could live in anything like comfort. Life, too, for rich and poor alike, was full of harrowing circumstances;

certificates had to be obtained from the authorities, and local bullies had to be conciliated, for even the humblest was not safe from denunciation. Bolder spirits found compensation in the excitements of political life; true, the Sections were forbidden to meet more than twice a week, but Sectional popular societies, much under Hébertist influence, were founded to evade the law. Women had their societies too, violent and quarrelsome – so quarrelsome that after a big street-fight they were suppressed by the Convention (30 Oct.).

The centre of interest in Paris was the Revolutionary Tribunal; it has been a centre of interest to the world ever since, for its dark records are illumined by many examples of heroism, loyalty, and innocence.

Month by month, as the laws of the Terror came into force, the prisons grew fuller and fuller, and the increase was all due to political prisoners. On September 2nd 1793 there were 1,640 prisoners and ten prisons. By January 1st 1794 there were 4,700, and in April the numbers reached 7,000, by which time there were thirty prisons, some of them only small houses of detention. The larger prisons, insanitary and overcrowded, were places of manifold discomforts and sickening smells. Round these prisons hung a host of relatives and friends, faithful and dauntless, eager to supply the wants of the prisoners, prompt to plead for them in any quarter where justice or pity might be looked for.

A decree (Oct. 10th) forbade communication with prisoners, except in writing, and then only about personal wants and domestic affairs; prisoners about to stand their trial were excepted. This law was not strictly kept, neither was another (Nov. 16th), that all prisoners must feed alike, the rich paying for the poor. Nowhere in Paris, in that time of dearth, was there better eating and drinking than in the prisons, and nowhere was there such good society. A common danger drew prisoners together, and gaols became schools of good manners, cheerfulness and fortitude.

All prisoners whose trial was imminent were taken to the Conciergerie, the prison of the Palais de Justice. The Revolutionary Tribunal, now organized in Sections, sat in two halls* in the Palace, and conducted simultaneous trials, several Judges sitting at each trial. Legal forms were observed; a preliminary examination of each prisoner took place before trial, and if, as sometimes happened, there was no case at all against him, he was released. During the trial, after each witness had been heard, the accused had an opportunity of defending himself briefly, with regard to that witness's

---

* One, in which most of the great trials took place, was the big Hall of the Paris Parlement; it was burnt by the Commune in 1871, and a Law-Court now occupies the exact site. The other, overlooking the river, was pulled down. The Tribunal did not sit on Sunday, nor, after Sunday was abolished, on its substitute, *décadi*.

347

evidence. But the appearance of fairness was delusive. The jurymen had been appointed by the Convention chiefly on account of their political opinions, and Fouquier-Tinville acquired the habit of packing them at important trials. The presiding Judges, Herman and Dumas, made no pretence of impartiality, and the callous Fouquier-Tinville was only concerned to obtain convictions; that was his business. Yet, in the earlier days, there were many acquittals of innocent persons who were also obscure. Only a small minority of those condemned could be called aristocrats, and many victims were of humble station. It must not be supposed that all were brave, for many were cowards, nor, that all were innocent; some were really guilty of high treason, some were fraudulent contractors, some were ruffianly terrorists. Many had broken the laws which forbade communication with an enemy country, by corresponding with emigre friends, or relatives, or employers, and by sending them money; for this they deserved some penalty, but they did not deserve death. The law (13 March 1794) forbidding any one to shelter a fugitive from justice on pain of death, was broken by numbers of the best and bravest in France. The Tribunal could sentence to prison or deportation, but deportation was not considered politic; "it is only the dead who never come back," said Barère.

Condemned prisoners returned to the Conciergerie

and were executed within twenty-four hours; on the day of their sentence if the trial ended early. This promptitude was, as we have said, intended to save them suffering. Before they left the prison, the executioners cut their hair short and tied their hands behind their backs. Carts were ready at the prison door, which opened into the Court in front of the Palace.* They took their slow way, over one of the bridges and along the quays, then north, into the rue Saint-Honoré, along that street past the Palais-Royal and the Jacobins, then down into the place de la Révolution by the rue Royale; the journey often took an hour and a half. The carts were escorted by gendarmes attached to the Tribunal, and Hanriot, who continued to command the National Guard, provided troops to keep order when necessary. The crowd was not always hostile, but unpopular prisoners were hooted and insulted. The scaffold stood on the Tuileries side of the plaster statue of Liberty in the centre of the square. There were always plenty of onlookers, and when the guillotine fell they waved hats and sticks, with cries of *Vive la République*! for the crowd believed that all who were executed were traitors.† People grew hardened to the sight of blood and

* The door still exists, on the right of the great staircase as you face it ; it no longer leads to the prison.
† I have not come across any contemporary mention of women knitting at executions, but there were *tricoteuses* in the gallery of the Jacobins.

death, and the amazing courage of the victims helped to disguise the horrors of the spectacle. Bodies and heads were interred in the ordinary burial ground of the Section, the cemetery belonging to the Madeleine church. The property of the condemned was confiscated by the nation, and became a source of revenue; this encouraged executions of the rich. In theory, at least, some provision was made for victims' families who were left destitute.

The first great trial of the autumn was the Queen's; Hébert had long been asking for her head. At the beginning of July the Comité de Salut public had separated her from her son, in consequence of rumours of a plot to carry him off and proclaim him King; on August 2nd she was transferred to the Conciergerie, leaving her young daughter in the care of the saintly Madame Elisabeth. The unhappy little Prince, now called Charles Capet, was already in the hands of a guardian appointed by the Commune: Simon, one of its members, a cordwainer of the Theatre-Français Section, who came, with his wife, to live in the Temple tower. They were a rough couple, and Simon, though probably not actively cruel, was determined to turn the child into a regular sans-culotte, as the Commune desired. He made him drunk, he taught him bad language and obscene songs; the boy, too young to resist, picked it all up and learnt to hate his own family.

When the Queen's trial was near, Hébert and Chaumette, to their eternal infamy, came to the Temple and drew from a tipsy child monstrous charges against his mother, which they passed on to Fouquier-Tinville.

Marie-Antoinette spent more than two months in the Conciergerie. Wasted with sorrow, she had lost all her beauty, but she still retained her charm and her majesty, and, even in the Conciergerie, found friends who plotted to save her. At her trial, which lasted two days and a night (Oct. 14-16), she behaved with great and simple dignity, never losing her presence of mind and answering prudently all questions put to her. She swept aside Hébert's charges with a disdain that gained her the admiration of the audience. Her counsel were Chauveau-Lagarde and Tronson-Ducoudray, 'official defenders' at the Tribunal, for whose courage and eloquence many a prisoner had cause to be grateful. They did their best, but nothing could have saved her, and in the early hours of October 16th she was condemned. She wrote a touching letter to Madame Elisabeth, repeating her husband's last wishes that their son should be bidden to take no vengeance for their death; and she kept her calm all through the terrible journey to the scaffold, hardly speaking to a constitutional priest who sat beside her in the cart, to whom she had refused to confess. Madame Elisabeth never received the farewell letter, which was found, later on,

among Fouquier-Tinville's papers. Her life too, innocent and harmless as she was, hung on a thread; Hébert
thirsted for her blood, and it was Robespierre who
once saved her when Hébert was calling, in the
Jacobins, for her trial.

After the Queen came the Girondins. Vergniaud and
some others had been impeached and the fugitive
deputies had been declared traitors (July 28th); yet the
Committee and the Convention had been loth to send
any of them for trial, though Hébert and the Jacobins
were clamouring for their heads. It was not till October
3rd that Amar, a cruel fanatic, reported for the Comité
de Sûreté generate, and obtained a decree sending
forty-one deputies, not all Girondins, before the
Revolutionary Tribunal. Some of these had already
escaped, Isnard, for instance, and Condorcet; some
were arrested as they left the Convention, and among
these were Ducos and Fonfrède. There was nothing
against these two but their friendship with Vergniaud,
and if they had ceased to take his part they might have
saved themselves; they preferred to share his condemnation. The arrest of sixty-four more deputies,* who
had signed protests against the dismemberment of the
Convention, was decreed at the same sitting, and of
these nearly sixty were caught and imprisoned. Osselin

* They are known as 'the seventy-three' or 'the seventy-five', from a
mistake in the list.

and Amar would have had them impeached then and there, but Robespierre saved them. He saved them again in February, when Hébert and the Jacobins were crying out for their heads.

On October 24th the great trial began. Brissot, as chief of the conspirators, occupied an arm-chair and twenty-one other deputies sat on benches raised on tiers; among them Vergniaud, Ducos, Fonfrède, Gensonné, Lasource, Fauchet, Carra, and Sillery, the friend of Égalité, who was not a Girondin. None of the accused had taken part in the rebellion, and their speeches and actions, however unwise they may have been, had not been unconstitutional. Yet all they had said or done was declared to have been part of a conspiracy against the Republic. The war into which they had plunged France, their attempts to prevent the revolution of the 10th August, their friendship with Dumouriez, and their conduct in many other matters, were regarded as proofs. The witnesses were their personal enemies, and Pache, Chaumette, Hébert, Fabre d'Églantine, and above all Chabot, were spiteful. Yet, as the trial proceeded, public sympathy began to turn to the side of the prisoners. Vergniaud was making a great impression, and their enemies feared that when the time came to hear the defence which each of the accused had carefully prepared, eloquence would prevail. On the fifth day Hébert made the

Jacobins tremble by affirming that Vergniaud and Ducos, at least, would be acquitted. He suggested an appeal to the Convention, and on the morrow (Oct. 29th) the Jacobins petitioned the Convention to give the jury power to stop a trial when they felt sufficiently enlightened. Osselin took this up, Robespierre amended the motion, Barère supported, and a law was made, that when a trial by the Revolutionary Tribunal lasted over three days, the President must ask the jury whether they had heard enough to be convinced; if they answered 'no', the trial must go on; if 'yes' the verdict must be given at once. On the morning of October 30th, the question was, accordingly, put to the jury, who answered that they were not yet satisfied. That same evening, however, they stopped the trial, before all the witnesses had been called or the defence heard, and soon after 11 p.m. they returned a verdict of guilty against all the accused. There was a stir in Court; the prisoners received their sentence with loud cries of indignation, and one of them, Valazé, stabbed himself to the heart with a knife he had concealed, and fell down dead. The rest were taken back to the Conciergerie, singing in chorus, as they walked, the first four lines of the Marseillaise, slightly altered. They supped together, simply, in the ancient chapel of the prison, where most of them had been confined, and throughout their last night they solaced themselves with snatches of song. Ducos, always cheerful, had enlivened their captivity with his wit and his verses, and he could still joke in the face of death. In the morning they were taken to the scaffold in four carts, the body of Valazé following in a fifth; a cold rain was falling, yet huge crowds had come out to gaze. Ducos and Fonfrède kissed each other as they got out of the cart, and their example was followed by the others. As they stood at the foot of the scaffold, waiting their turns, they sang the refrain of a popular patriotic song: "Death rather than slavery is the motto of the French." The whole execution took nearly three quarters of an hour, and Brissot was the last to die.

Two of the outlawed Girondins were captured and sent to the scaffold without trial: Gorsas on October 7th, the first deputy executed; Rabaut de Saint-Etienne early in December. Philippe Égalité followed the Girondins on November 6th, he had been contemptible in life but faced death courageously. Madame Roland, who had been in prison since June 2nd, came two days later, going to her execution with bright complexion and tasteful dress, composed and sympathetic, with words of cheer for her companion in the cart, a nervous downcast man; she even made him smile. Women were executed first, but wishing to spare him the dreadful sight, she asked to be guillotined second, and when Sanson, the executioner, demurred: "You wall not refuse the last request of a lady," she said, and he gave way. On the scaffold she turned to the Statue of Liberty with the famous words: "O Liberty, what crimes are committed in thy name!" Old Roland, when he heard of her death, went out into the high road and shot himself.

Two of the glories of the Constituent Assembly followed at brief intervals, and each might have made his escape, Bailly before his arrest, Barnave from prison, had he not felt that duty to his country required him to stay. Bailly was executed on November 11th, in the Champ de Mars, where he had displayed the red flag in July 1791. The populace hated him for this, and a cruel crowd heaped insults on him and forced the executioners to take down the guillotine and set it up nearer the river, outside the sacred ground. It was a morning of chilly showers and strong wind, yet through the long hours of agony Bailly maintained his old, dignified composure. "You are trembling, Bailly," said a scoffer when he shivered. "Yes, with the cold, my friend," he replied calmly.

Barnave, executed on November 29th, had been in prison in Dauphine since August 1792. Eloquent as ever, he made no attempt to save his own life, and deliberately spoke to the Revolutionary Tribunal with the language and ideas of the Constituent Assembly.

With him died the excellent Duport-Dutertre, the first Minister belonging to the Tiers-état; both nominally condemned for an imaginary plot, consisting in some good advice which the Minister, but not Barnave, had given the King.

Another young man of the highest promise, Custine, son of the General, a rising diplomatist, was sent to the Tribunal and the guillotine after a report by Robespierre. Other eminent victims during the winter months were Manuel; Girey-Dupre, the friend of Brissot; the Minister Lebrun; Dietrich, mayor of Strasbourg, in whose house the Marseillaise had first been sung; General Biron; Marshal Luckner, muddled to the last, and Lamourette. Clavière committed suicide in prison. Madame du Barry, who shrieked and begged for one more minute, must also be mentioned.

February 13th, 1794, is notable for the first 'amalgam', as it is called; i.e. the trying together of prisoners who had nothing to do with each other; a speedy method of dispatching business.

One of the accused, the notary Chaudot, was condemned for an act which had been legal when he did it.* His Section petitioned for him and the

---

* He had signed, because a second signature was required, papers of another notary concerning a loan which was being raised in Paris for the sons of George III.

357

Convention granted a reprieve and ordered a report. The legist Oudot, who made it, owned that Chaudot's act had been legal, but argued that the jury must have an intimate conviction of his guilt, or they would not have condemned him, and that the jury must know best. The Convention ordered the execution to proceed.

This blind faith in the jury explains why the justice of the Revolutionary Tribunal was believed in as a dogma.

While battles were raging and heads were falling, the revolutionaries were trying to make a clean sweep of the past. Everything which recalled royalty, or the feudal system, or 'superstition', must disappear. One decree (Aug. 1st) ordered the destruction of the Kings' tombs in the Abbey of Saint-Denis,* another (Aug. 6th) the destruction of all chateaux, but this decree was not carried out. Great havoc was worked all over France; statues were mutilated or destroyed, pictures and records were burnt. There were, nevertheless, intelligent men, both in the Convention and outside, who did their best to preserve beautiful and interesting objects for the nation, and a decree ordered the opening of the Louvre as a Museum of Art. A rage prevailed

---

* Bodies were exhumed and turned out of coffins, not for the sake of destruction, but to get the metal of the coffins for munitions; this was the case with the Kings' bodies.

for changing the names of streets, towns, villages, and individuals which smacked of royalty or 'superstition'; thus Saint-Denis became Franciade, the town of Saint-Pierre-le-Moustier became Brutus-le-Magnanime, and a man called Dubarry became Brutus-Bombier. Manners changed too; politeness was out of fashion and a slovenly dress was much affected. Every one was now plain *citoyen* or *citoyenne*, Monsieur, Madame, and other titles of courtesy having been dropped. Basire wanted the use of 'thou' to be made compulsory, but the Convention would not go further than an invitation, almost equivalent to a command (Oct. 31st). On August 1st the Convention broke with the old, complicated system of weights and measures, by adopting, in principle, the decimal system which is in use to this day: a change which was not carried out for some time. A still greater change came into force at once: a new Calendar, adopted on October 5th, the invention of the deputy Romme. The year was divided into twelve months of thirty days each and five extra days, called *sansculottides*, with a sixth every four years; the week, or *decade*, was ten days long, with a *décadi* instead of Sunday. The year began on September 22nd, the day on which the Convention had proclaimed a new era in 1792, and September 22nd 1793 was the first day of the year II. On October 24th new poetical names for the months, invented by Fabre d'Églantine, were adopted.* Each day of the year was given a name too, but was, in practice, known by a numeral of the *décade*; *primidi*, *duodi*, &c.

This Calendar was intended to help the nation to get rid of Christian 'superstition' by effacing Sundays and Saints' days. The Convention was not atheistic, though it contained atheists such as Anacharsis Cloots; the majority of deputies were deists, who believed that Christianity was politically impossible, since priests must needs be the supporters of Kings. The Constitutional Clergy were still paid by the State, but they were encouraged to break their vows by marrying, and even Bishops took wives. The practice of religion had become difficult, and there was much persecution. In the Departments, moreover, Representatives on Mission were trying to stamp out Christianity, and notable among them was Fouché, in la Nièvre (it was before he went to Lyon). Chaumette, on a visit to his home at Nevers, in September, met Fouché. Chaumette was more than half an atheist already, and he returned to Paris full of Fouché's new ideas, which, with the zealous support of Hébert and his friends, he began to put

---

* Autumn: Vendémiaire, Brumaire, Frimaire; from vintage, fog, frost.
  Winter: Nivose, Pluviose, Ventose; from snow, rain, wind.
  Spring: Germinal, Floréal, Prairial; from budding or sprouting, flower, meadow.
  Summer: Messidor, Thermidor, Fructidor; from reaping, heat, fruit.

into practice. The Commune was enthusiastic; its members adopted a measure of Fouché's which forbade worship outside churches, and ordered a report on funerals, and when Chaumette, on October 16th, read a long Regulation of Fouché's, they listened admiring. Fouché declared that 'the French nation could recognize no religion but that of universal morality', and he ordained that every citizen must be buried twenty-four hours after death in a cemetery with an inscription over the gate: "Death is an eternal sleep," and a statue of sleep among the graves. But the matter of funerals was not settled in Paris, for the Commune inclined to gloomy cemeteries while Chaumette wanted them gay with flowers, so that a man, as he said, 'might inhale the soul of his father from a rose.'

The antichristian movement spread, and curés began to write to the Convention, abjuring their religion and resigning their benefices. A demonstration gave vigour to the movement. Gobel, constitutional Bishop of Paris, was got hold of by Cloots, and on November 17th he and some of his higher Clergy were brought in triumph to the Bar of the Convention, by Department and Commune, to apostatize publicly. Momoro and Chaumette made speeches, Chaumette affirming proudly that 'Reason was resuming her empire', and Gobel was kissed and presented with a cap of Liberty.

It was not noticed that, though he renounced his Orders, he did not abjure his religion.

Fired by his example, several clerical deputies abjured; two Bishops, an Abbe and a Protestant minister, Julien of Toulouse, who said that he would worship no divinity but Liberty. Grégoire, Bishop of Blois, came in just then; he, however, bravely refused to renounce Orders or Religion. Other clerical deputies renounced later, Siéyes among them, and abjurations, in person or by letter, were daily received by the Convention. Whole Communes, too, renounced Christianity, bringing with them the spoils of their churches. From la Nievre came chests of Church plate sent by Fouché; a rich offering for an empty Treasury. The Paris Department and Commune seized the propitious moment to inaugurate a new kind of worship. A fête took place on *decadi*, 20th Brumaire (10th Nov.), in the cathedral of Notre-Dame. A symbolic mountain had been erected in the nave, with a small 'temple of Philosophy' on its summit. Two bands of white-robed maidens descended the mountain, to the sound of music, till they came to the altar of Reason, on which burned the torch of Truth; they bent low before it, and returned to the summit. Then the Goddess of Liberty, in the form of a beautiful woman, came down out of the temple, and took her seat upon a throne of greenery; hymns were sung to her, speeches were made, and she finally retired into the temple. It was all very decorous, and if it had not been daring, might have been thought dull. The performers, music, maidens, Goddess and all, were then taken to the Convention in procession. Chaumette was in his glory; by the help of Chabot he got a decree turning Notre-Dame into the Temple of Reason. The Goddess was kissed by the President and seated beside him, and the Convention marched off to attend a repetition of the service.

The worship of Reason became popular in Paris and other cities, and the fête in Notre-Dame served as a model for inaugural ceremonies; ceremonies which were sometimes enlivened by donkeys in vestments and bonfires of sacred objects. The presiding Goddesses, called usually Goddess of Liberty, but sometimes Goddess of Reason, were almost always young women of good character, and some of them were reluctant performers. There appear to be no contemporary records of orgies at these festivals,* neither was the worship necessarily atheistic, for a 'Supreme Being' was often worshipped as well as Reason. But the offerings of Church spoils, which poured in from Sections and towns and villages, were made the occasion for unseemly displays in the Bar

* The famous 'orgies' in St. Eustache, Paris, seem to rest on the sole authority of Grégoire, who is not to be trusted.

of the Convention, where the bringers, dressed in clerical vestments, capered and sang songs and jeered at religion.

Robespierre, a religiously-minded man, looked on for a time in silence, his soul filled with anger and disgust; at last he spoke out. On November 21st, in the Jacobins', when Hébert had been howling for blood and Momoro raging against priests, he answered by a tremendous attack on the antichristian campaign, in the course of which he declared that the Convention would always maintain freedom of worship, and uttered the words: "Atheism is aristocratic; the idea of a Great Being who watches over oppressed innocence and punishes triumphant crime, is entirely popular." At his bidding, three powerful Hébertists were forthwith expelled from the Club. He found an ally in Danton, who just then returned to Paris. Danton seized an occasion when the Convention had refused a petition for the stopping of clerical salaries, to represent the folly of driving priests into rebellion by hunger and persecution (Nov. 22nd). A few days later (Nov. 26th), he said it was time to put an end to "antireligious mascarades" in the Convention and to the monotonous speeches of "the priests of incredulity". He went further, by speaking of a future time of reconciliation, when the People, having triumphed over its enemies, could afford to be generous. The speeches of Robespierre and Danton made a sensation, and the

Convention gave up listening to abjurations. Chaumette saw that he had gone too far, and, after some hesitation, turned completely round. The Commune, in his absence, but previously excited by his eloquence, had passed a resolution to shut all churches and chapels which still remained open, with other persecuting measures, including a petition to the Convention to exclude priests from all kinds of employment (23rd Nov.). Chaumette, two days after, disclaimed responsibility, and made them repeal their resolution for the petition; but it was not till four days after this (Nov. 29th), when he saw how public opinion was going, that he wrung from the reluctant Commune a declaration that they never had intended, and never would intend, to interfere with, the freedom of public worship. Hébert, too, was forced to recant, and, after a second denunciation from Robespierre in the Jacobins' (28th Nov.), protested against the worship of Marat, and took to paying homage to Christianity in his journal. Robespierre crowned his work by persuading the Convention, on December 6th, to forbid all interference with public worship as long as it was conducted legally and unprovocatively. But Barère limited the effect of this decree, by getting a declaration made, that the Convention did not mean any disapproval of the measures already taken by the Representatives on Mission – one of whom was Fouché.

Maximilien Robespierre, known as 'the incorruptible',

small but not insignificant, and always neatly and appropriately dressed, inspired terror. Men trembled before the veiled glance of his spectacled eyes; at his denunciations, all the more alarming because they were often vague. But if he inspired terror, he also inspired admiration, and he was, as will have been seen, less of a terrorist than Collot or Billaud. Couthon and Saint-Just were his allies in the Committee,* and his younger brother, who supported him in the Convention, was successful without being cruel as a Representative on Mission. Robespierre must, none the less, bear the largest share of responsibility for the acts of the Committee of which he was the most important member, since it seems certain that he could have blocked any measure by a firm resistance.

He lived simply, in the house of Duplay, a well-to-do carpenter and joiner of the rue Saint-Honoré. The Duplays, a very worthy family, were his friends and adorers; the eldest daughter was his fiancée, the youngest was married to his friend, the deputy Lebas. Robespierre, in his rare leisure, would read poetry to the ladies or take them out for walks, and a small, admiring circle, was always ready to gather round him. All this helped to isolate a man nervous by nature, though not cowardly, prone to believe the worst of

* The three were sometimes called 'the Triumvirate'.

others, and obsessed by his own personality. He described himself as "one of the most suspicious and melancholy patriots" of the Revolution, and this is the key to much of his conduct. There were two sides to Robespierre, the practical man and the dreamer, and on both sides his genuine, if suspicious, patriotism made him uneasy. As a practical man he saw that in the Comité de Salut public lay the one hope of the Republic which he loved. But the Committee's existence was precarious, an attack might overthrow it; therefore he resented fiercely any attack or criticism, fearing lest it might lead to that disaster. As a dreamer, with visions of the brotherhood of man and convictions that the rights of property should be limited by the obligation not to injure others, he had aspirations after an ideal Republic, which were shared by Couthon and Saint-Just. When he looked around him, he saw a Republic, disorderly, corrupt, immoral, irreverent, far from ideal, and being no statesman, he imagined that the way to improve it was to remove forcibly all unworthy members. The enemies of his ideal Republic soon became, in his eyes, the enemies of France; he imagined them conspiring with the foreigner to ruin and degrade her. It was fatally easy to conspire with foreigners, as they abounded in Paris, attracted there by the Revolution. The Girondins had encouraged them; Robespierre, and with good cause, hated and suspected them.

Speaking in the Jacobins' a little later (8th Jan. 1794), he divided the enemies of the Republic into the *ultra-* and the *citra-* revolutionaries; those who went beyond the true line of revolutionary conduct into excesses which made the Revolution odious, and those who fell short of it into a 'moderatism' which belied the rule of Terror and encouraged the aristocrats. Hébert was the type of the one; Danton, who was known to regret in private the execution of the Girondins, necessarily became the type of the other. Robespierre did not yet distrust Danton, far from it, as he showed on December 3rd. The Jacobins were undergoing a 'scrutiny', in the course of which each member in turn had to prove his soundness or be expelled. Danton was attacked;* he defended himself to the satisfaction of the Club, and he was aided by Robespierre, who spoke in the strongest terms of his patriotism, his domestic virtues and his probity.

A series of complicated events weakened the position of both *ultra* and *citra,* and delivered them into the hands of Robespierre and the Committee. We will

---

* Danton was suspected of having amassed a fortune corruptly. He was a good man of business and bought property at Arcis-sur-Aube. His means have been minutely inquired into by modern historians, and it appears that he left rather more property than can be accounted for considering his income. It seems probable that he may have made some money by speculation; a practice abhorrent to conscientious revolutionaries.

mention first, though it did not come first in point of time, a blow for the *ultra*. Chaumette discredited himself. He was doing real services in the Commune: reforms in hospitals, the cruel flogging customary in schools abolished, efforts to purify the streets of Paris, for though he could not be called a moral man, he was great on morality. But he could not forget the days when the Commune had rivalled the Convention, and his ambition lured him into a false step.

The Revolutionary Committees in the Sections were arresting suspects freely, and patriots who displeased them found themselves no safer than royalists. No reasons had to be given for arresting, so that a man often did not know why he was put in prison, and such arbitrary arrests were a method of instilling terror approved of by Robespierre. Persecuted patriots and their friends were making loud complaints, and Chaumette saw a chance of asserting the power of the Commune beneficently. On December 1st he summoned the Revolutionary Committees to discuss a scheme of combined action with the Commune. This summons was outside the powers of the Commune, it also showed 'moderation', and the Convention annulled it (4th Dec.). Chaumette ate humble pie and was forgiven; but he had incurred the displeasure of the Sections, and was expelled from the Cordeliers' Club. He was never the same man again. Abjectly anxious now to keep within the law, he was reduced to denouncing the iniquities of shows of wild beasts, and dancing mountebanks. With the organization of the Revolutionary Government (4th Dec.), he had become a mere 'national agent', and the Commune was obliged to confine its acts to its own boundaries.

A short time before this, a scandal had cast discredit on some so-called 'moderates'. The Convention tried to repress financial speculation as injurious to the funds of the Republic, and certain well-known deputies, who passed for financial experts, Chabot, Julien of Toulouse and Delaunay of Angers, were wont to edify their colleagues by denouncing speculators, bankers, and companies, and threatening stern measures.

In reality these deputies were using their position to make money over the rise and fall of stocks, and, almost certainly, to obtain bribes. They were associated in their operations with some shady financiers, one of whom, the baron de Batz, was a royalist conspirator. They finally carried their daring so far as to alter the text of a bill, which the Convention had voted for the winding up of a lucrative concern called the India Company (8th Oct.); the falsified bill was published as a law, and no one noticed that it had been tampered with. But Chabot soon began to feel uneasy. Both he and Julien had been reproached with leniency to prisoners, and Chabot had lost his popularity by making a mercenary marriage with a young girl, sister of two Austrian Jew adventurers who called themselves Frey, were reputed rich, and professed hot patriotism. Therefore when, on November 9th, Osselin, who had drawn up the cruel laws on emigration, was himself impeached, without a hearing, for protecting a returned émigrée marquise, Chabot was alarmed; and on the following day he made the bold motion, that no deputy should be impeached until he had been heard in his own defence by the Convention. Basire, who was notoriously inclined to leniency, supported Chabot, exclaiming: "When is this butchery of deputies going to stop?" Thuriot half-supported, and the motion passed. It roused a resentful outcry, and before the Jacobins had time to petition against 'moderatism', the Convention, at Barère's instance, repealed the decree (12th Nov.). Chabot, Basire and Thuriot recanted miserably; it was a triumph for the Terrorists.

Chabot, now thoroughly frightened, came to the Comité de Sûreté générale on November 14th, with a packet of money and a confession. He spoke of a great plot, a 'Foreigners' Conspiracy' to corrupt the Convention. He divulged the machinations of Delaunay and his associates; he told how they had offered him a share in the spoils of the India Company; how they had given him the packet of money to corrupt Fabre d'Églantine, another deputy much concerned with

finance, whose signature to the falsified bill was necessary. He, Chabot, virtuous and patriotic, had not
offered the bribe, and had only appeared to fall in with
the schemes of the tempters that he might fathom the
plot. Basire confirmed Chabot; he had known about
Delaunay's corruption and had been offered his share
of the spoils; ignorant of finance, he had accepted
Chabot's version of a plot to be fathomed, and had
weakly and culpably held his tongue, but was not
otherwise guilty. The Committees had already heard
of the 'Foreigners' Conspiracy' from Fabre d'Églantine,
who had denounced it to a select circle in the autumn,
mentioning Chabot as one of the conspirators.* They
arrested Chabot, Basire and Delaunay on November
17th, Julien and de Batz escaped. As usual, no trouble
was taken to get to the bottom of the affair. The
Committees might well have suspected Fabre d'Églantine, who had signed the falsified decree although it
did not embody an amendment which he had himself
got voted; but he gave explanations which satisfied
them, and notwithstanding his bad reputation, his word
was believed. He did the Committees a service, on
December 17th, by denouncing Vincent, Ronsin (back
from Lyon), and Stanislas Maillard, for their intolerable
bullying of the people and unconcealed disdain of the

---

* This is the first appearance of 'the Foreigners' Conspiracy' in which
so many innocent people found themselves involved later.

Committee, to such effect that the Convention ordered the arrest of all three.

Danton had nothing to do with Chabot, who had sought Robespierre's advice before making his confession; and his strong position as a pillar of the Republic was further strengthened by his irreproachable conduct after his return; he supported the Committee loyally and consistently, and he did not put himself forward. Yet his position was being undermined by the conduct of three of his friends: Philippeaux, Camille Desmoulins and Fabre d'Églantine. The first two came into the field as champions of 'moderation.'

Philippeaux had returned from his mission to la Vendée, in October, boiling with indignation at the misdeeds and incapacity of Rossignol and Ronsin. He laid the facts before the Committee, and the Committee refused to act; they had but one explanation of any criticism of Rossignol: jealousy. Philippeaux, they said, had imbibed the views of dismissed aristocrat Generals, jealous of the brave sansculotte. Philippeaux, by denouncing Rossignol, incurred the deadly enmity of the Hébertists; he was insulted, derided by Hébert as 'Philippotin', and attacked in the Cordeliers' Club, but he refused to be silenced. At the beginning of December, when he was quite sure that the Committee would do nothing, he tried to force their hand by publishing the facts in a pamphlet; and when that failed to move them, he published other pamphlets. Unfortunately he was a journalist accustomed to the use of strong language, and though his statements were true, he put them in such an exaggerated way that they did not read like truth; he also, most unwisely, attacked the Committee as accomplices of Rossignol and Ronsin.

Hébert and other enemies carried the feud into the Jacobins' and attacked Philippeaux there. It was the time of the Jacobin 'Scrutiny', each sitting of the Club was a scene of denunciation, and Philippeaux found it hard to get a hearing, though Robespierre joined Danton in begging for quiet. Danton did not speak strongly in his friend's defence; he agreed with Robespierre that the attack on the Committee was serious, and said that he kept an open mind. A malicious and untruthful report on the affair was made in the Club by Collot, and Philippeaux was taunted with cowardice and shouted down when he tried to answer (5th Jan. 1794). This sickened him of the Jacobins and he turned to the Convention, making, on January 7th, formal accusations under twenty-six heads against Rossignol and Ronsin. His old enemy, Choudieu, declared at once that there was not a word of truth in his statements, and reported on the affair a month later, with the result that everything was referred to the incriminated Committee (Feb. 6th).

A second friend of Danton's, Camille Desmoulins,

was meanwhile making, not an attack on the Committee, but a criticism of the methods of the Terror. Camille, flighty and unstable, had joined in the cruelties of the Revolution; but when blood began to flow, his heart smote him. He had a special subject of remorse, because he had attacked the Girondins in two telling pamphlets, which had, he believed, inspired the accusations made against them, and, urged by conscience, he resolved to strike a blow for freedom. He had everything to lose, a happy home, a wife loving and beloved, when he took up his pen to write his last and most famous journal, *Le vieux Cordelier.** The Press was nominally free, but no paper dared to speak out; it was as much as a writer's life was worth.

Camille turned for help to his old school friend Robespierre. Robespierre, sympathetic and patronizing, looked over the first two numbers before they appeared; there was nothing in them to offend him, and the second contained an attack on Cloots and Chaumette which enabled him to get Cloots expelled from the Jacobins' (12th Dec.). The third number came out without Robespierre's sanction. In it, under the disguise of a description of the bad old times of the Roman Empire,

* The name, 'the *old* Cordelier', was an appeal from the Cordeliers' Club ruled by the Hébertists, to the days when the Théatre-Français Section had been the Cordeliers' District, with Danton and Camille prominent members of the local Assembly.

translated from Tacitus – times when every action, every quality, speech or silence, riches or poverty, brought men under suspicion – Camille presented a picture of the reign of Terror, the word 'suspect' recurring like a refrain. It would be difficult to exaggerate the impression made by the daring of this number, this voice among the dumb. As if this were not enough, Camille took up Philippeaux; he went about asking every one: "Have you read Philippeaux?" Camille's outspokenness, so his enemies said, encouraged the aristocrats to raise their heads again. They cited, as a proof, that two or three days after his No. 3 appeared, a large flock of women came to the Convention, imploring, with tears and cries, the release of their imprisoned relatives, whom they declared to be innocent (20th Dec.). The President, Voulland, a member of the Comité de Sûreté générale, answered them harshly, and Robespierre used cruel words; none the less he obtained a decree for what Camille called a 'Committee of Justice'; a Commission appointed to inquire into prisoners' cases and to report to the Government Committees, which would then release the innocent. This was a step in the right direction. Immediately after, appeared a yet more audacious number of *Le vieux Cordelier*, with a suggestion that a 'Committee of Clemency' should be appointed, and a pathetic appeal to Camille's dear and admired Robespierre to remember that 'love is stronger and more durable than fear'. Clemency! To the Terrorists the very name meant treason, and the huge sale of Camille's paper showed how dangerous he had grown. Already he had been described in the Jacobins' as 'very close to the guillotine'; he fell into deeper disgrace. Representatives on Mission wrote to protest; Barère denounced *Le vieux Cordelier* in the Convention, and Billaud, in spite of Robespierre, carried the repeal of the decree for the 'Committee of Justice' (Dec. 26th).

Camille's next number contained an attack on Hébert, so cutting that it drove Hébert to the tribune of the Jacobins' almost beside himself with rage (5th Jan. 1794). Camille was doing Robespierre's work here, added to which his journal was always full of praises of the Revolution, and Robespierre, though contemptuous, did not abandon him. When Camille was called upon to defend himself in the Jacobins' (7th Jan.) and professed that he really did not know what to think about Philippeaux, Robespierre rallied him on a love of the Classics so great that he had taken for Philippics what were only 'Philippotics'. He defended Camille as a privileged person, childish but well-intentioned; the erring numbers, he said, must be burnt. Camille replied by quoting Rousseau: "Burning is no answer" – an unlucky rejoinder which angered Robespierre. All the same, when, after hearing the numbers read, the Jacobins expelled Camille (10th Jan.), Robespierre insisted on their revoking the sentence. He played, indeed, a fine part in these stormy sittings of the Club, trying continually to turn the Jacobins' attention from personal quarrels to political questions. He forced them at last to discuss 'the crimes of the British Government' – and the attendance fell off.

Danton was friendly to Philippeaux, and, though he said nothing, was believed to be encouraging Camille. The third blow which fell on him was of a different kind and came through a friend who had never shown mercy: Fabre d'Églantine. One evening, in the Jacobins', Robespierre suddenly denounced, in a vague and terrific way, Fabre d'Églantine, "the man with the eyeglasses for ever in his hand," and four days later Fabre was arrested (Jan. 12th). For Delaunay's papers had been examined at last, and they did not bear out the explanations which Fabre had given. The business was extremely intricate and Fabre's guilt was not completely proved, but less suspicious men than the Committee might well feel convinced of it. Amar reported the arrest to the Convention with a confused account of the affair. Danton did not venture a defence of his friend, but moved that the accused should be heard at the Bar. This was prevented by Billaud and by Vadier, a heartless, sarcastic old man, member of the Comité de Sûreté générale. And when Danton pressed for a speedy report, Billaud threatened him:

"Woe to him who sat beside Fabre d'Églantine and is still his dupe!" It was, perhaps, from this moment that Billaud began to say to the startled Robespierre, in the privacy of the Committee, that Danton must be removed. Robespierre, at first, would not hear of it, but Billaud continued to press him.

There came a lull in the daily rush of events. On February 2nd Vincent and Ronsin were released; certain Sections had petitioned in their favour, and Danton pleaded for them, urging that both they and Philippeaux meant well. Danton would have had all republicans friends; he had good words even for Hébert.

On February 4th the Convention abolished slavery in the Colonies, a decree which was received with sincere rejoicing and celebrated by a fête.

In the middle of February, Robespierre and Couthon both fell ill, and it was Saint-Just who carried through a decree, doubtless inspired by Robespierre, giving the Comité de Sûreté générale power to release imprisoned patriots who could render a good account of their conduct since May 1st 1789. The enemies of the Revolution were to be kept in prison till peace, and then banished for ever; their property was to be sequestrated for the benefit of the Republic (26th Feb.)

Robespierre's illness marks the end of a period in his life. Hitherto he had been a Terrorist who kept a measure in terrorism; when he arose from his sick-bed he was a changed man; he had decided within his mind that he would abandon Danton, having convinced himself that Danton was a conspirator. No reasons can be given for this change in his opinion of Danton, beyond those we have already indicated, and they seem inadequate. Danton, who could move the people and dominate the Convention, was Robespierre's only rival and, perhaps unknown to himself, jealousy must have been working in his mind; the jealousy of the fanatic who believed he had a mission to purify the Republic and make it strong in righteousness. Danton stood in the way. What place could there be in Robespierre's ideal Republic for a man like Danton, jovial and sometimes coarse, opportunist, lenient, tolerant of evil-doers and accused by his enemies of corruption? Robespierre gave way to the temptation of believing evil of Danton.

Stories are told about this change, long conversations are reported; but all that seems to be known for certain is; that there was a growing coolness between the two men, due to Danton's disapproval of the Terror and wish to mitigate or end it, while Robespierre wished it to go on; that friends tried to bring them together; that they met for the last time, just before Robespierre consented to abandon Danton, at dinner in the house of a mutual friend, some miles out of Paris, and probably drove back together; the date of this meeting can only be inferred.

It was during Robespierre's illness that the Hébertists made their great false step. Vincent and Ronsin had come out of their prisons as insolent as ever; they had been holding receptions there, and feasting, and swaggering; and they had made lists of prisoners whom they proposed to release. The Jacobins refused to admit Vincent as a member, and the Hébertists concentrated their energies in the Cordeliers' Club. Part of their plan was to keep the people agitated by making the most of the scarcity of food, and as, at the moment, there was another food crisis, it was easy to spread alarm. Seditious writings were circulated in manuscript, and the Marat Section, of which Momoro was President, came in a body to the Commune one day (6th March), to denounce a plot to starve Paris. The speeches in the Cordeliers' had been growing more and more violent, and finally, on March 4th, the table of the Rights of Man which stood in their hall was solemnly veiled in black crape, in sign that those rights were being denied to the people. Then Vincent and Hébert surpassed themselves in denunciations; Carrier, back from Nantes,* remarked how sadly the Revolution

* Carrier was recalled on 8th February, on the representations of Jullien, a courageous boy of nineteen, protégé of Robespierre and special agent of the Committee in the West. Jullien went to Nantes to investigate, had a narrow escape from Carrier's vengeance, and wrote the Committee such a report that they recalled Carrier – politely and without censure.

had deteriorated with all this pity for the condemned, and demanded a "sacred insurrection", and Hébert at length cast prudence to the winds. Egged on by Momoro and Vincent, who urged him to speak out and told him that *Pere Duchesne* was dead – that journal having been comparatively tame of late – he plucked up courage enough to denounce Robespierre, and cried that an insurrection was necessary, and that the Cordeliers would not be the last to give the signal. Whereat the odious Vincent, seeing faces lengthen with fright, walked round, to 'unmask intriguers.'

When the Jacobins heard of this sitting they were indignant. Collot, however, always friendly to the Hébertists, engineered a reconciliation and took round a deputation to remonstrate (7th March). The Cordeliers, already repenting of their rashness, swore to remain united with the Jacobins, the crape veil was torn, and Hébert protested that the sitting had been falsely reported, and that 'insurrection' meant a closer union to obtain justice on traitors. The Jacobins received a deputation from the Cordeliers, and the reconciliation was complete. In the next two meetings of the Cordeliers, while Vincent continued to howl for blood, quite unconcerned, Hébert varied denunciations with assertions that the fatal sitting had meant nothing.

So the days slipped by till March 13th. On that day

Saint-Just reported in the Convention on a new manifestation of the 'Foreigners' Conspiracy'; the foreigner was trying to starve the people by manoeuvring to make food scarce and then laying the blame on the Convention; he was using, for this purpose, discredited men who would not shrink from desperate measures. Saint-Just touched, in passing, on the 'faction of the indulgent', who wished to save criminals, explaining it as another branch of the same great plot. That evening Robespierre and Couthon, now recovered, appeared in the Jacobins', and at night Hébert, Vincent, Ronsin, and Momoro were arrested.

Two days after, Hérault was arrested, together with another deputy, Simond, on an empty pretext of a visit to an imprisoned emigre. Hérault had become distasteful to his colleagues of the Comité de Salut public; he was a noble; he was also a libertine who led an unedifying life, and he was friends with a foreign intriguer allied to the Hébertists, named Proly. The Committee suspected Hérault, on very flimsy grounds, of betraying Government secrets to foreigners. Simond, formerly prominent in the Jacobins', had been a great denouncer. On 17th March Chaumette was arrested.

The arrest of the Hébertists was a risk, as no one knew how the people would take it; they took it quietly and believed all they were told about the new conspiracy. Congratulations began to pour into the Convention on the 'unmasking' of yet more traitors. Danton, too, gave the Committee his support in a fine speech (19th March). It was his last triumph.

The trial of the Hébertists began on the 21st March (1 Germinal). Twenty prisoners appeared; the majority were Hébertists: Hébert, Ronsin, Vincent, Momoro, Proly, and other adherents; but Anacharsis Cloots was merely a foreigner and an atheist, two others were concerned in a separate and crazy plot, and there was an old General who had repeated a rumour that the Cordeliers intended to set up Pache as a 'Grand Judge' by way of a dictator. Hébert, who occupied the armchair, was visibly broken, and it is said that his last night was troubled by terrific dreams; his friends showed no signs either of remorse or fear. All the accused but one man were condemned on the 4th Germinal (24th March), and executed the same evening. The crowds were bigger than ever, but the troops that Hanriot had provided were not needed, for the people seemed pleased at the execution.* Two days later, Ronsin's 'Revolutionary Army' was disbanded.

The ease with which the Committees, contrary to expectation, had disposed of the Hébertists, encouraged

---

* In consequence of complaints from the neighbourhood that the Madeleine Cemetery was getting overcrowded, the place of burial for the guillotined was moved to a cemetery in a corner of the Parc Monceaux, further north. (25th March.)

them to make their next and far more dangerous move. Hints had been thrown out. On the very day of Danton's last triumph, Barère had announced a report from Saint-Just on the whole conspiracy, declaring at the same time, that the Committee would never allow one faction to raise itself on the ruins of another. After the first day of Hébert's trial, Robespierre, in the Jacobins', had spoken darkly of a new faction, to be exposed when the time was ripe, and promised that the Committee would either save the people or perish. During the next day's sitting of the Convention (22nd March), in an address to the People, written by Barère, Justice and Probity were ostentatiously placed 'on the order of the day'. Danton's friends knew that he was in peril and warned him. He might have saved himself by an attack on the Committee, but he was too patriotic to make it; "better be guillotined than guillotine", as he said. Besides, a kind of lethargy seemed to have fallen on him of late, and even now he refused to believe in the possibility of an arrest. "They would not dare," he repeated, and when urged to fly; "Fly!" he cried, "Does one take one's country with one on the sole of one's foot?"

On the 10th Germinal (30th March) the Committees decided on the arrest. Robert Lindet refused to sign the order; Saint-André, who admired Danton and might have defended him, was absent on a Mission, as was Prieur de la Marne. Carnot thought it a pity, but he signed, and so did all the rest, except two members of the Comité de Sûreté générale. During the night, Danton, Lacroix, Desmoulins, and Philippeaux were arrested and taken to the Luxembourg, a palace used as a prison. When the agents of the Committees arrived, Danton was sitting up by his fireside waiting, and sometimes poking the fire moodily. Camille, who could not believe that Robespierre would forsake him, was correcting the proofs of a new number of his paper, containing his political creed: "I believe that Liberty is Justice . . . I believe that Liberty is Humanity."

Robespierre, the trusted friend, had been priming Saint-Just with notes, and a report was ready, venomous, perfidious; blackening the characters of Danton and Camille, putting a treasonous complexion on their actions. Saint-Just was vindictive; it is probable that he had never forgiven Camille for describing him in a pamphlet as 'carrying his head as if it were the Holy Sacrament'.

In the morning the arrest was reported to the Convention; the news came like a thunder-clap. Danton had many friends in the Assembly, but only one, the butcher Legendre, was bold enough to speak in his defence, protesting in simple but eloquent words his belief in Danton's probity, and demanding that the accused should be heard at the Bar. The President,

Tallien, a Dantonist, refused to let Legendre be interrupted, the motion was well received. The Committees saw themselves on the brink of ruin; if Danton were once allowed to speak, all was lost. Robespierre appeared in the tribune; he appealed to patriotism – no idols! no privileges! Neither Brissot, nor Chabot, nor Fabre d'Églantine had been heard at the Bar; the Convention must be great enough to break the rotten idol, Danton, lest he should crush France. He spoke of his own services; he too had sacrificed his friends, one after the other. Legendre collapsed. Barère, hearing murmurs round him of the dictatorship of the Committee, insisted that this was ridiculous, since the Committee was renewed monthly; Saint-Just read his report with calm conviction, and the Convention impeached the four deputies unanimously, for complicity with Orléans, Dumouriez, Fabre d'Églantine, and the enemies of the Republic.

The trial began on April 5th (13 Germinal) with fourteen prisoners, one of whom was Hérault. It was Robespierre's policy to discredit Danton, and in the Convention he had laid stress on his friendship with Fabre d'Églantine and Lacroix, for Lacroix was not respected, and had been accused of peculation during his mission to Belgium; true, he had denied it, and it was never proved. In pursuance of this policy, and with the deliberate intention of prejudicing Danton and his friends in the eyes of the public, Danton, Camille, Philippeaux, and Lacroix were tried with the men arrested for the India Company affair; Chabot, Basire, Delaunay, Chabot's two brothers-in-law, an ill-famed Army contractor, two foreigners, and Fabre, now weak with illness, who occupied the arm-chair as principal prisoner. Chabot had taken poison in prison, but, repenting, had called for help, and survived to be tried. He was not all evil, and when he had thought himself dying his mind was full of Basire: "Oh! poor Basire! What have *you* done?" he reiterated.

The prisoners were asked their name, age, and residence. Camille answered: "I am the same age as the sans-culotte Jesus"; Danton: "My residence will soon be in nothingness; as for my name, you will find it in the Pantheon of History." On the second day, General Westermann, from la Vendée, took his place beside the accused, and so, on the third, did Lhuillier, former 'procureur' of the Paris Department. Only one witness was heard, Cambon, whose evidence was favourable to Danton and Lacroix; the rest of the trial was occupied in reading the impeachments and in dialogues between the President and the accused. On the second day Danton, now thoroughly roused, got his chance, and defended himself with all the warmth of his picturesque eloquence. He grew angry when accused of having sold himself, and when the President rebuked him, saying that 'innocence was always calm', he burst out: "*I* sold! A man of my stamp is not to be bought!" His defence was making an impression, and some of the audience were clapping. Fouquier and Herman consulted together, they suspended Danton's defence on the pretext that his voice needed rest, and he was never allowed to continue it. On the third day (15 Germinal) Lacroix began to demand insistently that the witnesses for the defence, a number of deputies, should be called; other prisoners joined in, and several of them were defending themselves boldly and effectively. Fouquier and Herman wrote in haste to the Committee; the prisoners, they said, were raising such a storm, in demanding the calling of their witnesses, that the course of justice was interrupted; and this demand could not be legally refused without a decree. Saint-Just took the letter to the Convention; he did not read it, but declared that the prisoners were in open revolt – a sure proof of their guilt; that the Convention was in danger; that General Dillon, prisoner in the Luxembourg and a friend of Camille's, had just confessed that Lucile Desmoulins, Camille's devoted wife, had been paid "to stir up a movement to assassinate patriots and the Revolutionary Tribunal".*

* This is the first appearance of 'the Prison Conspiracy', supposed to be a part of the 'Foreigners' Conspiracy'. The two became stock accusations in the Revolutionary Tribunal.

He asked for a decree, that prisoners accused of conspiracy who resisted or insulted national Justice, should be removed from the Court. Billaud then had a letter read containing the deposition of one Laflotte, a prisoner in the Luxembourg, which described the new 'Prison Conspiracy'. The Convention voted Saint Just's motion.

The Comité de Sûreté générale was nervous about the trial. David, the painter, who was a member, hung about the Tribunal, and Vadier, who had said of Danton: "We must empty this stuffed turbot", was listening in a concealed nook. Amar and Voulland now entered with the decree. "Here is something to make you easy," said Amar, and Fouquier replied: "It was high time." The decree was read, and after a painful scene, the Court rose. On the 16th Germinal (April 5th), the prisoners began once more to demand their witnesses. It was the fourth day of the trial; Herman asked the jury whether they had heard enough, and the jury, after retiring to deliberate, answered that they had. Then the prisoners, knowing that all was over, gave vent to their rage and their despair; it is traditional that the voice of Danton in his wrath was heard across the river. The new decree was put in force, they were removed, and once more the jury retired. In the absence of the prisoners, the verdict was given and sentence pronounced; all but Lhuillier were condemned. "This time last year," said Danton in the Conciergerie, "I had the Revolutionary Tribunal instituted; but I ask pardon for it of God and of men."

At five o'clock the prisoners were taken to execution in three carts. Hérault was dignified; Danton, sad at times and at times disdainful, kept always his commanding air. Camille, excitable and vivacious to the end, yet proud of what he had done, held in his bound hands a lock of Lucile's hair; the crowds looked on, stupefied and mournful. The sun was setting in clouds when the scaffold was reached; Spring was early that year and a lilac bush on the Terrace of the Tuileries Gardens overlooking the guillotine, was in full leaf. The last to die was Danton; he murmured once, while he was waiting: "Oh! my wife, my beloved, I shall see thee again no more!" then checking himself: "Come Danton, no weakness!" He stood erect on the gory scaffold, lit up by the last rays of the sinking sun, and faced the executioner with a command: "You will show my head to the people; it is worth it."*

A third four days' trial, a supplement to the other two, followed. In an 'amalgam' of twenty-six persons, Chaumette and Gobel, once Bishop of Paris, stood side by side with Hébert's widow and other Hébertists; with General Dillon, the deputy Simond and Lucile

* These last savings of Danton are traditional.

Desmoulins, accused of taking part in the 'Prison Conspiracy'; with other unconnected prisoners, among whom were two Generals. Nineteen were condemned on the 24th Germinal (13th April) and executed the same evening. Lucile, young, fair, and innocent, was happy in the thought of rejoining her beloved Camille; the two widows, whose husbands had been enemies, had made friends in prison, and kissed each other before they mounted the scaffold. Gobel died as a penitent and Chaumette as a stoic.

The Convention invariably received congratulations from all over France on the discovery of each successive 'conspiracy'. It is noteworthy that the congratulations on the fall of Danton were not so numerous, and that hardly one came from Paris.

X

THE REIGN OF TERROR

III. Thermidor 6 April – 27 July 1794

With the death of Danton, the Terror entered on a new phase. The last hope of resisting it had been crushed; no one dared to criticize the Government, even kindly, and the editors of newspapers thought it safest to chronicle events without comments. It would be an error to attribute this acquiescence solely to fear. The great mass of Frenchmen endured what a contemporary historian* calls "this slavery, terrible but voluntary" because they believed that the existing Government could lead France to victory and safety, and saw no alternative but defeat. As the same historian continues: "They preferred the executioner's axe to the sword of hostile despots."

* Toulongeon, a 'Constituent' and a moderate man, who was, at the time, living in retirement. He says also: 'It is wrong to degrade a nation by imputing to it low motives and servile fear.'

Robespierre and the Comité de Salut public, having cleared enemies and rivals out of the way, began their work of regenerating the Republic. On the morrow of Danton's execution, Couthon promised reports on five subjects: the purification of public morality, the moral and political influence of the revolutionary action of the Government, the present object of the War, the functions of Representatives on Mission, and a proposed fête, dedicated to the Eternal.

The Government was strengthened by a reform of the Paris Commune. Chaumette had been succeeded by a friend of Robespierre's, Payan, an able man, given to long harangues.* In May, Pache was arrested, and the Committee appointed as Mayor another adherent of Robespierre's, Lescot-Fleuriot, one of Fouquier-Tinville's assistants. Certain obnoxious members were removed and their places were filled by nominees of the Committee. The Commune, with little to do, reduced the number of its sittings, and became a docile instrument in the Committee's hands. Government had also been strengthened by the abolition of the six Ministries (1st April), and the establishment, instead, of twelve 'executive commissions' to do the Ministers' work, appointed by the Committee (with the sanction of the Convention) and directly subordinate to it.

---

* In colloquial language, where Chaumette had 'gassed', Payan 'jawed'.

When Saint-Just made the first of the promised reports he produced a 'General Police law' which was finally adopted on April 16th. By this law all former nobles, as well as alien enemies, were forbidden to live in Paris and in fortified or coast towns, on pain of outlawry; they were excluded from popular societies and from the meetings of Communes and Sections. Some exceptions were made, and the Committee could 'requisition' any one whose talents were useful to the Republic.

Two other provisions of the law were meant to put an end to much local tyranny: Representatives on Mission were forbidden to delegate their powers, as they were in the habit of doing, and the power of requisitioning food-stuffs was restricted to the proper authorities.

Robespierre's path had been prepared, and on May 7th, in a famous report, packed with epigrams on his enemies, he argued earnestly against the 'arid' doctrines of Atheism and Annihilation in favour of a belief in God and a future life. Such a belief, he said, had nothing to do with priests and superstitions, and was alone able to exalt a nation; and he proposed a decree which was immediately voted: "The French people recognizes the existence of the Supreme Being and the immortality of the Soul. It recognizes that the true worship of the Supreme Being is the performance of the duties of man." A few days later, the Committee ordered that the inscription 'Temple of Reason' on the front of places of worship should be erased, and its place taken by the first sentence of the decree.

There was more in the decree. Robespierre proposed, as part of the national education, a whole series of public fêtes for the *décadi*; a sort of republican Saints' days, on which people were to make holiday, meet together, rejoice, and celebrate the Human Race, the French Nation, the Benefactors of Humanity, the Martyrs of Liberty, Liberty and Equality, Friendship, Thrift, Filial Piety, the various ages of man, Posterity, and similar abstractions. First of all was to come, a month later, a fête in honour of the Supreme Being.

These fêtes were an important part of Robespierre's programme. He intended to elevate the nation by providing amusements, pure, patriotic, and educative, and by allowing no others. The Convention had suppressed lotteries, and the police waged war on gambling. A careful eye was kept on all performances in the theatres, and at the same time free theatrical performances of an improving nature were given to the poor. The Committee was aware of the value of beauty in national life; at a time when money was badly needed, they preserved the royal parks and palaces, Versailles, Saint-Cloud, &c., expressly for the people, instead of selling them (5th May); they encouraged the arts, and had a great scheme for beautifying the Tuileries palace and gardens, which was never realized, through want of means.

Robespierre's decree was received by the bulk of the nation with thankfulness and admiration. Congratulations came from the Commune, from the Jacobins, from every part of France, and religion became popular once more. The journalists filled their pages with prayers and hymns and creeds; the Paris hawkers cried 'Prayers to the Eternal' in the streets. The fête, with a programme arranged by David, was awaited with joyful hopes, and fixed for June 8th.

Meanwhile the Terror went on. The Revolutionary Tribunal was more active than ever, for under the new 'General Police law' all prisoners accused of treason were cent to Paris for trial, and in consequence of this law, all the revolutionary tribunals and commissions in the Departments were suppressed, unless expressly continued by the Comité de Salut public (8th May). Hardly a trial, henceforth, lasted more than a day. Herman had been promoted to a post in the new 'Executive Commission' of Police, where he still served the Tribunal by supplying victims, his place as President was taken by Dumas, who is generally considered the cruellest man connected with the Tribunal. Another cruel Judge, Coffinhal, was prominent in these days; like Dumas, he was a strong adherent of Robespierre.

The Committee kept a tight hand over the Tribunal, and Fouquier-Tinville reported to them every evening when his work was done.

We can only mention some, even of the best-known, victims of the Tribunal. First, those condemned for specific deeds in the past. On the 20th April (1 Floréal), twenty-five Judges and Presidents of the Parlements of Paris and Toulouse, for having protested against the suppression of the Parlements by the Constituent Assembly. On June 14th a second 'batch' (it was the word used) of thirty was executed; one of them was Fréteau, the distinguished 'Constituent', who had been tried and acquitted by the Tribunal a month before; he had joined in suppressing the Parlements. On the 24th April, thirty-five inhabitants of Verdun, some for taking part in the surrender of the town in 1792, some for welcoming the Prussian conquerors afterwards. Among these last were seven young ladies who had gone with older relatives to visit the Prussian camp: two sets of three sisters and a friend. Thirty-three were guillotined, and the two youngest girls, who were seventeen, were sentenced to exposure in the pillory and twenty years' imprisonment. On the 3rd May, thirteen officers and soldiers of the Battalions of the Petits-Pères and the Filles-Saint-Thomas, for loyalty to the King on the 10th August. On the 8th May, twenty-eight Farmers-General. The Farmers-General had earned an evil name in past days, but most, if not all, of these prisoners were honest men who had worked hard and had not made excessive profits. They had been long in captivity and had rendered their accounts, but no one attempted to understand their defence. One of them was Lavoisier, the renowned chemist, an irreparable loss to science and to France.* Three of their assistants were sent to be tried with them, by mistake, and were snatched from the Tribunal, just in time, by a special decree. On the 3rd June, twenty-seven prominent citizens of Sedan, for supporting Lafayette in August 1792. On the other hand, ten Jacobins of le Mans, tried for supporting Philippeaux, were acquitted on 30th April.

For vague 'conspiracy', there fell, on the 22nd April, a 'batch' of thirteen, including the aged Malesherbes, Louis XVI's intrepid counsel, with three of his family; two former Duchesses; the famous orators of the Constituent Assembly, Thouret and Le Chapelier, d'Eprémesnil, their opponent, and a fourth 'Constituent'. Thouret had written, in prison, a republican History of France for his young son. On May 10th there were twenty-five condemned: a prominent member of the Paris Commune, Malesherbes' sister, the Minister

* The story that Lavoisier asked for some days' respite to finish an experiment, and was answered: "The Republic has no need of chemists", appears to be an invention of Bishop Grégoire's.

Montmorin's widow and son, five members of the
Loménie family, other nobles, ladies, faithful servants,
and Madame Elisabeth, who died as she had lived,
noble, brave, and sweet to the end. She had given wise
rules of conduct to the orphan niece whom she was
leaving alone in the Temple Tower; for her nephew
she could do nothing. In January Simon had left him,
to resume his place in the Commune, and the
Commune, with the approval of the Comité de Salut
public, had decided that a Governor was unnecessary
and that the members on duty at the Temple could
do all that was wanted. They were ordered to hand
over the child to their successors, daily, in his own
room, and to keep a careful account of his state of
health. As these members used to visit the young
Princess, it seems probable that they fulfilled their
duties to her brother, and that the story that his door
was walled up is not true. At the best, 'little Capet',
still under nine, was left much alone, with no teaching
and no outdoor air, in a darkened room which he was
expected to clean out himself; and the once lively and
promising child, depraved by Simon, sank slowly
towards the grave in dirt, disease, and apathy.

While Paris suffered, the Representatives on Mission
continued to spread the Terror over France: terror in
the Somme, where, a little earlier, André Dumont had
set out to extirpate Christianity, and threw numbers

of the inhabitants into prison. But though he raged and raved and wrote bloodthirsty letters to show his zeal, he had hardly any one executed.

Terror in Arras, where Lebon, an ex-priest, who used to watch executions and had horrible touches of joviality in his cruelty, superintended a revolutionary tribunal. This was one of the few kept on by the Comité de Salut public when they were suppressed, and Lebon established a branch of it in Cambrai. Complaints of Lebon's dark deeds reached the ears of the Committee and he was called to Paris to explain. Plausible and efficient, he secured the Committee's support, and returned to his tribunal in triumph. Yet the Committee remained uneasy, and in July the tribunal was suppressed and he was ordered to collect its records for examination.

Terror in Bordeaux. Here, through the winter, Tallien and Ysabeau had been the chief agents in carrying out the work of vengeance. They began fiercely; they changed the name of the Department from Gironde to Bec-d'Ambès, filled the prisons, set up a so-called 'military' commission of seven judges by way of revolutionary tribunal, and published an order that any person who pleaded for a prisoner should be treated as a suspect. By and by Tallien, who was young, handsome, and pleasure-loving, came under the spell of the beautiful Teresia Cabarrus, an aristocrat of Spanish birth, whom he afterwards married. She used her influence over him beneficently and saved many lives. The milder Ysabeau also loved pleasure and popularity, and as the military commission, known in the city as 'the seven deadly sins', was not unbribable, and often inflicted fines instead of condemning to death, the Terror waned. The demagogues of Bordeaux, balked of their prey, complained in Paris, and Tallien returned early in March to defend himself. Early in June, the Committee re-established the military commission, which had ceased sitting, with such a warning to do better, that it sprang into feverish activity. They also sent young Jullien, Robespierre's protégé, on a special mission to regenerate Bordeaux. The boy of nineteen, by a mandate from the Committee, dissolved the municipality of this great city and appointed a new one. He was not much concerned with the military commission, but was zealous in hunting out the fugitive Girondins concealed in the neighbourhood, whom Tallien had sought in vain. Guadet, Salle, Pétion, Buzot, and Barbaroux had for a long while been hidden by friends and relatives in the little town of Saint-Emilion – part of the time in cold, underground grottoes. Jullien's agents discovered Guadet and Salle in Guadet's father's house; they were taken to Bordeaux and executed there on June 19th, and six members of Guadet's family were executed in July. Barbaroux,

Pétion and Buzot, finding capture unavoidable, shot themselves in the fields; Barbaroux was found half-dead, taken to Bordeaux, and executed on June 25th. The bodies of the other two were found later, their faces partly eaten by dogs. So ended the Girondin leaders. The illustrious Condorcet was already dead; arrested as a suspect when wandering about in disguise, he had poisoned himself in prison on March 29th.

Terror in the ever-restless South. Barras and Fréron had been succeeded in Marseilles by Maignet, a friend of Couthon, much respected, popular, and a good administrator. Maignet had been blamed for leniency and was anxious to show his zeal. He received with dismay the news that all cases of treason were to be tried in Paris, for, as he wrote to Couthon, from Avignon to which he had moved, from twelve to fifteen thousand persons had been arrested for conspiracy in the Departments of Bouches-du-Rhone and Vaucluse, and it would take an army to convey them to the capital. At his suggestion, the Committee allowed him (10th May) to set up in Orange a 'popular commission' of five judges – a tribunal which became notorious for its severity. This was not all. The troublesome little town of Bédoin, in Vaucluse, cut down a tree of Liberty one night, and the citizens refused to give up the culprits. Maignet sent a revolutionary tribunal to the spot, and also orders that, after trial and execution of the guilty, the remaining inhabitants should be removed and their town burnt. These orders were carried out; sixty-five men and women were guillotined or shot, and on June 2nd the town was given to the flames. Both before and after the Terror, Maignet was a kindly man, as were many other Terrorists who, like him, were rendered inhuman by their fanatical zeal. The excuse they afterwards made, that fear of the guillotine drove them on, will not hold water, for the Committee did not persecute Representatives on Mission for leniency, and some of them carried out their stern errands without unnecessary cruelty. Their other excuse, that the Convention approved all their deeds, is valid. The Convention had been reduced to a pitiable condition, its function seemed to be to applaud what the Committees approved, pass the decrees they proposed, and cheer victories. Apart from this, business was petty and futile. The sitting on July 8th, for instance, was taken up with; (*a*) a report, addresses, and petitions, of no interest;(*b*) two offerings, one floral, from a gardener, one an allegorical picture by an old man; (*c*) a patriotic dialogue acted by two school-children.

While the Terror thus continued, the victories of the armies were rapidly taking away all the reasons which had brought it to pass. It is true that in la Vendée cruelty and ineptitude had once more stirred up rebellion.

Charette and some other chiefs were still in the field in lower Vendée; they met with a bad reverse in January 1794, when the Republicans took the Île de Noirmoutier and shot General d'Elbée whom they found there disabled from his old wound. La Rochejaquelein was killed in an obscure fight, early in January, but Stofflet soon gathered a band round him. Charette and Stofflet were both active, and towards the end of April they took an oath to support each other. The Chouans* had also to be reckoned with, lawless bands of smugglers across the Loire, who had been in insurrection for two years and had joined hands with the *Grande Armée* during its march to the north. Kléber had a plan for finishing with the Vendéens in a short time, but Kléber was thrust aside, and Turreau, the new Commander-in-Chief, was allowed to carry out his own plan. The devastation of la Vendée, ordered by the decree of 1st August 1793, had not yet been accomplished; Turreau resolved to do it systematically. He divided his Army into twenty columns, known, even at the time, as *colonnes infernales*, and sent them marching through the Vendéens' country, with orders to burn everything in the line of march, after removing food-stuffs and live stock, and to kill all who had taken part in the rebellion, men, women, and children. Some

* They got their name from the nickname of their original leader, Cottereau, who used as a signal the cry of an owl (Chouan).

Generals modified these orders – one who did his best to save the country was dismissed in consequence – but several carried them out with full rigour. Towns, villages, farms, mills, woods, were burnt. The column would bivouac for the night in a village, shoot the villagers in the morning, plunder, burn, and march on. Loyal villages were not spared. As to the loyal inhabitants, the Representatives on Mission tried to simplify the work of destruction by ordering their wholesale deportation, with the intimation that any who remained must expect to be shot. Thus the unhappy Vendéens of both sides were reduced to despair, and many rebels, sick of the war and ready to lay down their arms, saw nothing for it but to rejoin the bands of Stofflet and Charette.

Turreau's plan had never been expressly sanctioned by the Comité de Salut public, though they had allowed, and even supported it, because he promised to end the war in a fortnight. But when many fortnights had gone by and the war was no nearer ending, they realized at last that Turreau was almost as incapable as he was cruel, and removed him (13th May). Indeed, the eyes of the Committee were being gradually opened. Some months earlier, Billaud-Varenne, on a mission to Saint-Malo, had found Rossignol so stupid and so slack, that the Committee finally dismissed him with contumely (27th April). By mid-May, even Carnot had learnt that cruelty did not pay in la Vendée, and Lindet had perceived that it was madness to destroy a granary from which armies might be fed. The Committee changed its policy, and on May 21st invited the Vendéens to go back to their homes and families, lay down their arms, till the soil, gather in the harvest, and fear nothing; proclamations made later in la Vendée spoke of pardon for all who had been misled. The rebel armies replied aptly, that they had no longer homes and families to go to; nevertheless, under the auspices of the conciliatory General who had succeeded Turreau, the rebels in certain districts began to come in.

Let us glance at the foreign wars. If the Armies of the Alps and of Italy, which counted Bonaparte and Massena among their Generals, did not accomplish all that was expected of them, yet, by the end of July, they were holding important passes and menacing Turin. In the Eastern Pyrenees, General Dugommier drove the Spaniards off French soil and followed them into Catalonia; in the Western Pyrenees, General Muller invaded Guipuzcoa and captured Fontarabia and Saint-Sebastian at the beginning of August. Madrid trembled and the thoughts of the Spaniards turned towards peace.

At sea the Allies had the advantage. The British Fleet took Corsica, the French colony of Martinique, and part of Saint-Domingo, and blockaded French ports; and though Barère read out frequent lists of naval captures, Carnot began to fear famine. On June 1st ('the glorious first of June') a battle, hailed by both sides as a victory, took place between the British under Lord Howe and a French fleet escorting a large convoy. The French fleet was partially destroyed; the convoy escaped. When the extent of the French losses could no longer be concealed, Barère invented a story that the crew of the crippled *le Vengeur*, preferring death to surrender, had gone down into the deep with their ship, all flags flying. This was not true, but the inspiring legend became an article of faith, and a model of *le Vengeur* was hung up in the hall of the Convention.

On the north-eastern frontier, the jealousies and half-heartedness of Prussia and Austria once more made the task of the French Armies less difficult. A patriotic insurrection, under Kosciusko, had broken out in Poland; both the King of Prussia and the Emperor were intent on grabbing each his share of that country, and each wished to be able to move his armies eastwards. For this reason the King was anxious for peace and the Emperor not disinclined to it, and peace might perhaps have become possible, had not the Committee disregarded all approaches to negotiation which their agents in neutral countries indicated to them. The King of Prussia still kept his Army on the Rhine, because England and Holland were paying for it; the Emperor, more deeply involved, though he quitted his Army for Poland in June, could not leave his dominions in Belgium to be overrun by the French, and was obliged to continue the war with more or less vigour.

When the campaign opened, the Austrians still held three French border fortresses taken the previous Autumn: Condé, le Quesnoy, and Valenciennes; and Cobourg captured a fourth fortress, Landrecies, on 30th April, as a preliminary step to an invasion of France. Carnot, on his side, had resolved to strike a decisive blow in Belgium, and the Armies on the front were directed to operate in concert with Pichegru, who was commanding the Northern Army with Moreau as his second in command. Pichegru's object was the capture of Brussels; he won several actions, and on May 17th-18th Moreau, with inferior numbers, defeated Clerfayt before Turcoing. Yet it so happened that the campaign was decided by operations on the Sambre, undertaken at first as a demonstration or diversion. The Ardennes Army and a detachment of the Northern Army were together in the country between the Sambre and the Meuse; Kléber and Marceau were serving as Generals in these forces. In May came Saint-Just and Lebas on a mission.

Three times, egged on by Saint-Just, the two Armies crossed the Sambre; three times they were driven back by inferior Austrian forces; at the third trial they had begun to besiege Charleroi. Immediately after this third defeat, General Jourdan, who had been ordered by the Committee to march to their support with part of the Moselle Army, effected a junction and took command (3rd June). Jourdan himself did not succeed at first, and it was not till his second attempt – the fifth crossing of the Sambre and third siege – that he took Charleroi on June 25th, and defeated Cobourg on June 26th in the decisive battle of Fleurus.* The news of the victory was received with rapture in Paris, and by a decree Jourdan's gallant composite Army was renamed in gratitude 'the Sambre-et-Meuse' Army.

Marceau, who had fought with special valour, 'like a lion,' said Barère, became known as 'the lion' of this Army. Saint-Just, who had left the Army at the end of May, and had returned alone in June, on a fresh mission, was present at siege and battle, and greatly contributed to the success by his energetic measures. His haughty aloofness made him unpopular with the Generals, and he has been reproached for cruelty in restoring discipline; it does not appear, however, that he showed greater severity than would be considered necessary according to modern ideas. The victory of Fleurus, followed by others, opened the way to Brussels; the Austrians evacuated that city in haste,

---

* This battle is the first in which balloons were used for observation.

and detachments from the now united Armies of Pichegru and Jourdan entered Brussels on July 9th. Pichegru had already taken Ostend, on July 24th he took Antwerp. Belgium was won, the English and Dutch retreated into Holland, and early in August the Prussians were forced out of Trèves. Meanwhile General Scherer had been besieging the four border fortresses, the first of which he retook in July, the last at the end of August. It was a time of triumphs and Barère exaggerated them all; his lyric reports were called in jest 'Carmagnoles'.

We must now follow the course of events in Paris. In the early hours of May 23rd, sixteen days before the eagerly expected fête, a man named Admiral, after hanging about all the previous day in the hope of shooting Robespierre, lay in wait for Collot on the stairs of that deputy's flat, and shot at him twice, as he was returning, very late, from the Committee. The shots missed and Admiral was seized. This was alarming enough, but there was more to follow. Late on the evening of the same day, a quiet girl of nineteen, Cecile Renault, the daughter of a stationer, came to the Duplays' house and demanded to see Robespierre. She showed such contemptuous annoyance when told he was out, that the anxious Duplays had her arrested. When examined, this strange girl declared that she wished for a King, and that she had come to see

Robespierre because she 'wanted to know what a tyrant was like', but with no intention of harming him. Two small penknives were found in her pocket, and she had provided herself with a change of clothes, 'for prison', she said. Here was a plot indeed!

Barère in reporting (26th May), said that the two attempted assassinations were part of the great 'Foreigners' Conspiracy' engineered and financed by Pitt. He made the Convention pass a decree that, by way of reprisals, no English or Hanoverian prisoners should be taken. This insane decree, specially approved by Robespierre, was totally disregarded at the Front, where the Armies continued to carry on the war in the usual chivalrous manner. Robespierre and Collot received an ovation in the Jacobins' and ardent congratulations on their providential escape poured in from every quarter of the land.

The 20th Prairial (June 8th), the appointed day for the fête of the Supreme Being arrived. It was as lovely a summer's day as ever dawned, and with the dawn every one in Paris was up, decorating their house-fronts with green branches and tricolour flags, by order. By and by came the march of the Sections, gay with tricolour and white dresses and flowers and greenery, to the Tuileries Gardens, where each Section had its appointed place, for everything had been elaborately planned beforehand. It was not till midday that the

Convention appeared on a huge balcony constructed in front of the Palace, raised high on columns. Each deputy wore a tricolour sash and tricolour plumes in his hat, and carried a bouquet of flowers, fruit, and corn.* The neat figure of the President, Robespierre, clad in a coat of cornflower blue and nankin breeches, drew all eyes; he was radiant as he mounted a tribune in the balcony and gazed over the assembled multitude. He raised his hand, and there was a deep silence; he spoke, in harmonious and dignified words, of the objects for which they had come together, of the worship due to the Divinity, of patriotism and morality. Then the people, led by musicians, burst forth into a fine hymn with a simple tune, addressed to the Supreme Being, the 'Father of the Universe'; and when it was ended, Robespierre came down the balcony stairs, and with a blazing torch set fire to a formless and flimsy colossal statue of Atheism, inscribed 'the Foreigners' only Hope'; it flared up, disclosing a smaller and solider statue of Wisdom. After another fine speech from Robespierre, every one marched in procession to the Champ de Mars, where a huge Mountain, with rocks and grottoes complete, had been erected. The Mountain was speedily covered with selected representative parties from the Sections, of old and young together; at the

---

* The harvest was early and promising.

top stood the Convention, half way down were singers and orchestra. Incense smoked about the sacred hill and music resounded, ending with strophes to the air of the Marseillaise, in which all could join. The pageant concluded with a salvo of artillery.

Never was a fête more popular and more successful; yet, though Robespierre had been acclaimed by grateful multitudes, his heart, so light in the morning, was filled with wrath and gloom. On the balcony of the Tuileries, and again, on the march to the Champ de Mars, when he led the Convention and, by design or by accident, was left walking alone a few paces ahead of the foremost deputies, he had heard the deputies behind him muttering insults, taunts on his pre-eminence, blasphemies on the Supreme Being. There was red-haired Bourdon de l'Oise, an admirer of Danton, there was Lecointre of Versailles, fierce and independent men, both; there were other deputies, jealous, suspicious, scornful. Not yet was the way to the ideal Republic clear.

Two days later, on the 22nd Prairial (10th June), Couthon suddenly proposed to the startled Convention a terrible law for 'the perfecting of the Revolutionary Tribunal', which he had concocted with Robespierre. The preliminary examination of prisoners was suppressed. Official defenders were suppressed, for, said one article, "the law gives patriot jurymen, as defenders,

to calumniated patriots; it accords none to conspirators". Any proofs of guilt, proofs "material or moral",
that would satisfy the conscience of the jury would
suffice; it was no longer obligatory to call witnesses if
other evidence were forthcoming. Only seven jurymen
need sit. A long catalogue of actions which character-
ized 'enemies of the people' was given as a guide. The
only punishment the Tribunal could award was death.
The power to send conspirators for trial was vested
in the Convention, the two Government Committees,
Representatives on Mission, and the Public Prosecutor,
All laws in contradiction with the new law were
repealed.

Even the enslaved Convention sat aghast, and one
sturdy Montagnard cried that he would blow his brains
out if such a bill became law. Lecointre and Bourdon
de l'Oise demanded an adjournment, but Barère
declared that the bill was all in favour of patriots, and
Robespierre, armed with all his terrors, literally forced
the Convention to vote the whole law, article after
article. The next day, in the absence of the Committee,
the terrorized Convention took heart; the deputies
cared nothing for the wretched 'conspirators', but
perceived that if previous laws were repealed, deputies
could be sent to the Tribunal by the Committee without
being first impeached by the Convention. Bourdon de
l'Oise gave voice to the general feeling of insecurity,

and finally a decree put on record that the Convention had not meant, by the decree of the 22nd, to cede its inalienable and exclusive right of impeaching its own members. Further amendments were being voted the next day, when Couthon and Robespierre appeared, aggrieved and formidable. The Committee had been insulted by mistrust, said Couthon, they had never contemplated touching deputies; Bourdon, he sneered, talked as Pitt and Cobourg might. Robespierre, indignant and enigmatic, spoke of intriguers who wished to become party leaders. Bourdon protested, and Robespierre turned on him: "I did not name Bourdon; woe to him who names himself!" The bold Bourdon was silenced. Each deputy who had criticized the decree apologized and vowed that he meant no harm; all the amendments of the last two days were wiped out, and the law stood as originally voted. In this sitting Tallien was denounced by Robespierre for insulting agents of the Government, and when he explained that they were spying on him, Billaud called him an impudent liar.

The new law did little more than sanction what the Revolutionary Tribunal was already practising, for any evidence was admitted, and with the shortness of the trials the defence had become a mere farce. Yet even Fouquier-Tinville was shocked at the jury being cut down to seven, and remonstrated, nearly losing his place in consequence. There was no love lost between Robespierre and Fouquier.

Freed legally from all shackles, the Tribunal surpassed itself in activity, and whereas, up to the 23rd Prairial (11th June) 1,272 persons had been condemned to death, in the forty-seven days from June 11th to July 27th (inclusive) 1,366 were so condemned.

On June 9th, in consequence of complaints from the shopkeepers of the rue Saint-Honoré, the scaffold was moved to the place Saint-Antoine, by the ruins of the Bastille; on the 14th June it was moved further still, to a great square by the eastern gate of Paris, the 'Barrière du Trône renversé', now the place de la Nation. This made the journey of the condemned to the guillotine far longer. Their bodies were buried in eastern graveyards, nearly all in the little cemetery of Picpus.*

The lot of the prisoners grew harder. Food in Paris was scanty and bad, and as the long, hot summer went on, prison fare became worse and worse. The rule that all must feed alike was enforced, and in July common tables were set up. Communication with the outside world was cut off; visits of Police inspectors, to search for and confiscate knives, razors, scissors, jewellery, and assignats, vexed the prisoners, and the prospect

---

* As the ridiculous, though contemporary, statement is often made, that there was a tannery of human skins at Meudon, it had better be repeated that the bodies of the guillotined were all buried.

of the guillotine was daily more threatening. Yet they still kept up their courage, greeted the victories of the Republican armies with loyal enthusiasm, and went to death with the same gallant decorum, whatever their class or their age. Some were buoyed up by their religion, many by the belief that they were dying for their country, cowards caught courage from their fellow-sufferers. Members of the same family were often tried and executed together in these days, and found consolation in sharing the same fate. It was part of the policy of the Committee to keep republicans and aristocrats apart, lest they should learn sympathy; thus, when, in July, 'fraternal banquets' were instituted in the Sections, in which all citizens ate at common tables in the street, these banquets were discovered to be a 'conspiracy' and were stopped (16th July). In the prisons men of all ranks and opinions learnt at least tolerance, and often respect.

When Admiral and Cecile Renault were tried on the 29th Prairial (17th June), fifty-two others stood beside them. Admiral had known a man who knew the Baron de Batz, that arch-conspirator once denounced by Chabot as a leader in 'the Foreigners' Conspiracy', and some of the accused had really been connected with de Batz; others might have been connected, and others, again, were said to have joined in the 'Prison Conspiracy', which was all part of de Batz's plot. There were three of Cecile Renault's family; five former Police administrators of the Commune; the beautiful adventuress, Mme de Sainte-Amaranthe, who kept a gaming saloon in the Palais-Royal, with her son, a boy of seventeen, and her daughter and son-in-law; some Paris tradesmen; a group of nobles of high rank; a little servant-girl of eighteen. Old de Sombreuil was there with a son; his daughter, who had saved him once in the September massacres, was now in prison. After a trial lasting from three to five hours, all were condemned. They were taken to the guillotine dressed in red shirts, because two of them had attempted the lives of deputies, and with them seven other prisoners were executed. This huge execution made a great impression, and one which was unfavourable to Robespierre.

Since the last half of May, the Tribunal had been helped to speed up its ghastly work by two 'Popular Commissions' appointed by the Government Committees and sitting in the Museum (the Louvre). Their business was to go through the prisons, sifting out the innocent and the guilty summarily (law of 13th March). They had another function; by the 'General Police law' of April 16th, any person living without an occupation, who complained of the Republic, was to be deported to Guiana, and the 'Popular Commissions' had to decide on all such cases. They reported each day to the Comité de Salut public, which passed and signed their lists for deportation or for trial, after a cursory glance at them. So carelessly were the lists compiled that some prisoners appeared on lists both for trial and for deportation, and in two days the Committee signed lists containing the names of 459 persons sent for instant trial, of whom at least twenty had been guillotined already. The Committee had grown reckless in its hurry, and the Tribunal committed gross irregularities. Thus, the Judges occasionally signed the day's death-sentences before the names of the condemned were filled in; Fouquier-Tinville added extra names to lists of prisoners up for trial, without any formalities, and prisoners were not carefully identified, one being taken for the other. On July 19th, for instance, a boy of seventeen was tried and executed instead of his father.

In the middle of June, a still more expeditious way of emptying the prisons was discovered: the extension of trials for 'the Prison Conspiracy' that imaginary plot among the prisoners to escape and overthrow the Republic. It began in Bicêtre, the convicts' jail, where one prisoner denounced his fellows for plotting. The result of the consequent inquiry was so successful that Herman, with his Ministerial 'Executive Commission' of Police, was ordered by the Committee (June 25th) to search out conspiracies in all the prisons. Spies, called *mouions*, were found, or placed, in a prison; they betrayed the unguarded talk of one or two prisoners, and any one in that prison whom the authorities wished to get rid of was entangled in the web. Seventy-three prisoners from Bicêtre were executed in two batches, on June 16th and 26th; these were mostly criminals under sentence, and many were quite young; it had become a common thing to execute boys and girls of seventeen and eighteen. The next prison visited was the aristocratic Luxembourg; here Herman soon prepared a list of 154 names; the Committee sent them all for instant trial, and Dumas was making preparations for one gigantic 'batch', when Fouquier-Tinville stopped it by remonstrating with the Committee. They were tried in three batches, on July 7th, 9th, and 10th, and all but nine were condemned. A fourth batch of eighteen followed on July 22nd, the 4th Thermidor. On the 5th Thermidor, forty-six prisoners from les Carmes were condemned; on the 6th, 7th, and 8th Thermidor, seventy-three prisoners from Saint-Lazare, in three batches, and on the 8th Thermidor thirty prisoners from other prisons were also sentenced. Many distinguished men fell in these holocausts, many noble ladies; we can only mention: from Bicêtre, Osselin, the deputy, who was awaiting deportation there. From the Luxembourg, three generations of ladies of the de Noailles family; the abbe de Fenelon, aged eighty, worthy member of the great Fenelon's family, and friend and protector of the little

Savoyard chimney-sweeps of Paris; a boy of fourteen who was sentenced to twenty years' imprisonment. From les Carmes, General Beauharnais. From Saint-Lazare, the famous poet André Chenier, and a father who allowed himself to be executed in his son's place, Loiserolles. In the meanwhile the Tribunal was trying other prisoners as before, and had condemned in one day (June 27th) a Marshal of France, de Mouchy, and his wife; two widowed duchesses de Biron; and Prince Victor de Broglie, 'Constituent' and General. Another well-known Constituent, Gossin, was executed (4 Thermidor) because Fouquier-Tinville had carelessly put the official paper which proved his innocence into the wrong dossier.*

Robespierre had not identified himself personally with these last butcheries. It can hardly be argued from this that he disapproved, as he made no protest; moreover his friends and supporters, Herman and Dumas, were conspicuous in promoting them. It is difficult to know what really happened in the Committee, because the accounts given by interested witnesses after Robespierre's death are untrustworthy, but this much

---

* It is worthy of note that in the height of the Terror (July 9th) a decree was passed for the provisional release of labourers and artisans belonging to small towns and country districts, provided they were not accused of treason. The reason was that harvest and other work was suffering through the numbers in prison.

seems clear: The Committee had long been overworked and want of sleep made tempers short. To all outward appearance the members worked together in harmony, but in the privacy of the Committee there were scenes of angry recrimination. Taunts of 'Dictator' had been flung in Robespierre's teeth, and it is likely that members in a passion threatened one another with the guillotine. When the summer came, bringing day after day of excessive heat, the irritation grew It was impossible to conceal this state of things completely, and rumours of dissensions reached the public and even spread to foreign countries. Robespierre and Carnot detested each other, and all the more when Carnot treated Saint-Just shabbily on his last mission to the Armies. Robespierre hated Collot and Billaud as Hébertists, and they hated him as a religious reformer, as did Vadier, Amar, and other members of the Comité de Sûreté générale. Saint-André and Prieur de la Marne were usually absent on missions, Prieur de la Cote-d'Or supported Carnot, Lindet was neutral, and Barère, the one member who was always good-tempered, had not yet taken a side. They all said afterwards that they abominated the 22nd Prairial law, and doubtless they were offended at Robespierre's high-handed way of springing it on them, but they worked it with zeal, and there seems little doubt that his law on the Supreme Being was the greater offence.

Soon after carrying the 22nd Prairial law, Robespierre, hurt and angry, ceased to take an active part in the work of the Committee, but it is certain, from the number of orders which he signed, that he must have continued to attend the meetings. Saint-Just was absent with the Armies, Couthon did not attend assiduously, and for a short time Robespierre's enemies had it all their own way. It is not probable, whatever they said afterwards, that they had as yet conceived the idea of getting rid of him. On the night of June 28th Saint-Just returned, fresh from the field of Fleurus, and a few days later Robespierre ceased even to attend the Committee, though he still looked in occasionally to sign orders. Neither did he speak in the Convention. His retirement was a great tactical mistake, for he lost his hold over Committee and Convention.

Robespierre had enemies outside the Committee too and, to his honour, they were a cruel and conscience-less set, some of them suspected of peculation on missions. He had already had his knife into Fouché, the butcher of Lyon, into Barras and Fréron, the butchers of Marseilles and Toulon, into Tallien and Leonard Bourdon and Bourdon de l'Oise. These men, and others too, began to realize that their lives were insecure, and that they were followed about by spies.

A period of more or less veiled hostilities began with an anti-religious demonstration on the part of the Committees. There lived in Paris a crazy old woman, Catherine Théot, who called herself the Mother of God, and had gathered round her a little sect of devotees. She prophesied the coming of a Messiah, and scoffers whispered that Robespierre, the restorer of Religion, must be he. It happened also that the aged dame's chief supporter, Dom Gerle, a crackbrained, harmless enthusiast and a 'Constituent', was a protégé of Robespierre's. All this gave a chance for a covert attack on Robespierre; the silly sect was transformed into a big conspiracy, and on June 15th cynical old Vadier reported on it for the two Committees. Without once mentioning Robespierre's name, he cleverly cast scorn and ridicule on religion by sneers at persecuting priests, and by a description of the sect and its ceremonies so ludicrous that the Convention rocked with laughter. A number of the Sect were sent for trial, but Robespierre, much to his credit, interfered in the Committee to save them, so that the affair went no further.

Another device of Robespierre's enemies was to increase the natural panic prevalent among deputies, by talking much about lists of deputies doomed to the guillotine, drawn up by Robespierre. Rumours and conjectures as to who was on Robespierre's next list were rife, and quite a number of deputies never slept at home for fear of being arrested in the night. In fact

Robespierre's enemies started the legend which represents him as the only author of the severities of the Revolution, and thirsting indiscriminately for blood; accusations which caused him great distress.

Robespierre, on his side, was active in the Jacobins', in person and through his supporters. Fouché was President, and one evening (11th June) when Fouché was vilifying Chaumette, Robespierre demanded explanations. A duel of words ensued, in the course of which Robespierre, who himself never lost a chance of blackening Danton, reproached Fouché with throwing mud at the grave of his old associate, and fairly tore him in pieces. Fouché ceased to attend the Club not long after, was denounced by Robespierre as a conspirator, and expelled (14th July). He became a conspirator in earnest by promoting combined action against Robespierre. At other times Robespierre, in the Jacobins' would denounce conspiracies to divide patriots in his old, vague way; he would complain of persecutions, of how he was called Dictator and tyrant. But he never breathed a word about dissensions in the Committee. His followers were less cautious. Dumas proposed to purify the Convention; Couthon protested that the Convention would never be subjugated by four or five villains (21st July), and declared that five or six deputies, gorged with plunder and dripping with blood, were agents of the Foreigner (24th July). This

was a pretty plain warning, both to the Committee and
to Tallien and his like. It came, too, in the middle of
an attempt at a rapprochement. For, on July 22nd (4
Thermidor) Saint-Just was charged by the Committees
to make a report on the situation of the Republic, and
the next day there was a meeting of both Committees,
at which Robespierre appeared to give explanations.
Saint-Just defended Robespierre, and told how it had
come to his knowledge that the enemy was counting
on their quarrels to bring about the overthrow of the
Terror. Robespierre seems to have given the names of
the deputies whom he wished to be removed – and
they were not members of the Committees. His
colleagues were obviously afraid of him in his presence,
for Billaud, who had been calling him 'Pisistratus', said
to him: "We are your friends, we have always marched
together."

But Robespierre had determined to speak out, and
was already preparing a long and elaborate discourse,
which he delivered in the Convention on the 8th
Thermidor (26th July). As a declaration of war it was
singularly ineffective: complaints of persecution and
calumny, especially of the calumny that he aspired to
be Dictator; eloquent passages on virtue and Religion
– "No, Chaumette, no, Fouché; death is not an eternal
sleep . . . Death is the beginning of immortality";
criticisms of the Terror in its useless persecution of

patriots; veiled criticisms of the Comité de Salut public; open denunciations of the wicked agents of the Comité de Sûreté générale; denunciations of Cambon and the Finance Committee.* The rest was vague, and the Committees felt themselves threatened indiscriminately. The usual applause followed the speech, and the printing of it was voted; so was Couthon's proposal to send it to every Commune in the Republic; but the Convention no longer trembled at Robespierre's nod, and objections were afterwards raised. Such a speech, it was said, should not go out to the country before an inquiry had been made into the charges it contained. Robespierre, when called on to say whom he meant, refused to divulge more, and the decree to send the speech out was repealed, to his obvious chagrin.

In the evening he read the same speech to the Jacobins, who received it with immense enthusiasm. He called it his last will and testament, and declared that if his efforts to purify the Convention failed, he would drink hemlock. "I will drink it with you!" cried David, and Dumas threatened all who would not listen to Robespierre with the fate of Hébert and Danton.

* This outrageous denunciation of Cambon and the Finance Committee, as traitors and cheats, came just after they had finished the great work of getting all the creditors of the Nation inscribed alphabetically in one book, the *Grand livre de la dette nationale* (2nd July), which henceforward constituted a creditor's sole title to the debt. This simplification got rid of masses of papers, cumbrous and complicated.

Collot and Billaud shouted attacks on Robespierre's speech against a hostile demonstration, in which cries of *a la guillotine!* were heard, and after Couthon had talked about conspirators there were more cries of "Conspirators to the guillotine!" When Collot and Billaud returned to the Committee, they found the members working round the table, Saint-Just writing at the report which he was to deliver the next morning. Again there was an angry scene, Saint-Just maintaining a provoking 'marble' calm, and when the others left him at 5 a.m. he was still writing. He had warned his colleagues that he should 'go deep', and he did. His report, which shows what some of Robespierre's intentions were, contained an indictment of four members of the Committee: Barère, Carnot, Collot, and Billaud; he accused all four of making the reputation of the Committee serve their own ambition, and was sarcastic over the way in which, after the soldiers had won the victories, the Government (Barère and Carnot) had seized upon the glory. He accused Collot and Billaud of a plot to clear out some members of the Committee, and to destroy the Revolutionary Tribunal and the Paris Commune. He proposed no measures against them, but asked for an inquiry.

Robespierre had made the fatal mistake of threatening instead of striking. In the hot cloudy morning of the 9th Thermidor (27th July), the two Committees called in Fouché, probably for a last consultation, and prepared for a life and death struggle. They knew the dangers: Hanriot, who disposed of the National Guard, was devoted to Robespierre, so were the Commune and the Jacobins, so was the Revolutionary Tribunal.

The Convention opened. It was a critical moment when Saint-Just appeared in the tribune at 11.30 and began reading his report: "I belong to no faction; I will fight them all." Tallien, taking his life in his hands, sprang up to interrupt him, spurred not only by his own danger, but by thoughts of his fair Cabarrus now in prison, under the shadow of the guillotine. He cried that the veil which hid the strange divisions in the Government must be torn; the Convention applauded. Billaud was already on his feet, telling of the plot against the Convention in the Jacobins', protesting that they would all die rather than live under a tyrant, accusing Robespierre, recounting that he had protected Hanriot* and had wished to spare Hébert and Danton. He spoke in a hubbub; Lebas was shouted down, Robespierre rushed to the tribune, but Tallien was before him, assuring his colleagues that the veil had now been torn. He brandished a poniard which he had brought to stab the new Cromwell if the Convention refused to impeach him; he demanded the

* Hanriot had been implicated vaguely and distantly, by a witness, in the Flébert conspiracy.

arrest of Hanriot and his Staff. It was voted, as was the arrest of Dumas. Barère spoke; it is said that he had come down with two speeches in his pocket and produced the anti-Robespierre discourse. Vadier accused Robespierre of leniency to traitors; Bourdon de l'Oise chimed in. And all this time Robespierre was endeavouring at intervals to speak, and always his enemies prevented him; he must not gain the ear of the Convention or all might yet be lost. Cool at first, he grew angry, and shouted at Collot, who was presiding: "President of Brigands!" His voice became hoarse with effort, and a friend of Danton's, Gamier de l'Aube, cried: "the blood of Danton chokes him!" An obscure member proposed his arrest, and it was voted unanimously. But Robespierre's closest friends stood by him nobly. His brother and Lebas, neither of them implicated, claimed to share his arrest. Couthon was doomed, so was Saint-Just, who might possibly have saved himself earlier if he had abandoned his report; they made no effort. The arrest of all four was decreed; they walked to the Bar with Robespierre and were taken off to the rooms of the Comité de Sûreté générale,* where they were given dinner. The

* The Comité de Sûreté générale sat in a house adjoining the Pavillon de Marsan, at the north end of the Tuileries Palace; the Comité de Salut public sat in the Pavilion de Flore, at the south end of the Tuileries.

431

sitting was suspended for two hours, at five o'clock, and the arrested deputies were sent to separate prisons before seven.

In the Tribunal, Dumas had been arrested while presiding; another Judge took his place, and forty-five prisoners were duly condemned. Disturbances were reported in the Saint-Antoine quarter, through which the carts must pass, but Fouquier-Tinville refused to put off the execution, and it took place as usual.

Had Robespierre been tried by the Revolutionary Tribunal, it is quite likely that he would have been acquitted, as Marat was. His friends prevented a trial by hastening to the rescue as soon as his danger was known. The Commune met at 5.30, summoned by Lescot-Fleuriot and Payan, and Hanriot was already calling out some of the National Guard, so that the place de Grève was soon full of artillery, ready to defend the Commune. Payan was a man of action, and under his guidance measures were rapidly taken: a proclamation invited the people of Paris to rise and save the patriotic deputies persecuted by villains; the orders of the Committees were defied; the tocsin was rung to call all good citizens to the Hôtel de Ville; the Sections were convoked; an Executive Committee was chosen, &c. The Jacobins were asked for aid and sympathy, and a large meeting of the Club was only too anxious to give them; frequent deputations passed to and fro, ending with the coming of a number of Jacobins to the Commune.

The last word lay, of course, with the Sections; whichever side secured the support of the majority must win. Here the situation was uncertain, for though few Sections actually came to the Hôtel de Ville to swear fealty, many were understood to be wavering, and the Commune was hopeful. The Convention was, as yet, very insufficiently guarded, and a bold stroke might have ended the business; there was, however, no one to make it. Hanriot had no plans, and he was drunk, for though a sober man, he had taken a glass to inspirit him for the occasion. With an idea of rescuing the imprisoned deputies, he led a squadron of mounted gendarmerie, brandishing swords and arresting passers by, straight to the court outside the Comité de Sûreté générale; here his own gendarmes arrested him and handed him over to this Committee. He had not been long a prisoner when the judge Coffinhal, who was very active that night, came from the Commune with a detachment of artillery, invested the Committee's rooms, and snatched him away in triumph, at about 8.30. Rescue did not make Hanriot more resourceful, and his chief idea still was to rush about, inciting the people and the National Guards to rise.

One great object of the Commune was the release

of the five deputies and Dumas. This was easily effected, as the Police Administrators of the Commune were still paramount in the prisons. Owing to their orders, the Luxembourg jailers refused to receive Robespierre, and all the others were released from their prisons at various times, Couthon, the last, at 1 a.m. The Police Administrators took Robespierre to their office in the Mayor's house, close by the Palais de Justice, where he arrived at about 8.30, and was heartily cheered. If he had gone at once to the Commune, harangued the people and given a lead, he might have roused Paris to drive his enemies out of the Convention, as the Girondins had been driven. He preferred to stay quietly in the hands of the Police, where his position was perfectly legal, for he was full of conscientious scruples about causing an insurrection, full of respect for the outward forms of Law. Messengers from the Commune implored him to come – Coffinhal was one – he would not move. At length, feeling, doubtless, that to keep away was to betray the people who had risen in his behalf,* he gave way, and appeared in the Hôtel de Ville at about 10.30. His brother was already there; Lebas joined them, and later on Saint-Just, and the two Robespierres with Saint-Just wrote a note to summon Couthon. But Robespierre,

* This was the argument he used in summoning Couthon.

who probably sat with the Executive Committee in a room apart, took no active measures on his own behalf, and an appeal to his own Section, the Piques, to rally round the Commune, is signed with the first letters of his name, as though he had hesitated and broken off in the middle. When Couthon arrived, after 1 a.m., he began to bestir himself. He entered the hall where the General Council sat, with Couthon, Saint-Just, and Lebas, and was greeted with a burst of applause. He and Couthon talked of writing to the Armies, in the name of the French People; he bade a gendarme go down and speak to the people. It was too late, the troops of the Convention were already entering the Square below.

For meanwhile the Convention had been acting with vigour. There were anxious moments when it was reported that Hanriot had been carried off and that the Comité de Sûreté générale was invested by artillery, and the deputies vowed to die at their posts; but Hanriot and his troops moved away and the peril passed. News was brought that the Commune was in insurrection; the mayor, with all the rebellious members of the Commune were promptly outlawed. Hanriot was outlawed; Robespierre and the arrested prisoners who had escaped were outlawed. Barras was appointed to the command of the Paris National Guard, with Fréron, the two Bourdons, and other deputies to help him; this was an excellent measure, for Barras was a firm and capable man, of an imposing presence. He took the lead at once, and was soon able to announce that there were plenty of loyal troops round the Convention, and that he was making preparations to march on the Hôtel de Ville.

Loyal deputations soon made it apparent that the majority of the Sections was more or less on the side of the Convention, and the decrees outlawing Robespierre and the Commune, which Barras took care to announce far and wide, rallied wavering Sections and brought hostile ones over, till finally there were barely three Sections on the Commune's side. The Sections had learnt from experience, that the only safe course was to stick to the Convention, and that the most popular deputies might at any moment be branded as traitors. The outlawry decrees reached the artillery guarding the Hôtel de Ville; at the same time the Sections called their gunners home, and the troops of the Commune melted away. When the united forces of two Sections, under Leonard Bourdon, reached the place de Grève at about 2 a.m., they found it deserted. They seized the abandoned guns, and a party of fifty prepared to storm the upper stories of the Hôtel de Ville, where the Commune sat. They were on the steps outside, when a body fell among them, from an upper window; it was the younger Robespierre, who had jumped when he realized that all was lost; he was taken up half dead. They mounted the stairs; two pistol shots had been heard, and, entering an inner room, they found Lebas and Robespierre lying on the ground. Lebas was dead, he had obviously shot himself; Robespierre, still alive, was shot through the lower jaw. Hanriot was missing; Coffinhal, in a fury with him for losing the day through his drunkenness, had flung him out of the window into a filthy little courtyard, where he lay till he was found by gendarmes early in the afternoon. Coffinhal escaped. The prisoners were secured, and Leonard Bourdon brought into the Convention a gendarme who claimed to have shot Robespierre. Whether he had, is a question which has not been completely settled, but all the probabilities point to an attempt at suicide on Robespierre's part. Immediately after, Legendre brought the keys of the Jacobin Club, the doors of which he had locked after turning every one out.

Robespierre was carried to the Tuileries, and laid on a big table in the audience room of the Comité de Salut public. There he lay for hours, with a box under his head, speechless but fully conscious; his clothes, the very same that he had worn at the Fête of the Supreme Being, all bloodstained, torn and dishevelled. Curious spectators who had come to have a look surrounded him; they taunted and insulted him. Saint-Just, Dumas, and Payan were brought in, and taken off by and by to the Conciergerie, Saint-Just pale, but without a hair awry. At about 5 a.m. two doctors were called in to patch up Robespierre for the guillotine. They dressed his wound and bound up his head, but his enemies dared not have him moved, lest he should die, and he was left on the table for some five more hours of agony and insult. At length he was sent to the Conciergerie, accompanied by the two doctors. Young Robespierre was brought there too, still alive, and Couthon, who had been found lying, much injured, on the quay by the river.

The Revolutionary Tribunal sat. There was no trial, for the prisoners were outlaws, and all that had to be done was to establish their identity. Twenty-two were sentenced; Robespierre and his brother, Couthon, Saint-Just, Dumas, Lescot-Fleuriot and Payan, Hanriot and another General of the National Guard, the young man who had presided at the Jacobins' in the night, and twelve members of the Commune, one of whom was Simon. Fouquier-Tinville, with his usual indifference, went through his task almost unmoved; not quite, for when it came to the turn of Lescot-Fleuriot, who was his friend, Fouquier left the room. The scaffold was moved back to the place de la Révolution, and the twenty-two were taken thither in the evening. The crowds were enormous and showed no pity; the prisoners were received with jeers and execrations and signs of cruel joy. Robespierre's enemies had taken care to spread about that a seal with a fleur-de-lys had been found on the table of the Commune, showing that the rebellion had been a royalist conspiracy, and this increased the hostility of credulous spectators. It is said that the carts were halted, on purpose, before the Duplays' house, empty now, for the Duplays, involved in Robespierre's ruin, had all been arrested. Towards seven o'clock the guillotine was reached. Robespierre, weak as he was, walked up the scaffold steps; it is traditional that when the executioner tore roughly at the bandage round his head, a scream of pain escaped him. He was not the last to be beheaded, that honour was reserved for the Mayor, Lescot-Fleuriot. The bodies were buried in the cemetery where Danton lay.

No mercy was shown to the vanquished. On the 11th Thermidor seventy men were guillotined, the largest number ever executed by the Tribunal at one time; on the 12th, twelve men followed them; all but four of these two 'batches' were members of the Commune. These unfortunate men, some of whom had been members for only a few weeks, were hunted down like rats, and no attempt was made to discriminate between degrees of guilt. A few others managed to escape. Coffinhal was taken and executed on the

18th (5th Aug.). He had hidden in an island on the Seine till, driven by hunger, he sought refuge with a friend, who betrayed him.

Robespierre's enemies, in compassing his fall, had not been moved by ideas of justice or compassion; nevertheless there was joy in the prisons. The prisoners had heard the tocsin and knew by various signs that something was happening, and they had spent the night of the 9th Thermidor in expectation of a massacre. Gradually the news came through to them that Robespierre had fallen; hope sprang up once more, and they embraced each other with tears of joy.

XI

FAMINE AND VENGEANCE
29TH JULY 1794 –
NOVEMBER 1795

After the fall of Robespierre no man was left powerful enough to make Convention and nation tremble before him, and France shook off, as it were, the nightmare of the Terror. What need was there for all this restraint? The pretext for the Terror had been the danger of the country, and now, as every one knew, the victorious armies of the Republic were dreaded by Europe. France became herself again, and therefore speech was free. Those who had friends in prison pleaded and schemed for their release as of old; the torpid Press burst into life, and a swarm of pamphlets and placards began to appear. There was much talk about re-establishing the freedom of the Press; an unnecessary measure, because the Press had, in theory, remained free, and had been restrained by fear alone.

When the coalition of Robespierre's enemies known as 'the Thermidoriens' overthrew him, they had, as we have said, no intention of ending the Terror which made government so much easier; nevertheless they felt that the Terror must be regulated and that certain abuses must be stopped. So the despotism of the Government Committees was curbed by a decree, that in each Committee of the Convention a quarter of the members must retire monthly, their places being filled by new members elected by the Convention (29th July). The Committees were re-organized on this basis, with some limitations to the powers of the Comité de Salut public (24th Aug.). Retiring members of the two Government Committees were not re-eligible for a month.

Paris, too, was curbed. Never again must a Commune of Paris rival the Convention. The Commune had ceased to exist, by the death or outlawry of its members, and the Convention put the local government of Paris into the hands of the ministerial 'Executive Commissions' and of Police Administrators of its own appointing (31 Aug.). The Sections were limited to one sitting in a *decade* and payment for attendance was suppressed. The office of Commander-in-Chief of the Paris National Guard was once more abolished.

Again, there were too many prisoners, so the Comité de Sûreté générale was given power to release political prisoners who were not 'suspects' in the legal sense (5th Aug.), and the Revolutionary Committees, those fillers of prisons, were ordered to inform arrested persons of the reason of their arrest (5th Aug.). Further, the number of these Committees was greatly reduced (24th Aug.). Paris which had possessed forty-eight was left with twelve.

From the first it was evident that there were two parties among the Thermidoriens; the Terrorists pure and simple and the men inclined to modify the methods of the Terror, and that the Convention supported now one of these parties and now the other. This was especially clear when the Revolutionary Tribunal was in question. There was no difficulty about repealing (on 1st Aug.) the monstrous law of the 22nd Prairial; that law was Robespierre's and Couthon's work. The rest was contentious matter. Billaud prevented the suspension of the Tribunal before it had finished with the Commune (11 Therm.), but reforms were felt to be necessary, and Barère presented a list of names for a new and better Tribunal. Whom should he propose as Public Prosecutor of this new Tribunal, but the man identified with all the iniquities of the old: Fouquier-Tinville. This was too much, and the Convention decreed Fouquier's arrest (1st Aug.).

Then Merlin de Douai presented a bill for the organization of the reformed Tribunal, doing away with the optional ending of trials after the third day, and his bill was voted (9th Aug.). The next day, when he was reading the final wording of his bill, two Terrorists persuaded the Convention to restore the Tribunal, with a new list of members, exactly as it had been organized before the 22nd Prairial, when, so one of them, Duhem, observed, it had produced such happy results. The Tribunal thus constituted was installed (12th Aug.); yet, though some of the old members had been kept, and though it carried out the same cruel laws, the new Tribunal showed a new spirit, and trials were fair. Bourdon de l'Oise had managed to secure for it the power of acquitting when treason had been technically committed without evil intention, and this power was largely used. In four months forty-six prisoners were sentenced to death, while, roughly speaking, eighteen times as many were acquitted, or released after an inquiry.

The release of prisoners was a frequent cause of strife in the Convention. A good many were released by the Comité de Sûreté générale in the early days, and some aristocrats got out, which caused consternation among the Terrorists, who pictured dangerous émigrés pouring out by the score to plot the ruin of the Republic. Such alarms were needless, for the prisons only emptied gradually; at the end of September there were still nearly five thousand prisoners in Paris; by the end of December, however, the extra prisons had been suppressed, and this although many of the minor tyrants of the Terror had been arrested.

The Terrorists might struggle their hardest, but conscience was stirring in the nation and in the Convention, and a reaction was bound to come. The logical French mind never shows finer than in repairing a wrong, once it is fully recognized as such, and slowly, but inevitably, wrongs were repaired. Sad to say, as often happens in reactions, justice was accompanied by discriminating vengeance, and her work was mainly carried out by unworthy instruments.

The Convention was much to be pitied at this time. The deputies, who had most of them started full of the hopes and ideals of the Revolution, became aware of prisons unjustly filled, of innocent blood shed, of colleagues cowardly abandoned. Some had taken an active part in these crimes, many had applauded, nearly all had acquiesced. They could not face it; they could not believe that they, so well intentioned, had allowed such things to be done, and the easiest way of casting off a general sense of guilt was to lay all the blame on Robespierre. So Robespierre's memory was daily execrated in speeches, the evil he had done was exaggerated, ridiculous stories about his orgies and his secret royalism were invented to discredit him, and every one explained how much they had always disliked him. But Robespierre's misdeeds, real and imaginary, would not cover individual lapses, and fresh cruelties done by Representatives on Mission were continually coming to light. The deputies concerned fortified themselves by boasting of their humanity, just as Legendre, who had collapsed before Robespierre, boasted of how he had defended Danton. Many members, base in their remorse, tried to salve a guilty conscience by fierce attacks on fellow-sinners, and debate after debate turned to a stormy interchange of horrible recriminations. One member, Boudin, a merciful man, was brave enough to say, when pleading for mutual pardon, that he accused himself of not having had spirit enough to protest and die: "I saw only an ignominious death brought on by a useless resistance, and I had not the courage to go to the scaffold accompanied by the curses of the people." The Convention applauded, and continued to recriminate. Barère spoke once of the enormous ditch of hatred dividing the members of the Convention from one another, and after Thermidor that ditch was wider than ever.

There were no great leaders left to guide the Convention through the period of reaction, no great orators, nothing but a set of talented and competent men of the second rank. Oratory soon sank to a very low level. Barère and a few men of the old school could still be eloquent, and other deputies could still say what they meant, in altercation or when doing business. But when there was any occasion for display, meaning was drowned in a torrent of wearisome set phrases; a prisoner invariably 'languished' or 'groaned in fetters', an emigre 'tore the bosom of his country', and a Terrorist 'watered the soil with blood.'

Tallien, his friends, and allies, are known as Thermidoriens of the Right, and some of them had left their seats upon the Mountain to take up their position on that side. They were as conspicuous in their new role as they had formerly been in their revolutionary violence; pleasure-loving and self-indulgent men, most of them, without fixed principles, now on this side, now on that. Tallien, Fréron, Bourdon de l'Oise, and André Dumont seemed usually to plead for mercy out of hatred and to call for justice out of spite. No past services to the Republic weighed for an instant with this party. Tallien and Fréron each conducted a newspaper, and Fréron's *Orateur du Penple*, filled with savage attacks on Terrorists, had considerable influence. In the Convention, Fréron once made the senseless motion to pull down the Hôtel de Ville because it had harboured Robespierre. Tallien, thin and sallow, elegant in appearance and modest in deportment, was much under the influence of his wife, Teresia Cabarrus, who did not care for the Republic. The fine-looking Barras, a powerful member of the party, seldom made speeches. Lecointre was, at least, sincere, but his grotesque appearance made it difficult to take him seriously.

Legendre, sincere too, was perhaps the best of this party; he had modelled himself on Danton and was sometimes really eloquent in a rough way. Dubois-Crancé, Merlin de Thionville, and the fluent and fluid Thuriot were always to the fore and rather less violent.

In the Centre, a whole set of useful and distinguished members, once "toads of the Marsh" (*crapauds du marais*), emerged and worked in the Committees, and since the Comité de Salut public was still the Government, a knot of them may be said to have ruled France for more than a year. Cambacérès was one, an able legist, skilful in managing the Convention and personally selfish. Another was Siéves. It is said that when asked what he had done during the Terror he answered: "I kept alive." Others, 'Constituents' like Siéyes, were Boissy d'Anglas, handsome and impressive, who, while keeping quiet, had used his influence generously to soften the lot of victims, and two lawyers, Treilhard and the hard-headed, active-minded Alsatian, Reubell. With them worked Merlin de Douai, glad to use his talents in furthering less inhuman ideas. Between the two chief parties stood a young man, Thibaudeau, a fluent speaker who had the ear of the Convention, and tried to be fair to both sides; he held, therefore, a unique position.

On the Left were the old members of the Committees, haggard and hollow-eyed from their long labours and sleepless nights. They had been too deeply involved in the Terror to escape denunciation for long, and it came at the end of August (29th) when Lecointre charged seven of them with complicity in Robespierre's crimes, making a number of definite accusations. A sturdy defence from Billaud, an appeal by other members for unity, and a reminder of the great services rendered by the accused, caused the accusations to be thrust aside. But on the morrow, the Convention, feeling that the affair must be thrashed out, made Lecointre read the documents on which he based his charges. Lecointre had got much of his information from Fouquier-Tinville's account of his dealings with the Committees; this prejudiced his case and, after a long debate, it was decreed that the accusations were calumnious. Nevertheless when, two days later, the Committee was partially renewed and Barère went out by lot, Billaud and Collot resigned. Carnot and Lindet, as yet undenounced, were too useful to part with. Henceforth the accused members lived under a cloud, though they bore themselves proudly with the air of dethroned Kings; Legendre took up the accusations a month later, and it was almost a relief to them when, at the end of December (27th), after much debating, a commission of twenty-one deputies was appointed to examine Lecointre's charges against Barère, Collot, Billaud, and Vadier; the three others (Amar, David, Voulland) were dropped out. Carnot and Prieur of the Cote-d'Or rallied boldly to their colleagues' side, protesting that the Committee had always acted together. The accused members had by this time persuaded themselves that they had plotted to attack Robespierre some six months before Thermidor gave them their chance. Carnot's defence, when he was himself denounced later on, was that, in the press of urgent business, members of the Committee signed orders for which other members were responsible, as a mere matter of form and without reading them, and so were not aware of what was going on; a singular excuse when life and death were concerned.

The accused Committee-men were supported through thick and thin by the bulk of the Left, the remains of the Mountain; men of principles and convictions, austere and honest if wrongheaded, who feared, with some reason, that in a reaction the Republic might perish. Most of them had served on missions, for the Mountain never spared itself; some, like Cambon and Romme, had distinguished themselves in other ways.

Duhem, a cadaverous doctor who had been an admirer of Marat's, was the most clamorous of the party.* They did not lag behind the Right in denunciations and opposed all measures of mercy, though outside the Convention many of them were kindly. A good number of them were staunch Jacobins, and dominated the Club, from which Robespierre's friends had been eliminated. Under their guidance, the Club petitioned the Convention for the continuance of revolutionary government, and expelled Tallien and Fréron, who were trying to get a foothold. Jacobin speeches were full of threats, as they had been under the Terror, and Carrier attended the meetings; the Jacobins even made the mistake of linking their cause with his. All this made the Committees uneasy, and when, at the beginning of November, Billaud, in the course of a violent speech in the Club, remarked that, though patriots were now silent, "the lion is not dead when he sleeps, and when he wakes he exterminates all his enemies," the Committees felt that it was time to make an end. A mob, probably encouraged, besieged the Club doors and bullied the Jacobins; the Committees seized the pretext, and on November 12th 1794 the Jacobins' Club was closed by a decree, for ever, as it proved. In the following Spring another decree ordained that the

* To Duhem's credit, he tried to save the little Prince in the Temple by getting him banished.

premises should be turned into a market. The suppression of the Club was a blow to the Montagnards; Paris, in general, approved.

The day before the Jacobins' was closed, Carrier was arrested; his position since the fall of Robespierre, his enemy, had seemed secure, but his crimes were beginning to find him out. In the Autumn of 1793, the Nantes Revolutionary Committee had, with his consent, sent up to the Revolutionary Tribunal 132 well-off citizens of that place, accused of 'federalism'. Only ninety-seven of them arrived in Paris, survivors of a forty days' journey of dreadful hardships, and Fouquier-Tinville, moved for once by pity, saved their lives by continually postponing their trial. At length, reduced yet further to ninety-three, they appeared before the reformed Tribunal. Meanwhile the Nantes Revolutionary Committee had also been sent to Paris for trial, and its members were fetched from prison to give evidence against their former victims. But along with the ninety-three citizens was tried an old enemy of the Nantes Revolutionary Committee, Tronjolly, a prominent Nantes lawyer, skilful and bold, who managed to turn the trial into an attack on the Nantes Revolutionary Committee and Carrier. To crown this strange trial where the accused turned accusers, the jury acquitted some of the defendants and found the others guilty of conspiracy, but without evil intentions, which amounted to an acquittal (14th Sep.). Carrier had given evidence, denying all knowledge of crimes in Nantes.

The trial of the Nantes Revolutionary Committee had thus become necessary, and started on October 16th with fourteen accused. The horrors of Nantes, as yet imperfectly known, began to be revealed to the public,* and, as the days went on, fresh men implicated were put beside the prisoners for trial, till the number swelled finally to thirty-three. At every turn the prisoners were pleading that Carrier had ordered this, that Carrier had bidden them do that, and demanding that he should be called. By and by the jury began to demand the same, and then the audience, till the Court rang with shouts of "Carrier! Carrier!" It was brought home to the Convention that an inquiry must be made.

The newly roused conscience of the Convention was still strong, and Carrier was treated with scrupulous fairness. A commission of deputies was appointed to sift the matter, and he was given every opportunity to explain his conduct to them. They chose the Montagnard Romme to make their report. Romme, though loth to condemn Carrier, was a just man, and reported in favour of Carrier's impeachment. Carrier was put under arrest, after a patient hearing; he was given time to

---

* They were undoubtedly exaggerated by many witnesses, but, with all allowance for exaggeration, the record remains black and terrible.

prepare his defence, and heard again on three separate days. He struggled vigorously against his impending doom, defying his accusers to produce his written orders; he vowed that he had had nothing to do with cruelties; but it must be observed that he did not consider cruel, the execution, by any method, of prisoners convicted by any kind of Court. The Convention decreed his impeachment in the early hours of November 24th, and of the 500 deputies who voted, not one voted in his favour. He joined his fellow criminals before the Revolutionary Tribunal, and twenty days later he and two others were condemned to death (16th December). They were executed in the place de Grève,* Carrier, to the last, showing no signs of remorse or fear.

Two of the other prisoners were acquitted, twenty-eight more, among them villains guilty of inhuman crimes, were got off by their advocates on the ground that they had committed them without treasonable intentions. The public indignation was so strong that the Convention decreed the renewal of the Tribunal, and debated sending the twenty-eight before an ordinary tribunal (18th Dec.). The organization of a new and further reformed tribunal was decreed on December 28th (8 Nivose). In its first three months

---

* Where all executions took place at this time.

this tribunal only condemned one person to death; its chief work was the trial of the second great criminal, Fouquier-Tinville.

Fouquier, like Carrier, struggled hard for his life, and like Carrier he was indignant that his services to the Republic should be so ill requited. He was tried with twenty-nine other members of the old Revolutionary Tribunal, with whom were joined two members of the 'Executive Commission' of Police, who had arranged much of the infamous Prison Conspiracy (one of them was Herman, once President of the Tribunal), the Police Administrator of Bicêtre who had assisted, four *moutons* (prison spies) and two jailers. When the harrowing stories of victims were told by survivors, the hearts of the audience were torn by pity, and many wept; but Fouquier, no whit abashed, continued to defend himself with professional skill, alert and resourceful. His chief plea was, that in all he did he was only carrying out the orders of the Committees; he had, in reality, allowed many irregularities independent of the Committees. After a trial lasting nearly six weeks, Fouquier, Herman, and fourteen others were condemned to death on May 6th 1795, the rest were acquitted. On the following morning three carts conveyed the condemned men to the place de Grève, amid the execrations of the crowd. Fouquier, unquailing to the end, was executed last, the

455

last man guillotined by sentence of the Revolutionary Tribunal. The days of that Tribunal were already numbered, and on May 31st it was definitely suppressed, and the Convention decreed that henceforth persons accused of treason should be tried by the ordinary Courts.

A third great criminal still remained: Lebon. The Convention appointed a commission to examine into the charges against him, and heard him in his own defence; but he was not fairly treated, for he was denied access to some of his papers. He was impeached on July 10th, 1795, sent before the Arras tribunal, and executed at Arras on October 16th.

Punishment was not the only expiation demanded by justice, and side by side with punishment went reparation. As soon as it was realized that 'the seventy-three' Girondin deputies, in prison or in hiding, were innocent, a report was asked for. Thuriot protested that their return would rend the Convention, Tallien that May 31st had been consecrated as an annual festival and must not be disturbed; but after a report by Merlin de Douai, 'the seventy-three' were recalled (8th Dec., 1794), and though the Convention lost some peace, it gained a number of members who were strong republicans without being Terrorists. But if 'the seventy-three' who had protested against the expulsion of the chief Girondins were innocent, what of the chief Girondins themselves, the outlaws who had escaped the guillotine and were already petitioning to return? Here there was more resistance, and Merlin de Douai reported, for the Committees, that their return must not be allowed (17th Dec.). Their friends did not abandon their cause, and in less than three months had talked their enemies over. Siéyes now spoke of their "honourable exile", Merlin turned completely round, the decrees against the Girondins were all repealed (March 8th, 1795), and the annual fête on May 31st was abolished. The proscribed Girondins came out of their hiding-places, and the Right gained what it sadly needed, some leaders of character. There was Lanjuinais, indomitable and upright, who soon became the most respected member of the Convention; there was Larevellière, deformed, determined and virtuous; and if Isnard was vindictive, Louvet played a noble part. Saved from death by the devotion of his wife, after long wanderings and hairbreadth escapes, he had learnt only generosity, and co-operated loyally with the colleagues who had outlawed him. He was, besides, a genuine orator.

Thus, to the honour of the Convention, the Girondins were recalled; very bitter, some of them, but they had had a lesson and no longer made themselves impossible. Their leading members helped on the work of reparation powerfully.

But if the colleagues who survived were innocent, what of the colleagues who had perished? The question had arisen, long before, over the confiscated property of the condemned.

Should not the property of innocent victims of all the Revolutionary Tribunals be restored to their families? There were great difficulties in the way; much of the property had been sold; and then, who should decide which victims were innocent? It was always best to let sleeping dogs lie, and the task of revising all the sentences of the various revolutionary tribunals was too gigantic to contemplate. Yet, month by month, the idea of restoration gained ground. Lanjuinais got over one difficulty by arguing that, guilty or innocent, the victims of the Tribunals had not had a fair trial, and restoration was voted on May 3rd, 1795. Where property had been sold, the heirs must content themselves with compensation, and there was to be no restoration of the property of the Bourbons, of Mme Dubarry, and of the men outlawed on the 9th Thermidor. This measure, very bold in the state of the finances, reflects great credit on the Convention.

Reparation did not end here, and, a month later, it was decreed that a funeral fête for the 'friends of Liberty' who had died on the scaffold should be held on the 3rd October, the anniversary of the wholesale impeachment of the Girondins. It was celebrated by the Convention with solemn music, and on the list of 'martyrs" names read out, appeared not only the Girondins, but Manuel, Philippeaux and Camille Desmoulins.

Another wrong set right was the persecution of Religion, which had continued despite Robespierre's efforts. This was a difficult matter, for many deputies were violently anti-Christian. On September 18th, 1794, Cambon, anxious to suppress all Religion because it was costly, had persuaded the Convention to vote that the Republic would no longer pay the expenses of any form of worship.* But in February 1795 (the 21st) a step towards toleration was taken. Boissy d'Anglas, reporting for the Committees, said, that though man, when enlightened, would outgrow the need for Religion, it was at present wanted by the unhappy and the igno-rant, and was, moreover, encouraged by persecution. On these grounds he obtained a decree, restating the old law that public worship must not be molested, with provisions that every sign of it must be confined strictly to the interior of the appointed buildings. Some country places hereupon took back their churches, interpreting the decree as a permission, and it became evident that,

---

* Priests and nuns whose salaried posts had been suppressed had been granted a pension, provided they took the civic oath; a small pension was now continued to all in this case, to keep them from starving.

elsewhere, the withholding of churches was causing great discontent. Lanjuinais, a religious man, came to the rescue, and on his Report it was decreed, on May 30th, that all places of worship in use on September 22nd, 1792, should be restored to Communes or Sections of Communes for religious purposes, the State retaining the ownership. The laws of no payment by the State, and no signs of worship outside buildings continued in force, as did the laws regarding priests, and *décadi* still took legally the place of Sunday.

Many other laws of the Terror fell into disuse and some were gradually repealed, but over decrees concerning émigrés there was no slackening, and a law of November 15th, 1794, ordained that "the émigrés are banished for ever from French Territory", and awarded death to any emigre over sixteen who returned. Local lists of émigrés were made, and, from these, general monthly lists were compiled and published. Any one who found himself on the list, even by mistake, stood in peril of arrest and trial, and had to take instant steps to get his name removed. From now on, it became the business of friends of émigrés to endeavour to gain the ear of some one with influence who could get émigrés struck off the lists. The Convention was always reluctant to show mercy to any émigrés, even to poor peasants who had been driven by the Terror from the frontier Departments.

We must now turn to Paris in the winter of 1794-5. Reaction here took an odious form, in the shape of a band of well-to-do young men who ought to have been fighting, shirkers who had been called up and had managed to evade going to the Front; many of them had succeeded in getting themselves requisitioned by some Government department. They are known as the *Jeunesse dorée* (gilded youth). Fréron was their great protector, and told them in his paper that their business was to avenge the deaths of women and children. They haunted public places, armed with sticks and wearing green cravats and high black coat-collars, and when they saw a Jacobin they set on him. This led to many frays, in which the *Jeunesse* sometimes got the worst of it. Marat was still officially a demi-god, his remains had been solemnly taken to the Pantheon in September* and his bust was put up in all the theatres. At the end of January 1795, the *Jeunesse* began knocking down these busts, to the scandal of some of the audience and the joy of others; and there was so much excitement and so many rows over Marat's busts in theatres and cafes, that the Committees ordered their removal. In a short time most of the busts and monuments of Marat in Paris had been demolished. The *Jeunesse* also took up a song against Terrorists which had come out

* Mirabeau's corpse was turned out on the occasion.

in January; violent words set to a catchy tune which lent itself to bawling, and whenever the Marseillaise was sung they howled it down with this song, *Le Réveil du Peuple,* for the *Jeunesse* was anything but patriotic. In the height of the reaction the Marseillaise, identified with Terrorists, was almost banned in Paris, and the *Réveil du Peuple* took its place.

The remains of Society in Paris gathered itself together again, lived in as much luxury as the times allowed* – for there were still rich people – dressed expensively, frequented concerts, danced and enjoyed itself, forgetful of the past. Mme Tallien was the reigning queen, ready, as always, to do a good turn and get an emigre struck off the list, and there her virtues ended.

The poor of Paris, hungry and wretched, felt this gaiety and extravagance as an insult to their woes. Scarcity of food had become actual dearth. Bread was the staple food of the Parisians, and though the price of bread was kept low by a subsidy, there was not enough bread to go round; other food-stuffs were mostly beyond their means. Their bread, too, was nastier than ever, black, and so sticky that if a piece was thrown at the wall it clung there. Yet dainty loaves and cakes were displayed in fashionable shops, and the

---

* As yet, no one dared to keep a private carriage.

rich could get white flour by paying heavily, for there was no longer a Commune to enforce regulations.

The dearth was the same in many parts of the Republic, though in some districts there was abundance. Populous towns were often on the verge of starvation, the Comité de Salut public grew more and more anxious, and Representatives on Mission were often desperate. The 'maximum' had become a dead letter, because owners could not be got to sell at the fixed prices; it was abolished on December 23rd, 1794, and the free circulation of grains was decreed. This improved matters in some districts, but the prices of all kinds of food rose, and often, when owners were willing to sell corn, the countryfolk, fearful of famine, refused to let it leave the place. Corn-wagons destined for Paris were pillaged by starving towns on the way, and riots over food were frequent. At Nantes, in December 1794, there was so little food that the troops gave up part of their rations to feed the poor. Paris was, at least, allowed to buy as much bad bread as there was, but Amiens was on scanty rations for months, and reduced one day to two ounces of rice.

To make things worse, assignats were always sinking in value, and though wages rose, they did not keep pace with prices. In May 1795 a Paris carpenter with three children published his budget. He and his wife earned between them twenty francs a day, and could not live on less than twenty-five.

On the top of starvation came all the miseries of one of the coldest winters ever known in Europe, rivalling the icy winter of 1788-9. Forty-one consecutive days of hard frost began in mid-December, and, through it all, women must stand shivering in queues for hours, to secure the daily portion of food or fuel for their families.

To the soldiers of the Republic, ill fed and half clad, the winter brought disease and suffering; it brought also glory. The Autumn Campaign had carried the victorious armies still farther. In Spain there had been advances, and the brave Dugommier had fallen in battle. In Italy there had been much fighting with little result, and Bonaparte had been suspended by the Committee as a protégé of the younger Robespierre. In the East, Jourdan had forced the passage of the Roer in a great battle on October 2nd, and had compelled the Austrians to recross the Rhine; the French had entered Cologne (Oct. 6th); Marceau had driven the Austrians out of Coblentz; Kléber had besieged and taken Maestricht; and the Prussians, retreating before the Rhine and Moselle Armies, had recrossed the Rhine at Bingen. The only places remaining to the Allies on the left bank of the Rhine, at the end of the year, were the fortified towns of

Luxembourg and Mayence. The old idea that the Republic would never be secure till France had her 'natural frontiers' of mountain, sea and river, revived in the minds of the Committee and became dominant. France, they decided, must annex Belgium and all the country up to the left bank of the Rhine. So they ordered their Armies to besiege Luxembourg and Mayence, regardless of the bitter winter. They had grown accustomed to expect daily feats of valour and endurance from the soldiers, though they were no longer able to provide for their wants. The Armies lived, as they best could, on requisitions from the impoverished inhabitants of the occupied countries.

The two sieges went on through the winter. Huge works were raised round Mayence and fights took place daily; but as the town could be reinforced from the right bank of the Rhine, the siege was useless as well as costly. The Generals were all against it, but Mayence was the key of the German Empire, and the Committee was inexorable. About half the besiegers and number-less horses died of cold and misery before Mayence.

Meanwhile Pichegru and Moreau had advanced to the borders of Holland, the Allies (Dutch, English and Germans) retreating before them. The Stadtholder of Holland would fain have treated with the Republic for peace, but the Committee would not hear of it. Holland was on the brink of a revolution; it must be invaded, and they ordered Pichegru forward. Here the winter was all in favour of the French, for the rivers froze as they had not frozen for a century, and on January 8th-10th, 1795, Pichegru was able to cross the Waal, artillery and all. Once across, he marched from success to success, all easy. The Stadtholder retired to England, revolution ensued in Amsterdam, and the French were welcomed as deliverers. They entered Amsterdam on January 20th; they entered Rotterdam and the Hague; a detachment of cavalry captured the Dutch fleet frozen in the Texel. Pichegru's well-disciplined and needy soldiers, who did not pillage in the midst of abundance, won golden opinions.

The fruits of the campaigns of 1794 were reaped by the Committee of 1795, in a series of triumphant peace-treaties, all ratified by the Convention. First one with Tuscany, signed on the 9th February 1795. Next a treaty with Prussia, negotiated at Bale by Barthélemy, the French Minister in Switzerland, a good diplomat of the old school, and signed on 5th April 1795. It was followed by a second treaty, amplifying the first. The King of Prussia allowed France to remain in occupation of the Rhine-lands till a general peace, and in return the neutrality of certain northern states of the German Empire was to be respected. Next came a treaty with Holland. Here the soldiers had prepared the Dutch to expect generous dealing, and had provisionally granted terms which the Committee wished to repudiate. Siéyes was especially voracious; he wanted to extort huge sums of money, he wanted to annex Zeeland. The Representatives on Mission in Holland besought the Committee not to drive the Dutch to desperation, since, after the thaw, Pichegru's Army, dispersed through Holland, was at their mercy; the Committee would not listen to advice. At length, when the Dutch still refused to be bullied into signing a treaty, Siéyes and Reubell were sent to the Hague, and, on the spot, abandoned some of their pretensions. A treaty of peace and alliance with the Dutch Republic was signed there on May 16th; Holland paid a large indemnity in coin, with other subsidies, allowed the French to keep Dutch Flanders and Maestricht, and consented to a joint occupation of Flushing, which commanded the Scheldt.

Peace with Spain followed, also negotiated by Barthélemy, and signed at Bale on July 22nd. The French conquests in Spain were given back, and in return France received the Spanish part of Saint-Domingo. A month after came a treaty with Hesse-Cassel. The Committee might have had peace with all Europe if they had given up their system of 'natural frontiers', but they did not desire peace. There was not bread enough in France to feed the armies if they were disbanded; and then, who knew what successful Generals might attempt in peace time? The Committee, which contained no statesmen, found it easier to go on fighting. Belgium, Luxembourg,* and other small States were annexed on October 1st.

One peace, at almost any price, the Committee did sincerely desire, peace in la Vendée, and for a time they thought they had ensured it. As it was, peace was coming gradually; the policy of the old Committee had been reversed, the refugees had been allowed to return, and humane Representatives on Mission were trying to pacify the country by allowing priests to conduct public worship. Although Charette and Stofflet, quarrelling as usual, were still active in the field, and the bands of Chouans were still at their deadly work in Brittany, the military situation was promising. Canclaux was once more commanding the Western Army, Hoche† was in command of the Brest Army, and a display of force by good Generals, combined with conciliation, might have ended the rebellion. At this juncture, the Committee induced the Convention to vote an amnesty; a decree that all rebels who brought in their arms within a month should never be molested in the future (2nd December, 1794). Five Representatives, to be joined by others on the spot, were sent to carry

---

* Luxembourg, after a long siege, had capitulated in June 1795.
† Hoche had been released after the 9th Thermidor. He had a narrow escape, for he was in the Conciergerie during the height of the Terror.

out the amnesty. The Committee, expecting an invasion from England, were so anxious for peace quickly, that they would not wait for a slower, surer peace. The Representatives got into touch with Charette and with a royalist agent, Cormatin, an adventurer who gave himself out to be leader of all the Chouans. Conferences were arranged; they were held in a tent at la Jaunaye, a lonely castle near Nantes, and on February 17th, 1795, an agreement was reached. The Vendéens and Chouans, by their leaders, submitted to the Republic and promised never to bear arms against it; and in return they were promised an amnesty for every one, freedom and protection for religion, restoration of their property and other benefits, while, with singularly misplaced trust, they were not required to give up their arms. Indeed, the chiefs were to help organize their followers into Territorial Guards, to be paid by the State. Charette, Cormatin, and all the leaders present signed this 'Pacification of la Jaunaye'. At another conference, in April, the same terms were signed by Chouan chiefs. Stofflet did not sign till May. Thus peace seemed to have been secured, but, in truth, the time for making peace had not yet come.

These were not the only diplomatic successes of the Committee. France was resuming her place among the nations, and the Convention, drilled beforehand, received ceremoniously not only envoys from some of the Powers with whom treaties were made, but the envoys of two friendly neutrals: Monroe, from the United States of America in August 1794, and de Stael, from Sweden, in April 1795. Madame de Stael opened her salon again, and exercised an influence, liberal and generous, over a wide political circle.

Yet the position of the Committee, even of the Convention, was not secure, and interspersed with successes came a series of grave perils.

The first crisis was in Germinal (March-April). Paris was restless, the politicians of the Sections were anxious about the fate of the 'patriots' imprisoned since Thermidor, and their fate seemed linked with the fate of Barère, Collot, Billaud, and Vadier, over which the Convention itself was torn in two. The Commission appointed to report on them had recommended their impeachment (March 2nd, 1795), and they had been put under arrest in their own houses; all but Vadier, who had escaped. The others defended themselves tenaciously in the Convention, the Mountain came to their help, Lindet and Carnot were dragged in, old incidents were raked up, every one must have his say on every point, and the affair threatened to go on for months. At the same time life was becoming intolerable to the unhappy poor of Paris. Winter was over, but Spring did not bring more food; the crowds at the bakers' were bigger than ever and, worst of all,

Boissy d'Anglas, reporting for the Committee, on March 15th, said that it was high time that favoured Paris should share in the privations of the Departments; Paris too must be rationed; 1 lb. of bread daily, per head. This was decreed, with a concession to manual workers of lb., and Boissy was known to the people ever after as 'Boissy-Famine'. Their attitude was threatening, and a stern 'police law', with the object of putting down incitements to sedition and violence (21st March), had no effect.

After a prelude of several petitions, some political, demanding the Constitution of 1793 as a remedy, some merely wretched, demanding bread, a great mob surrounded the Convention on the morning of the 12th Germinal (1st April), and a multitude of men, women and children forced their way past the guards and into the hall, crying: "Bread! Bread!" Some of the men had "Bread and the Constitution of 1793" written round their hats, and, through the hubbub, politicians from the Sections made speeches, demanding that Constitution and the release of imprisoned patriots. But the hungry, unpolitical part of the mob, in which women and children were conspicuous, kept crying: "Bread! Bread!" and to every attempt to move them they answered: "Bread! Bread!" More forced their way in, till the hall was full to suffocation, and at one o'clock the Committees had the tocsin rung, to call loyal citizens to the help of the Convention. But the mob had not come with evil intentions, a few firm words from Barras set them moving at last, and the hall was cleared. The Convention, left to itself, voted the instant deportation of Barère, Billaud, and Collot, on the supposition that they must have been concerned in causing the rising. Barras was more practical; Pichegru happened to be in Paris, and Barras got him made temporary Commander-in-Chief of the Paris National Guard. In that capacity Pichegru put down ensuing disturbances swiftly and smoothly. There was trouble the next day, when a crowd at the city barrier stopped the carriage conveying Barère and the others, and took them back to the Committees, insisting that they must have a proper trial. But the crowd was dispersed, and the Committees sent the three deputies off again.*

The Convention had been thoroughly alarmed, and vengeance fell on the Mountain. The Montagnards had shown an indiscreet sympathy with the mob; and when it was proposed to prosecute the instigators of the rising they had refused to vote; and when André Dumont proposed the deportation of Barère, they demanded a vote by roll-call and rushed to sign their

---

* All three, with Vadier, were impeached later; Collot and Billaud were already on their way to Cayenne, and Barère managed to escape both deportation and arrest.

demand. This was enough to convince credulous colleagues of their complicity in the rising; the arrest of eight Montagnard deputies was voted at once (12th Germinal), and on the 16th Germinal the arrest of nine more. Among the seventeen were Leonard Bourdon, Choudieu, Duhem, Cambon, Lecointre, Thuriot, and Maignet who was thrown in, as a Terrorist merely. Cambon escaped. The arrested deputies were sent away from Paris to fortresses. On the 21st Germinal (10th April) the Convention decreed that all men known to have taken part in any "horrors committed under the tyranny which preceded the 9th Thermidor" (i.e. Terrorists) were to be disarmed, both in Paris and in the Departments. The definition was conveniently vague.

For seven weeks after the rising Paris was outwardly peaceful and inwardly simmering with discontent. No relief came to the hungry people; they did not even get their ration regularly, as Paris was living from hand to mouth with hardly any stores to fall back upon, and the day's provision of flour sometimes arrived too late to be made into bread, causing rations to run short. Before the end of the third week in May, the faubourgs of Saint-Antoine and Saint-Marceau were ripe for another explosion. On the evening of the 19th May frequent groups, mostly of women, gathered; they were heard lamenting Robespierre, and complaining that the

Convention was starving the people. A 'Plan of Insurrection' was widely circulated; it contained demands for bread, the Constitution of 1793, the release of imprisoned patriots, and a new Assembly. On the morning of the 20th May, the 1st Prairial, the tocsin rang and the faubourgs marched upon the Convention.

The attack was opened in the hall by a number of fierce and brazen women* who filled a gallery, shouting for bread, laughing scornfully, and insulting the Convention, till the deputies could stand it no longer and had the gallery cleared by a show of whips. Already a sound of blows was heard on the door to the President's left; the door resisted long, plaster fell, hinges cracked, and at length, at about half-past one, the mob burst in. By the opposite door, in rushed the Guards of the Convention, and pushed the invaders clean out of the hall. The mob made a second onslaught and was repulsed a second time, with the help of National Guards from a loyal Section, and in a brief interval of comparative calm, gendarmes began to seize insurgents in the corridors. Soon fresh cries were heard; the mob had gathered again, and at about half-past three burst in irresistible, through both doors, filling the hall; workmen came pressing in, and National Guards in uniform, from the disaffected Sections, and

* At this time bands of such women were to be met in the streets.

a great quantity of women. National Guards from the
loyal Sections entered with them, all mixed in confusion. Many of the insurgent men were armed with
guns, pikes, or swords, and, as in the last rising, bore
inscribed round their hats: "Bread and the Constitution
of 1793." There was firing at the doors, where resisting
deputies were knocked down and badly hurt; there
were scuffles by the tribune, and one deputy, Féraud,
coming pluckily to the help of a youth in danger, was
thrown on the tribune stairs and dragged into the
corridor, where he was murdered by a woman fury
and others.* Several hours of chaos and tumult
followed, and through it all Boissy d'Anglas, who was
presiding, sat in his chair steady as a rock, unflinching,
though firearms were often levelled at his head. From
the tribune a man in uniform read the 'Plan of
Insurrection', but the aimless mob in possession
seemed to have no leaders. By and by the severed head
of Féraud was brought in on a pike; the bearer halted
before the President. Boissy faced the ghastly sight
with unmoved firmness.†

At about eight o'clock the President in office, old
Vernier, a Girondin, relieved Boissy in the chair. Most
of the deputies had fled in panic, only a few of the

---

* Féraud was in no way obnoxious to the mob; he was little known,
having spent most of his time with the armies, on mission.
† The story that he saluted the head gravely appears to be an addition.

stoutest-hearted remaining; Lanjuinais was one, but they were chiefly Montagnards. The mob, tired at last of shouting, began to ask for a roll-call of members. Some of the Montagnards conceived the unfortunate idea that further bloodshed could be prevented and the mob be induced to move away, if the remains of the Convention appeared to grant their demands. Vernier seemed to grasp this plan; he called the deputies round him and told them to vote by lifting their hats. A little circle of Montagnard deputies proposed popular measures, one by one, the other Montagnards lifted their hats, and Vernier declared that the measures were carried. Lanjuinais did not vote. In this manner was voted the release of imprisoned patriots and of the deputies arrested in Germinal; the forbidding of all kinds of fancy bread; and finally, as the Committees had not been heard of since the morning and might be supposed dead or imprisoned, the dismissal of the unpopular Comité de Sûreté generate, four Montagnards being appointed to fill its place. At this moment members of the Committee in question appeared, and after them came National Guards. Two hours before, this same Committee had got together the whole battalion of the loyal Lepeletier Section with its guns, and had them ready and waiting; but it was not till eleven o'clock, when the insurgents were beginning to retire, that the order to clear the hall was given. The drums beat, and after a short resistance the mob was driven out of the Tuileries.

The Convention returned, thirsting blindly for vengeance. The doors were shut that the faithless deputies who had encouraged the mob might not escape, and the arrest of fourteen Montagnards was decreed; nine for the evening's work, five accused of cruelty on missions. Vernier, who had presided over the fatal debate, was not even blamed; a clear proof that the Committees were seizing a pretext for getting rid of their enemies.

The mob had only retired for the night, and on the following day the insurrection was more dangerous than ever. The three rebel Sections of Saint-Antoine, overpowering all resistance, ranged themselves before the Tuileries, a dense, impenetrable mass of humanity; the loyal Sections surrounded them. There came a moment when the rebel gunners turned their guns on the Palace, and then, to the horror of all good citizens, the gunners of the loyal Sections, suddenly siding with the rebels, turned their guns too. The deputies sat expecting death, when, all at once, the Sections began to fraternize; loyalty carried the day and persuaded rebellion to abstain from violence, but not before the Convention had promised to take steps towards putting the Constitution of 1793 in force.

On the 3rd Prairial the mob rescued the man who

had carried about Féraud's head, as he was being taken to execution, and it was not till the 4th that the insurrection was put down. An unsuccessful attempt on the faubourg Saint-Antoine in the morning, by the Sections aided by the *Jeunesse dorée*, armed for the occasion, led to the calling in of the regular troops in the afternoon. The command of the troops was given to General Menou, a 'Constituent', the Sections were ordered to march with him, the faubourg was surrounded, and the inhabitants laid down their arms.

The vengeance of the Convention was swift and cruel. A military commission of five was appointed to try offenders – a court with no jury, where neither counsel nor written defences were heard – and insurgent heads were soon falling in the place de la Révolution. Thirteen deputies arrested on the 1st Prairial had been impeached on the 2nd, together with nearly all those arrested in Germinal, and, to the shame of the Convention and in defiance of the laws, eleven deputies accused of encouraging the rising were sent before the Military Commission (8th Prairial); not without protests from Lanjuinais and Louvet. Of the eleven, one committed suicide and two escaped, Prieur de la Marne and another. The rest were tried; and though they were guilty, at worst, of an error of judgement, and innocent of all complicity in the rising, six of them were condemned to death on June 17th. These six were all well-known and had all served on missions to the armies. Romme, the savant, inventor of the new Calendar, was one; and the most interesting was Goujon, a young idealist of promise, unstained by cruelty, noted for his height and his strength, and with a head like St. John in pictures. They had resolved not to suffer execution and had managed to conceal two knives. With these and the blade of a pair of scissors, the whole six stabbed themselves on the stairs leading out of the Court room. Three were dead before their guards could reach them; the other three were conveyed, dying, to the guillotine. The six are known to History as 'the last of the Montagnards.'

The Mountain had, indeed, ceased to exist as a fighting party. Within a fortnight of the rising the arrest of twenty-seven other prominent Montagnards had been decreed, and of the members of the Government Committees on the 9th Thermidor, all but three were dead, imprisoned, or in hiding. Lindet had been arrested; Carnot, on the brink of arrest, was spared because he had 'organized victory'. The Terrorists, real and supposed, had been disarmed, and the turbulent faubourgs raised their heads in revolt no more. The reaction grew savage, and not only former oppressors were, in their turn, oppressed; any ardent republican, even of the kindliest, might be called a 'Terrorist' and treated as such.

In the South a new 'white Terror' took the place of the 'red Terror'. Already, earlier in the year, bands had formed at Lyon and Marseilles, calling themselves *Compagnie de Jesus* and *Compagnons du Soleil*, whose object was to punish Terrorists; which they did by isolated murders and by massacres of prisoners. Lyon started the prison massacres in May; the Marseilles *Compagnons du Soleil* were responsible for two, one at Aix and one in the Fort Saint-Jean at Marseilles (5th June). There were murders and massacres in many other places, indeed it was reported to the Convention, in October, that scenes of blood had taken place in ten Departments and thirty cities. Tarascon, in the summer, had two massacres by night, in a prison on the Rhone, and the murderers threw the corpses of their victims into the river. The local authorities did nothing, and some Representatives on Mission encouraged the murderous 'companies'. As no one cared to denounce the assassins, and as no official enquiries were made, the number of their victims will never be known. The Convention, much disturbed, ordered prosecutions, but took few steps to stop the atrocities. In October Fréron was sent to Marseilles, perhaps on the principle of 'set a thief to catch a thief', and effectually put an end to murder and massacre.

The 'white Terror' was supposed to be connected

with a revival of royalism and royalist conspiracies. Emigres had slipped back over the eastern border and were making centres of royalism; there was a royalist agency in Paris itself; an agent of Pitt's in Switzerland, Wickham, passed his time in forwarding and financing futile royalist plots, and both he and the émigrés confidently expected south-eastern France to rise against the Republic. Out-and-out royalists hoped, as the Princes did, for a restoration of absolute monarchy; for the Princes continued to believe that the Revolution had been engineered by a few wicked men. Constitutional royalists hoped for a restoration of the constitutional monarchy, with the little Louis XVII as King, and an enlightened Regency.

Their hopes came to an end with the death of the young Prince on June 8th. After Thermidor the child had been less unkindly treated, and though the Comité de Sûreté générale thought it necessary to deny indignantly a newspaper report that 'little Capet' was to be educated, guardians were appointed to look after him. These guardians did as much as they dared for the sick boy, whom they were compelled to leave alone at night. They found him crippled by disease, and very silent – so much changed that a controversy has raged ever since as to whether the child really was the Dauphin. Before his death he was attended by good doctors who had formerly known him by sight. They were satisfied of his identity, and satisfied Mme de Tourzel, his governess.

If royalist plots were futile in the East, they were extremely serious in the West. Charette broke his pact in June, without any warning, and appeared in arms again; other chiefs did the same, for, with few exceptions, the Vendéen and Chouan leaders had signed the agreement with the Republic without any intention of keeping it, and merely to gain time and drill their followers, while Puisaye, an agent of the comte d'Artois, prepared in England an expedition of émigrés to Brittany. Pitt's Government had long since promised help; help was now forthcoming, and on June 27th a small British fleet landed a Division of émigrés, commanded by d'Hervilly, on a lonely beach in Quiberon Bay, not far from Vannes, in Brittany. A second Division was to follow, and, later, some British troops. The landing-place had been kept a secret, and the few Republicans on the spot were easily routed; the émigrés were speedily joined by numbers of Chouans, and under good leaders a big rebellion might have been started.

But the witless émigrés always bungled their affairs. D'Hervilly and Puisaye were both in command of the expedition, and d'Hervilly's regiments, recruited in England, had been filled up with pressed French prisoners of war, republicans, and therefore hostile to the enterprise. Against Puisaye's wishes, d'Hervilly insisted on staying by the coast, where the British fleet could support him; and the émigrés established themselves in the peninsula of Quiberon, a long tongue of land joined to the mainland, with which it runs fairly parallel, by a long, narrow neck known as Quiberon Beach. A fort at the farther end of the neck blocked and guarded the entrance to the peninsula. Hoche, in whose command Quiberon lay, compared the émigrés' position to that of rats in a trap.

Hoche made his preparations with his usual consummate ability, and at the news of the invasion the Convention sent Tallien to help him, giving him unlimited powers. Hoche took up his position on Quiberon Beach, and there repulsed an attack of the émigrés, in which d'Hervilly was mortally wounded. The leadership of their army now devolved on Puisaye, aided by the young de Sombreuil* who had just landed with the second Division of émigrés.

With the help of republican deserters from Quiberon, who acted as guides, Hoche surprised the guardian fort on the night of July 20th-21st; a risky adventure which was completely successful. Once the fort was in his hands, he had only to march forward, sweeping the peninsula. The pressed soldiers deserted, ruining

* Brother of the heroic Mlle de Sombreuil who saved her father's life in the September massacres.

the defence, and nothing was left to the émigrés but to embark. Puisaye was one of the first to seek the ships, leaving Sombreuil in charge. The fleet came as close in as the Admiral dared, to fire in support of the émigrés, and boats and shallops were sent to take them off; but the sea was rough and, in the confusion, many among the crowds who rushed headlong to the shore were drowned. Sombreuil, whose task it was to protect the embarkation, though gallant, had no military skill; he was driven back and back, right to the end of the peninsula, where he and his small band of émigrés were forced to surrender. It is often said that they capitulated; in truth there was no capitulation, and there could be none, because they were at Hoche's mercy. The Republicans took nearly twelve thousand prisoners; of these more than half, including a large number of women and children, were released; the rest were tried by various military commissions, which acquitted the pressed soldiers and nearly all the Chouans. Of the emigre nobles, 364, many of them once officers in Army or Navy, were condemned to death, after fair trials, and shot; Sombreuil was one of the first. The émigrés died pitied and lamented by the whole country-side; every one would fain have saved them, and many were helped to escape. Sympathy was, however, of little avail, the law had to be carried out, and an attempt by a Representative on Mission to save a number of émigrés who were mere boys was foiled by the Committee.*

The danger of an invasion was not yet over. Charette, who had been appointed by the Princes Commander-in-Chief of the Catholic royal Army, was in communication with the foreigner, and in August protected the landing, by the British, of a large quantity of arms and ammunition. Stofflet, jealous of Charette's honours, was still neutral, but the Chouans were all up and out, and it needed only the presence of a Prince of the Blood royal to revive a promising rebellion. A Prince was coming; escorted by a British fleet, the comte d'Artois embarked at Portsmouth, arrived off the coast by Quiberon early in September, and by the beginning of October was established, with his court and over 5,000 British troops, on the small Île d'Yeu, off the coast of la Vendée, and preparing to land with the help of the British and Charette. But Hoche, now in command of the Western Army, was there to oppose him, and took care to make a landing impossible. In vain Charette approached the shore; the landing was postponed. The Prince could have landed

* There are still Frenchmen who believe that the expedition to Quiberon was planned by the English with a view of crippling the French Navy by abandoning the émigrés, some of whom had been naval officers, and might have returned to serve their country under Napoleon, when experienced naval officers were badly wanted.

quietly by himself from a boat, if he had wished, but he had no intention of sharing the vagabond life and the risks of his followers. Charette, already defeated by the Republicans, judged it useless to keep his troops together and disbanded them, betaking himself to the woods with some three hundred horsemen. The Prince left the Île d'Yeu for England on November 18th. Before he left he sent Charette a sword and a friendly letter. Charette returned a rude message and broke the sword across his knee.

The rest of the story belongs to the history of the Directoire. The Directors had learnt wisdom, and at the end of December 1795 they appointed Hoche Commander-in-Chief of all the three Armies in the West, and gave him powers to pacify the country which amounted to a dictatorship. He used these powers nobly, and showed that he was not only a great soldier but a statesman. While taking all military measures against the rebels, he set himself to conciliate the inhabitants; Religion was protected, priests were won over to friendliness, peasants taken in arms were sent back to their homes, and pacific proclamations were widely distributed. Early in 1796 he let it be known that if Charette and the émigrés wished to leave France, he would give them passports and means to reach a foreign land. Charette refused to go. Stofflet took up arms again at the end of January 1796; within a month he had been taken and shot. Charette was not captured till a month later; he was taken to Nantes and shot there on March 29th, after a trial. The Chouans took longer to subdue, but, at the end of June 1796, Hoche could write to the Directors: "The war, I venture to say, is finished."

XII

THE END OF THE CONVENTION 23RD JUNE – 26TH OCTOBER 1795

Although circumstances had rendered it impossible to put the much vaunted Constitution of 1793 in force, the Convention had by no means given up the idea of doing so when the country was more settled, and because this Constitution was admittedly sketchy and left many points undecided, a Commission of eleven was elected towards the end of April 1795, to draw up what were called the 'organic laws' which would fill in the sketch. After the revolt of Prairial, the attention of the Convention was turned to the Constitution in earnest, and it did not take the Commission of eleven long to discover what they probably knew already, that the Constitution of 1793 was quite unworkable. Therefore, instead of 'organic laws', they produced, on June 23rd, a new Constitution. Boissy d'Anglas, extremely popular since the insurrection, reported for them; the whole Commission, he boldly declared, had found that the Constitution of 1793, "dictated by tyranny and accepted by fear", was nothing but "the organization of Anarchy", and must be abandoned. The Convention, from which the stalwarts of the Mountain had been eliminated, applauded.

The new Constitution, framed with thoughtful care, was discussed in the same spirit. The later Convention was at its best in these interesting debates, and showed real anxiety to avoid previous mistakes and to found a stable government.

Perpetual agitations must cease. An article of the Constitution ordained that no assembly of citizens must be called a 'popular society', and all existing popular societies and Clubs were dissolved by a decree, on August 23rd. To cool hot heads, the Declaration of Rights, which prefaced the Constitution, was succeeded by a Declaration of Duties, including the golden rule.

Paris must not raise her head too high. The Department of Paris became Department of the Seine, and the city was divided afresh into twelve 'arrondissements', each containing four of the old Sections, and each with a mayor and Council; Police administration was central. Other large cities were similarly divided, in proportion to the population.

There must be a check on sudden changes. Two Chambers were established; a 'Council of Five Hundred', which alone could introduce laws, and a 'Council of Seniors', two-hundred-and-fifty married men over forty, serving as an upper Chamber, which accepted laws or rejected them. The same voters elected both Councils, and the old system of election in two steps was kept. A small property qualification was required to obtain the suffrage. To secure continuity of policy, the two Councils must never be entirely renewed; accordingly, one-third of the members of each Council retired yearly, and their places were filled at an annual election; retiring members might be re-elected for a second period of three years. With regard to local government the administrations of Departments were kept, because they had always resisted changes, and Districts were suppressed.

The executive power was vested in a Directory (Directoire) of five, elected by the Councils, and the Directors retired in rotation, one each year. They appointed their own Ministers and, together, had most of the powers of a constitutional monarch, but not a veto on the laws.

The banishment in perpetuity of émigrés was made an article of the Constitution. This 'Constitution of the year three', as it is called, was finally adopted on August 17th.

One thing remained to do. Mindful of how the work of the Constituent Assembly had been ruined by its successor, the Convention was resolved that this should not happen again, and the deputies, in their eagerness to avoid their predecessors' error, rushed into the opposite extreme, and determined to secure a very large majority in the new Councils. How could this be done, except by a decree? The members of the Convention were re-eligible, and popular deputies were certain to be elected, but everyone was aware that the great mass of deputies was equally certain to fail of election. It was therefore decreed, on the 5th Fructidor (Aug. 22nd), that five hundred members of the Convention, roughly two-thirds, must sit in the Councils, and, to keep up a pretence of election, that they must be chosen by the Electoral Assemblies. Another decree (13th Fructidor) fixed the method of forcing them on the 'Electors'. It was also decreed that if, despite these precautions, the full five hundred were not chosen, the Convention should itself elect the remainder. Deputies impeached or under arrest were declared not eligible. These decrees were issued as an annex to the Constitution, and the Primary Assemblies were summoned to meet early in September, in order to accept or reject the Constitution and to choose their 'Electors'.

The decrees came as an unpleasant surprise to the

country. All moderate men were heartily sick of the Revolution, with its accompaniments of famine, no trade and a worthless currency; and just as they were hoping to get rid of the Convention which had brought these evils upon them, they learnt that their unloved rulers were taking a new lease of life. A good many men were angry, besides, at being deprived of their freedom of choice. The Constitution was well, though not enthusiastically, received by the Primary Assemblies and was accepted by a very large majority;* the decrees of the 5th and 13th Fructidor, though generally disliked, were also accepted, but by a majority not so large, more than a tenth of the voters rejecting them. On the 23rd September most of the results were known, and the Convention, without waiting for the rest to come in, declared that both Constitution and decrees were the law of the land, and summoned the Electoral Assemblies for the 12th October.

In Paris the two decrees were especially unpopular, and there were other grievances. Towards the end of June the Committees had begun to show some leniency towards imprisoned Jacobins, some intention to have the reasons of their arrest inquired into. Certain reactionary Sections foresaw the release of their old oppressors, and hastened to the Convention with angry

---

* For this time only, the suffrage was unrestricted, and all who had voted in the last Primary Assemblies were admitted to vote in these.

petitions against 'indulgence'. Another grievance was, that the Convention having lately decreed the establishment of a camp near Paris, with a view to protecting the arrival of provisions, troops were arriving in the outskirts and were seen in the city itself. This also was the subject of insolent petitions.

When the Primary Assemblies met, the Sections saw their chance – it must be remembered that the Primary Assembly in each Section was composed of the same men exactly as the Sectional Assembly, but sitting in a different and more imposing capacity. So the Sections behaved as they had behaved in their palmy days: discussed any matters they chose, regardless of decrees to the contrary, passed resolutions condemning the Convention, declared their sittings permanent, communicated with each other, and sent emissaries into the country. With mutual encouragement, all but one, the Quinze-Vingts Section, rejected the decrees of the 5th and 13th Fructidor. One Section took the lead: Lepeletier, rich and prosperous,* the very Section which had come to the help of the Convention in the Prairial rising. Across the river the Theatre-Français Section was prominent.

The disaffected Sections are often called 'royalist'; it should, however, be noted that 'royalist' and 'terrorist'

* Formerly called 'Bibliothèque'; the National Library was in its territory.

were words much bandied about between opposing parties at this time, and neither word means what one would suppose. The Sections probably contained few men, even among their leaders, who definitely wished to re-establish the Monarchy; the majority looked no further than the overthrow of the Convention. But the discontented were egged on by royalist writers of newspapers, they were used, as the 'Federalists' had been used, by plotters who linked the royalist cause with theirs, and a Committee of émigrés in Bale had high hopes of the Sections. Civil war might have resulted if the movement had spread, but it is impossible to believe that any great number of Frenchmen would have accepted a Bourbon Monarchy, much less an unconstitutional monarchy, which was all that the Bourbons would have granted. And what alternative to the Bourbons was there?

Disaffection soon turned into revolt. On October 2nd (10th Vendémiaire), when most of the Sections had chosen their 'Electors', the Lepeletier Section ordered all the 'Electors' to meet the next day in the hall of the Theatre-Français (now the Odeon), in flat defiance of the Convention, which had not summoned the electoral Assemblies till the 12th. Fifteen Sections responded by sending their 'Electors' to the Theatre-Français on October 3rd, and this meeting passed a resolution not to recognize the Convention as a

Convention any longer. The Convention ordered the 'Electors' to separate at once, and the officials who arrived at night to proclaim this decree were hooted and hustled by the crowd round the theatre.

The Committees had called in the small body of regular troops from the camp near Paris, and these were reinforced by National Guards, of whom the Quinze-Vingts Section, part of the Faubourg Saint-Antoine, sent a large detachment, for this Section was now conspicuously loyal. But the forces of the Convention were still so insufficient that arms were distributed to a number of 'patriots', old partakers in revolts, who had rallied round the Convention at the appeal of the Committees; Paris believed that some of them had even been released from prison for the purpose. They were formed into a 'patriots' battalion' – a proceeding which alarmed and irritated the Sections still further, and helped to make lukewarm Sections take up arms. On their side, the disaffected Sections declared themselves in rebellion against the Convention, and beat their drums all night to call up their National Guards; they could no longer ring the tocsin, as bells had been removed.

General Menou, who had gained such credit in Prairial, was at the head of the Convention's forces, and on the 4th October (12th Vendémiaire) the Committees ordered him to surround the head-quarters of the Lepeletier Section, the convent of the

Filles-Saint-Thomas, and arrest the rebel leaders. Menou did not at all like fighting alongside of the battalion of 'patriots', and he liked still less the idea of shedding the blood of the citizens who had marched at his side in Prairial. He delayed so long that it was evening before his troops set out, and when he reached the rebel head-quarters, the Representative on Mission who accompanied him parleyed instead of acting, and made an agreement that if the forces of the Section dispersed, Menou would withdraw his. The Section made a pretence of dispersing, Menou withdrew his troops speedily and unwarily, and the Section returned. In haste and alarm the Committees dismissed Menou and set Barras in his place. The services of several Generals then in Paris were put at Barras' disposal, and Barras made one of them, General Bonaparte, his second in command, and had the good sense to give him his full confidence.

The 13th Vendémiaire (5th Oct.) dawned with more drum beating in the Sections. The rebels were about 25,000 strong, and they too had Army Generals among their leaders, the chief in command being General Danican who had fought in la Vendée. The object of the Sections was to rush the Tuileries, by an attack from the rue Saint-Honoré and other approaches on the north side of the river. Barras ordered his men to remain strictly on the defensive.

The Sections had hardly a gun; they had given them up after the Prairial revolt, and a new organization of the National Guard, Artillery and all, had not yet been completed. Before dawn, the Lepeletier Section had sent a detachment to seize the guns in the camp near Paris, only to find that Barras had just secured them. These guns were brought into the Tuileries, and Bonaparte posted both them and the troops, with science and skill, at strategic points round the Palace.

At 4.30 in the afternoon the Sections began the attack, and a good deal of fighting ensued, but though the rebel fire did much damage to the forces of the Convention, every onslaught was eventually stopped by the artillery, which swept advancing columns with grape-shot. One of the strongest rebel positions was the church of Saint-Roch in the rue Saint-Honoré, and before this a battle raged, in the course of which the Sections compelled the Republicans to abandon their gun for a time. It soon became apparent, however, that the efforts of the Sections were not meeting with success, and Danican, with other leaders, resolved to try an attack from the south side of the river. Their forces were marching in a column by the Quai Voltaire, towards the bridge, when Bonaparte's guns, placed along the quays by the Tuileries, caught them, and dispersed them with a cross fire of grape-shot. In vain one gallant young leader attempted to re-form his scattered ranks; every one fled, and Danican, who showed himself incompetent throughout, with the rest. By six o'clock the rebel attacks had ceased, and the Sections were now on the defensive. They still held important positions, and prolonged the fight by firing from houses and throwing up barricades; but their positions were turned, one by one, and after the church of Saint-Roch had been taken, early in the morning of the 14th, all resistance ceased.

The Convention, now near its end, did not punish the revolt severely. Three Military Courts were set up to try ringleaders, and between them condemned forty-six to death; only three executions took place, for the other condemned were still at large, and no trouble was taken to hunt up fugitives. The Military Courts acquitted prisoners whenever it was possible, and among others they acquitted General Menou. One of the three executed was Lemaitre, a leader in the Sections who was a genuine royalist conspirator. His treasonable correspondence was found to contain mention of many deputies on whom the émigrés were building their usual wild and fallacious hopes.

The last days of the Convention were darkened by Tallien's mischief and spite. Tallien and his friends, becoming aware that the reaction which they had promoted was going too far for their own security, went suddenly over to the Left, and resumed their seats on the Mountain. Tallien had been suspected of joining in royalist intrigues, and anxious to give the remains of the Mountain a proof of his zeal, he called for a private sitting, and used the Lemaitre correspondence to denounce Lanjuinais, Boissy d'Anglas, and other prominent deputies for complicity in the Vendémiaire rising (15th Oct.). Lanjuinais and Boissy were triumphantly cleared on the spot, but the arrest of two of the others, both Thermidoriens of the Right, was decreed the next day. Tallien's prestige suffered so little that, on October 22nd, he was chosen one of a Commission of five, appointed to report on the dangerous situation of the Republic and to propose remedies. The Mountain began to raise its head.* The new Legislature had been summoned to meet on October 27th (5th Brumaire); it was whispered about that Tallien, in reporting for the five, would propose, in view of the unsettled state of France, to annul the elections and postpone the meeting of the two Councils. Thibaudeau learnt this; like all reasonable men he saw that what France needed was a settled government, and he foiled Tallien by making, before Tallien reported, an attack on his character, conduct and plans, so scathing that Tallien was reduced to

---

* The Mountain had been further diminished by the arrest, early in August, of ten more members, chiefly for cruelty on missions. Fouché was one.

denying the intentions imputed to him (23rd Oct.). Thus was this disgrace averted from the Convention. On the 24th October Tallien reported, and he and his Commission succeeded in getting a law passed, reminiscent of the Terror, which ordered the instant carrying out of the decrees against the always troublesome refractory priests, and excluded from public functions, till a general peace, all close relatives of émigrés, whether by blood or by marriage.2 This law did not apply to the members of the three Assemblies: Constituent, Legislative and Convention.

These last days were not all spent in anger and violence. Much laborious work had been done in the various Committees (for instance on the penal code), and now, as the end approached, useful constructive laws for securing uniformity of weights and measures and for fostering the Arts and Sciences were hastily passed, these being objects to which the Convention had devoted attention. Together with them, a definite organization of part of the great scheme of national education, which had, at various times, been the subject of many debates, was completed. On the last day, the 4th Brumaire (26th Oct.), after electing the hundred-and-five members required to fill up the five-hundred who were to go on into the Councils, the Convention, as its last act, decreed an amnesty for all offences connected with the Revolution, unless they were also offences against the ordinary laws. Emigres and refractory priests were excepted. The same decree abolished the death penalty as soon as a general peace should be declared, and changed the name of the place de la Révolution into place de la Concorde. It had already been decreed, some four months previously, that no more executions should take place in this square. In consequence of the amnesty sixty-seven deputies, under arrest or in hiding, were free to return to their homes.

Another prisoner released soon after, was the young Princess in the Temple tower. After her brother's death she had been more kindly treated, and before long her friends were allowed to visit her. Strange to say, they found her well-grown and healthy, after more than a year of solitary confinement. In December she was exchanged for the four deputies and the Minister of War, whom Dumouriez had handed over to the Austrians, and for a fifth deputy who had been taken prisoner, Drouet, the man who had stopped the King at Varennes. The Comité de Salut public had negotiated the exchange.

The Convention left to its successors a legacy of war, with poor prospects of peace, for the 1795 campaign ended with reverses. Pichegru had been given command of the Rhine and Moselle Armies, and the Committee decided that both he and Jourdan must cross the Rhine and carry the war into a new country, where there would be more food for the troops. For three months French and Austrians watched each other from opposite banks of the Rhine, waiting for an opportunity to cross. Several circumstances made a crossing peculiarly difficult for the French; for one thing, Mayence still held out, and they did not care to advance, leaving that fortress in their rear; for another they had no horses for transport, as nearly all the horses had been killed in the siege of Mayence; neither had they money to buy food and equipment, coin being hard to come by and assignats having sunk so low as to be almost worthless. Pichegru, the Committee's favourite General, disgusted at the incompetence of his own Government, lent an ear to the proposals of the prince de Conde, who wanted him to join forces with the émigrés and restore the Monarchy, promising him a Marshal's baton and other rewards. Pichegru committed no overt act of treason, but when, at length, Jourdan crossed the Rhine near Dusseldorf on September 6th, and advanced successfully, he was slow in supporting him. He crossed, himself, at Mannheim on September 20th, too late, attacked the Austrians near Heidelberg, was defeated and obliged to retreat. Clerfayt made a junction with Wurmser, and the Austrians were soon able to render Jourdan's position so dangerous that, though undefeated, he too had to retreat, and re-crossed the Rhine in the third week of October. Clerfayt relieved Mayence and took possession of the great siege works. Jourdan's retreat exposed Pichegru, who retired in his turn, before it was necessary, abandoning Mannheim. In vain the insatiable Committee ordered fresh attacks; the armies of Jourdan and Pichegru were in no condition to attack, as they had no transport. In consequence of privations discipline was relaxed, and the Generals were heart-broken, for they could not keep their starving men from pillage. The campaign of 1795, which had cost so many lives and so much suffering, ended much where it began. The Austrians, too, were in a bad plight, and an armistice, negotiated between Marceau and the Austrian General opposite him, at the end of December, was extended to all the French and Austrian armies, and lasted three months.

The career of Marceau belongs almost entirely to the Revolution, for he was mortally wounded in September 1796, when engaged in protecting a retreat. This wonderful young man of twenty-seven was not only beloved by the French Army, he had endeared himself to the inhabitants of the Rhine-land by his humanity, and to his enemies by his courteous chivalry. He died a prisoner in the Austrians' hands, carefully tended and sincerely lamented, and his body was escorted by Austrian troops, with all funeral honours, to the French lines, where it was solemnly handed over. He was buried at Coblentz.

Hoche and Marceau! The Revolution was barely over, and already the glories and ideals of France were embodied no longer in her orators but in her soldiers.

No constitutional government can have been further removed from the early ideals of the Revolution than was the government of the Directoire, marked as it was by national bankruptcy, relaxation of morals, perpetual war, lust of conquest, and flagrant breaches of the Constitution; ending as it did in military rule.

National bankruptcy, for what Mirabeau had dreaded came to pass under the Directoire. The Government, it must be remembered, paid most of its debts in assignats; and the Convention started a bankruptcy, on July 31st 1793, by repudiating assignats over a certain sum issued in the King's days and bearing his effigy. The Directoire, after issuing in March 1796 a new kind of paper money, *mandats territoriaux*, gave up the struggle to impose it when 'mandats' sank almost as low as assignats, and in July 1796 a law was passed relieving creditors from the obligation of accepting assignats or mandats. This end, when it came, was a relief to the public, for, paper money being worthless, there was no longer anything to lose on it, and coin reappeared. A further stage of bankruptcy followed in September 1797, when a law was made that the creditors of the nation should continue to be paid interest on one-third of the debt owed them, while the other two-thirds should be paid off in certain securities. These securities were of so little value, that the decree amounted practically to a repudiation of nearly two-thirds of the national debt.

Relaxation of morals. The Legislative Assembly had allowed divorce and made it easy, the Convention made it still easier,* so easy that, before the Convention ended, the resulting scandals had become great enough to cause the suspension of two laws (Aug. 1795). The impulse had been given, the dissolute society of the Directoire slighted the marriage bond, and, with Barras at its head, lived only for pleasure and display, courted rich financiers who flourished while the nation went bankrupt, and expressed its extravagance and profligacy in the bizarre forms and the indecency of its dress. Yet, side by side with these glittering circles, existed another world of respectable bourgeois homes, making little show and practising the ancient family virtues.

Perpetual war, for the Directoire was afraid to make peace. The Government eked out the resources of

* This easy divorce saved many families from total ruin. The property of an émigré and his wife was sequestrated the wife often stayed in France and divorced him, whereupon her legal portion of the property was restored to her, and she and the children lived on that. To attached couples such a divorce was merely nominal, a pretence to be kept up in public, and they were reunited at the earliest opportunity.

France with the spoils of other countries. Besides, they dared not disband their armies, and above all, they dared not leave their Generals unoccupied. What could ordinary men like the Directors do with two men of genius such as Bonaparte and Hoche?

Lust of conquest. Here the Directoire carried on the tradition of the Comité de Salut public of 1795, and, with Bonaparte to help their ambitions, began to remodel Europe. In 1796, through Barras's influence, Bonaparte was given the command of the Army of Italy, and the great General first began to show all his powers in a marvellous campaign, unprecedented in warfare, in which he imposed peace on Sardinia and wrested Milan and Lombardy from Austria. By degrees Italy was moulded into Republics dependent on France – Rome, snatched from the Pope was one – and, as if to show how empty was the pretext of bringing republican freedom to the nations, Holland, the allied Republic, was made dependent; Berne and part of Switzerland were forced into a Helvetian Republic; the neutral Republic of Geneva was annexed; and another neutral Republic, the oldest in Europe, Venice, which had been seized by Bonaparte, was handed over to the Austrians by the treaty of Campo Formio (1797) as a compensation for Belgium.

Breaches of the Constitution; these may be exemplified in a very short sketch. The five Directors elected by the Councils in 1795 were all 'regicides', i.e. they had voted for the death of the King. This was the one unpardonable sin in the eyes of the royalists, and a pledge that the Directors would never betray the Republic. Larevellière, Reubell, Letourneur (a military man and member of the Comité de Salut public), Barras and Carnot were chosen; Siéyes had refused. These men did not lack ability nor good intentions, there was much to respect in Carnot, all except Barras were worthy, and Reubell had some force. But they were not inspiring personalities, nor did they make good figure-heads. The Convention had arranged for Directors, Councils, Ministers, Judges, and every one connected with the Government, a set of theatrical costumes, compounded in varying proportions of cassock, tunic, toga, mantle, and plumed head-gear. These they were obliged to wear, and Barras alone among the Directors could carry off his dress; the virtuous Larevellière looked ridiculous in his, and exposed himself to further ridicule by his earnest patronage of a dreary sect of Deists, calling themselves 'Theophilanthropists.'

For more than a year and a half, though the newly elected third of the two Councils was in opposition, the two-thirds majority of old members of the Convention supported the Directors, as they had supported the Comité de Salut public, and all went well;

Directors and Councils pulled together, kept on the old course, and weathered conspiracies. But when the first annual elections took place in May 1797, and a third of the two Councils, consisting of half the old members of the Convention, retired by lot, the fatal flaw in the Constitution became apparent. In their place the country elected men hostile to the Directors; Constitutionalists eager to return to a more liberal policy, royalists even, though royalists in secret. Pichegru, who had lost his command after the 1795 campaign, was elected, and became President of the Council of Five Hundred. The opposition, thus reinforced, now commanded a large majority, while the Directors were still almost the same body. Only one, Letourneur, had gone out by lot, and in his place the renewed Councils elected Barthélemy, the former Minister of France in Switzerland, a Constitutionalist. The Councils now proceeded to make government impossible for the Directors, not merely by opposition but by hanging up finance bills. It became a question whether Councils or Directors should go to the wall, and Reubell, Barras, and Larevellière, believing that a royalist plot to upset the Republic was at the bottom of the opposition, resolved on making a *coup d'État* with the help of the Military. Carnot was hostile to illegality, Barthélemy they considered an enemy. The approval of both Hoche and Bonaparte had to be obtained, for the Directors were in the position of small boys in whose neighbourhood two powerful schoolmasters are stationed. The approval was given; Hoche sent his aide-de-camp; Bonaparte sent Augereau to manage operations. On the 18th Fructidor of the year V (4th Sept. 1797), very early in the morning, troops surrounded the Tuileries, where the Councils sat, and Augereau arrested deputies obnoxious to the Directors, as they arrived. Many, happily, had been warned in time and stayed away. Carnot and Barthélemy were marked for arrest too, but Carnot escaped. The Directors now secured from the two Councils a law declaring the elections of forty-nine Departments null and void, and sentencing to deportation, without trial, sixty-five prominent political men, comprising the two Directors, fifty-three members of the Councils, and ten others. Only seventeen of them were caught, and these were deported to Cayenne, with much rough and cruel treatment. Seven of them died there.*

After this gross act of tyranny, the Directoire, dependent henceforth on the Military, lost all claim to be considered a constitutional government.

Hoche, the only man who might have rivalled Bonaparte and kept him in check, died of illness just after the *coup d'État* (19th Sept. 1797), and in the

* Pichegru, one of the deported, escaped; so did Barthélemy.

following year the Directors were glad to rid themselves of Bonaparte for a while, by allowing him to go off on an expedition to Egypt (May 1798), with a view of striking a blow at the power of Britain in the East. In his absence the Directors got into fresh difficulties. They failed to secure a majority in the Councils by more annulling of elections, and in June 1799 the Councils, in their turn, declared the election of one Director void, and forced two others, Larevelliere and Merlin de Douai, to resign. Reubell had gone out, by lot, and Barras was the only one left of the original five. Meanwhile the Armies of the Republic had been meeting with reverses, and the military situation was once more so serious that the Directors wrote to Bonaparte recalling him. Bonaparte had not waited to be recalled. Hearing how things stood in France, he had sailed before the letter arrived. On reaching Paris he found that Sieycs, now one of the Directors, was planning for him to overturn the Government. With Siéyes' help he made his *coup d'État* on the 18th and 19th Brumaire of the year VIII (9th and 10th Nov. 1799), by dispersing the two Councils and forcing the Directors to resign. France hailed him as a deliverer who came to bring peace and settled government, and there was general joy when he became First Consul under a new Constitution, the 'Constitution of the year eight'. Illusions about Napoleon Bonaparte's disinterested love of Liberty were short-lived, and when he began to encroach there were no men left strong enough to resist him. The Terror had ruined the Revolution and Liberty, by destroying so many men of talent, character, and courage; it had removed the leading men who could have guided the Republic, it had removed also the honest and determined men with lesser gifts, who would have formed an opposition.

Thus the Revolution, after an opening full of hope and promise, pursued a tragic path, and ended, as far as such a great and fruitful movement could end, in a tragedy. Yet it does not follow that the ideas with which it started must necessarily have brought about this result. Tragedy came through definite mistakes, these mistakes were avoidable, and had they been avoided the course of events might well have been other than it was.

ENDEAVOUR INK

Endeavour Ink is an imprint of Endeavour Press.

If you enjoyed *A History of the French Revolution* check out Endeavour Press's eBooks here:
www.endeavourpress.com

For weekly updates on our free and discounted eBooks sign up to our newsletter:
www.endeavourpress.com

Follow us on Twitter:
@EndeavourPress